CENTER
STREET

LARGE
PRINT

Also by Michael Savage published by Center Street:

God, Faith, and Reason

Government Zero

Scorched Earth

Stop the Coming Civil War

Trump's War

Teddy and Me

STOP MASS HYSTERIA

AMERICA'S INSANITY FROM THE SALEM WITCH TRIALS TO THE TRUMP WITCH HUNT

MICHAEL SAVAGE

CENTER STREET

LARGE PRINT

This book is dedicated to the men and women of law enforcement who are on the front lines protecting the rest of us from the violent, radical, left wing street criminals whose goal is to tear our society into pieces.

Center Street
Hachette Book Group
1290 Avenue of the Americas, New York, NY 10104
centerstreet.com
twitter.com/centerstreet

First Edition: October 2018

Center Street is a division of Hachette Book Group, Inc. The Center Street name and logo are trademarks of Hachette Book Group, Inc.

The publisher is not responsible for websites (or their content) that are not owned by the publisher.

The Hachette Speakers Bureau provides a wide range of authors for speaking events. To find out more, go to www.HachetteSpeakersBureau.com or call (866) 376-6591.

Print book interior design by Timothy Shaner, NightandDayDesign.biz

Library of Congress Cataloging-in-Publication Data has been applied for.

ISBNs: 978-1-5460-8293-4 (hardcover), 978-1-5460-8290-3 (ebook), 978-1-5460-7606-3 (large print)

Printed in the United States of America

LSC-C

10 9 8 7 6 5 4 3 2 1

CONTENTS

CONTENTS

CONTENTS

CONTENTS

1.

WE'VE REACHED
A NEW MASS HYSTERIA
INFLECTION POINT

atred is in the air. We are living in an age of hate, in which mental pollution is worse than air pollution. The most accessible and comprehensive of all unifying agents, hatred is spreading like a virus into all-too-willing hosts. It unifies knee-jerk liberals, no matter what their other differences. Hatred of conservatives, Trump, and his voters is just one of many cases of mass hysteria infecting American society today, but it is likely the most destructive.

As I write these words, three of the most malicious acts in living memory have been perpetrated by agents of the left. First, AntiFA—that group of lawless, self-styled, antifascist anarchists masquerading as "activists"—has published the home

addresses of agents from Immigration and Customs Enforcement (ICE),[1] essentially guaranteeing
that these hardworking, law-abiding, honest, and
decent men and women will be harassed at levels
no citizen should be forced to endure. And that's if
they're lucky. With these cowardly, masked goons,
violence against our public servants is inevitable.

The second obscenity was the odious suggestion
by Peter Fonda, brother of the infamous Hanoi
Jane, son of the onetime gray-listed communist
sympathizer Henry Fonda, that Barron Trump,
son of the president of the United States, be locked
in a cage with pedophiles.[2] It's appropriate that, in
this stoner's view, the real animal is the one outside
the cage.

Flip that for a moment. Can you imagine what
would have happened to anyone who tweeted that
kind of sentiment about the daughters of Barack
Obama? Chuck Schumer, Nancy Pelosi, and every
shockable Democrat on Capitol Hill would have
been calling for blood.

The third obscenity is courtesy of mad California congresswoman Maxine Waters, who screamed
to an audience at a toy drive that they should harass
President Donald Trump and the people who work
for him. "If you see anybody from that Cabinet...
you get out and you create a crowd and you push

back on them...."[3] She has decided, apparently, that God is on her side. Maybe she heard that from a burning bush. Or a burning tire at a riot... the kind caused by the kind of incendiary, high-decibel, hysterical rhetoric of which she is so fond.

Where is the outrage? More important, where is the humanity? Where is the *decency*?

It is gone. It is lost in the sea of mass hysteria that dominates our world in a way and at a level that history has never before seen. Can it be stopped before we have an actual civil war? Can it be stopped before America is lost?

The question is a real one.

On the same day as those earthquakes hit the cheering mainstream media, President Trump—after just one day of bad social media and press—issued an executive order that terminated the administration's policy of splitting migrant families.[4] Mind you, the policy was designed to stop criminals, to prevent individuals from crossing our borders illegally. For these people, children were just the props to make leftist hearts bleed and to let the lawbreakers take advantage of the benefits of living in this country.

I was initially disappointed in the president. But then I thought about what he said: "We're keeping families together and this will solve that problem.

At the same time we are keeping a very powerful border and there continues to be zero tolerance."

There was a storm of protest from the left, one that the media would have fanned so that the smoke of that fire would obscure every goal President Trump has for this nation. He made a disagreeable decision, one that went against the law and his own ideals. He made a *political* decision. Maybe that's why he may turn out to be the greatest commander in chief of our era.

Trump put statesmanship above the desires of his electorate. You know, if President Richard Nixon had done that when the Watergate scandal broke—owned up to an environment he created that allowed for corruption—he might never have had to resign. It would not have defined his administration and obscured his real achievements.

The president capitulated so that we could get off this topic and try to solve the problem of illegal immigration and anchor babies through legislation, which, of course, the Democrats have been stonewalling in an effort to poison Trump to voters. Care for the illegal immigrants? That's not even on the Democrats' radar.

The jury is out on whether the president, by putting out this fire, can turn to stopping the bigger one: our porous and ineffective borders. My fear—and my gut—tell me that the social virus of all-consuming hate of the left is impervious to dispassionate reason, just as physical viruses are impervious to antibiotics.

The left does not just hate President Trump. They hate this nation.

In this book, I will expose the many contemporary and historical cases of mass hysteria, going as far back as Columbus. Whether the mass movement is run by Farrakhan, Hitler, Stalin, Mao, Castro, Moses, Abraham, Isaac, Muhammad—it doesn't matter. The cause and the symptoms are the same.

I've found that virtually all mass movements rely upon hatred, with perhaps the exception of modern Christianity. In the beginning, Christianity was not born of nor was it spread by the gospel of hatred. Christianity was born of love and spread through the gospel of love, overcoming the gospels of hatred in the past and during our time. Can you say the same about other religions?

In *The True Believer*, Eric Hoffer wrote, "Mass movements can rise and spread without belief in a God, but never without belief in a devil." He posited that the strength of the mass movement was proportionate to the "vividness and tangibility of its devil,"[5] an insight not lost on Adolf Hitler. Hitler once said that if the Jew did not exist, "We should have then to invent him. It is essential to have a tangible enemy, not merely an abstract one."[6]

Hoffer relates the story of a Japanese mission, visiting Berlin in 1932 to study the National Socialist movement, lamenting they had no "devil" equivalent to the Jews in their own country.[7] Chiang Kai-shek had the same problem in galvanizing his mass movement when he failed to replace the vanquished Japanese with a new devil.[8]

The new "Jews" for progressives are Trump and his supporters. The hatred for Trump is at the same fever pitch as was the hatred for Jews in early Nazi Germany. The patriarchy, the family, the church, white people, the police, the military, capitalism, conservatives—the Bible itself—are all hate piñatas for hysterical progressives. They attack anyone and anything the liberal media tell them to hate.

As Thomas Jefferson wrote, "I really look with commiseration over the great body of my fellow citizens who, reading newspapers, live and die in the belief that they have known something of what has been passing in the world in their time."[9] That's just as true today. Do television viewers really know what's been passing in the world in their time because they watch the news? I don't care what channel it is. Is what you see on ABC, CBS, NBC,

CNN, and MSNBC really representative of what has been passing in the world in your time?

No, it's a snapshot. It's not a movie. Whether you know it or not, you're living through a mass hysteria primarily of the left, but not solely of the left. How absurd they have become in their hatred of Donald Trump and those who voted for him. Their hatred has reached a fever pitch comparable to mass movements in totalitarian states.

Hatred has now become mainstream, especially on CNN and MSNBC. FOX does not use hatred as a unifying principle. But the news czar of CNN was apparently raised on the mother's milk of hatred, because it's all his marionettes spew. Whoever it is that runs NBC must also have been suckled at the breast of hatred, because that's all you hear from MSNBC's mouthpieces. It's their stock-in-trade.

Samuel Johnson, one of my favorite essayists, wrote the following in 1780: "Every man has a right to utter what he thinks truth, and every other man has a right to knock him down for it. Martyrdom is the test."[10] Now, what does he mean by "martyrdom is the test"? Are you willing to die for your beliefs? Let's hope you don't have to, but anyone can shoot off their mouth.

You know which side you're on by who you

hate. If you hate Trump, you also hate white people—with impunity, by the way. From there you conclude that all people who voted for Trump are racists, which on its face is absurd, but your unhinged hatred and anger allow you to believe it. And you go on watching and listening to hate shows that preach that anything they disapprove of is racist.

Today the word *racist* is used the way *communist* was used in the early 1950s. They used to smear people by saying, "Are you now or have you ever been a communist or a communist sympathizer?" And now these left-wingers play a new game, which is, "Are you now or have you ever been a racist?" That's the one word that fits all they hate.

Ironically, while there certainly were people wrongly accused of being communists during the so-called Red scares, the accusations of communism or sympathy with communism during the mid-twentieth century were mostly true. The Venona Project proved communists had infiltrated Hollywood, newspapers, academia, and even the government.[11] At least two members of Franklin Delano Roosevelt's administration, Alger Hiss and Harry Dexter White, were Soviet spies![12]

Today, however, while racism certainly exists, and some people are rightly called out for it, the accusations of racism against anyone and everyone who criticizes a non-Caucasian person in any way are mostly unfounded. While African Americans and other minorities suffered real inequities during the first half of the twentieth century—virtually all institutional racism by some level of government—that fight was won. Today, the idea that "people of color" are disadvantaged is just another case of mass hysteria, propagated mostly by people who have no one's best interests at heart but their own.

So, if you voted for Trump, fill in the blank. You're a racist. If you believe in the Second Amendment and own guns, you're a racist. If you believe in the traditional family, the traditional institution of marriage, or the church, you're a homophobe. If you are a person who achieved some degree of financial success, you're a "capitalist pig" who hates poor people. If you support the police, you're a racist who hates blacks. If you support the military, you're a mass murderer. If you go to a NASCAR race, well, fill in the blank.

Certain things hold true. No matter what changes, they remain the same. Many examples of covert racism in America today can be seen in the newspapers, which is why they're going out of business. By and large, the primary readers of newspapers are old "progressive" or self-described "liberal" white people. And so they appeal to them with their propaganda sheets attacking police, patriotism, the traditional family, the military, and one race in particular. For example, newspapers in San Francisco don't exist anymore. When I moved here, there were two good newspapers: the *San Francisco Chronicle* and the *Examiner.* But they died. They died because they submitted to covert propaganda.

For example, rarely do they show pictures of criminals unless the criminal is Caucasian. The physical characteristics of a "minority" criminal are almost never described. Neither are the names or religious affiliations of terrorists released, until it is impossible to conceal them any longer.

On June 4, 2018, the Supreme Court, in a landmark 7–2 decision, said that the misnamed Colorado Civil Rights Commission had trampled on the rights of a Colorado baker who declined to make a cake for a gay couple. "The Commission's hostility was inconsistent with the First Amendment's guarantee that our laws be applied in a manner that is neutral toward religion," wrote Justice Anthony Kennedy in his majority opinion.[13] What we learned—what history failed to teach us, but the Constitution ultimately did—is that mass hysteria cannot, must not, and will not be tolerated in this nation.

Did the newspapers across the nation celebrate

this affirmation of one of our most basic, cherished freedoms? Of course not. Instead, they blared, "IN A NARROW MARGIN SUPREME COURT RULES IN FAVOR OF CHRISTIAN BAKERS." The vote was 7–2. Only editors in the grip of liberal mass hysteria could call that margin "narrow."

A few months ago, a headline I posted on my website, MichaelSavage.com, screamed, "FASCIST LIBS IN UK ARREST ANTI-IMMIGRATION PROTESTER, IMPOSE TOTAL PRESS SILENCE! LIBERALISM WILL BRING ABOUT A CIVIL WAR HERE IF THIS IS TRIED."[14] They had arrested the anti-immigration protester and activist Tommy Robinson, head of the English Defense League, without charges. The judge then imposed a total press blackout on the arrest. They redacted the charges, saying they will be shown to the public after he is released from prison.

A van full of police officers pulled up and told Robinson to stop live-streaming, even though he wasn't disturbing the peace in any way. This is an example of the religion of liberalism run amok. It's what happens when a religious fervor takes over a political movement, something that is happening all over the West among antipopulist, antinationalist, and, in America's case, anti-Trump mobs.

This book covers not only the present madness, but similar instances of mass hysteria going all the way back to 1492. It is an attempt to stop the mass hysteria of our time before it leads to a civil war.

In short, today's mass hysteria must end before it ends us.

2.

THE HISTORY AND MECHANICS OF MASS HYSTERIA

The run-up to the 2018 U.S. midterm elections has proven that the voices of mass hysteria now control the news media and social media with everything from vile tweets to Bolshevik-like marches. They are attempting to corrupt our political system with undocumented voters and uninformed rhetoric to demonize President Trump, Republicans, and conservative thinking in general. If they are allowed to triumph, if Congress is lost to the Democrats, Trump will be impeached, and all his work will be undone.

So will the future of our nation.

The bases for fomenting and maintaining hysteria have been in place long before there was an America. Only the goals and slogans have changed.

That is why I have chosen to write about history. It is scary to see how little we have learned over time, and I hope—with your help—we can start to change that. If we do not, then we will again prove true George Santayana's chilling but prescient statement: "Those who cannot remember the past are condemned to repeat it."[1]

This book is about the past, the present, and the future. If you listen to my radio program, *The Savage Nation*, then you know I am very, very concerned about the mass hysteria choking our nation. It is manifested in shouting and bullying that prevents dialogue and hardens adversarial stances. We will be discussing the many forms mass hysteria has always taken, but here are three topics you will instantly recognize:

Guns. Donald Trump. Russophobia.

Gun control is an area where mass hysteria has trumped sound regulation. The left exploits horrors like school shootings—a mental illness and pharmaceutical issue, not a gun issue—as opportunities to repeal the Second Amendment. This is using mass hysteria, trying to implement regulation based on emotional reactions to traumatic events.

As we have seen throughout American history,

guns have a place. Many of the events that led to the founding of our country would not have occurred if the colonists hadn't kept weapons. The Founding Fathers knew this when they included the Second Amendment in the Bill of Rights. We cannot, must not, and will not let the left weaken us, opening us up to tyranny with cheap emotional ploys designed to generate mass hysteria.

As for President Donald Trump, is there a figure who has been so consistently, maniacally, and wrongly reviled as the forty-fifth president? Every commander in chief, like every human being, makes mistakes. But the way the mainstream media and social media fan the hate, this effective leader is not only called the Antichrist, he is called a bigot, a misogynist, an Islamophobe, a hater—the list is nearly endless. Most of those are agenda-driven lies. No one in the media will give him credit for what he is: a leader.

His administration has accomplished more in nearly two years than Obama managed in eight. But people make obscene gestures when they see him, have chest pains when they hear him, spit when someone mentions his name favorably. That is mass hysteria at work.

I had my own brush with this madness when

President Trump invited me to visit him in the Oval Office this past April. We discussed a topic about which I am passionate: a ban on the catastrophic and inhumane hunting of elephants. About ten minutes into our meeting, a red button flashed on his desk. I thought—I feared—that it was a nuclear launch button. I asked, half-joking, "Mr. President, did you just launch a nuclear weapon?"

The president laughed and answered, "Yeah, I launched an atomic bomb." Then he waited a moment—with what professional entertainers would call perfect comic timing—and added, "No. I'm ordering a Diet Coke."

He asked if I wanted one. I laughed. It was self-effacing and funny. How did the Trump-hating mainstream media play it?

"President Trump Jokes About Launching Nukes with Talk Show Host Michael Savage."[2]

They will say anything, twist any event, distort any fact, spin any achievement, to make him appear incompetent, dangerous, and hateful. None of it is true. All people can, and should, have differences of opinion. But the media contemptibly uses mass hysteria to transform disagreements into psychotic breaks.

The insanity over Russophobia is unlike anything we have witnessed in a half century. Without evidence, with just bold propaganda, half our population[3] has decided that Russia controlled the 2016 presidential election. No one can quite articulate how or why Russia did this, not even individuals investigating the claim—which, of course, was promulgated by the losing party and magnified thousands of times by the corrupt, degenerate left-wing media.

I'm not sure readers will even remember that Special Counsel Robert Mueller's own "witch hunt," as the president calls it, was begun to investigate Russian interference in the election and whether any members of the Trump campaign "colluded" with Russia. As of this writing, it has been going on for more than a year, at the cost of tens of millions of dollars, and hasn't produced any evidence of such collusion.[4] Not able to do so, it has morphed into a personal vendetta against the president and anyone associated with him.

The Mueller investigation has become so protracted and far afield of its original purpose that even Mark Penn, pollster and adviser to former president Bill Clinton and political strategist for Hillary Clinton in 2008, has called for its end. In an op-ed for the *Hill,* Penn wrote, "Rather than a fair, limited and impartial investigation, the Mueller investigation became a partisan, open-ended inquisition that, by its precedent, is a threat to all those who ever want to participate in a national campaign or an administration again."

Even the story that former Trump campaign manager Paul Manafort engaged in collusion with Russian officials is falling apart. Manafort has been indicted on money-laundering and tax evasion charges unrelated to the Trump campaign, in an effort to pressure him to turn state's evidence against the president or former members of his campaign. But according to the *Washington Times*, when Manafort's attorney, Kevin Downing, asked the special counsel's office during mandatory discovery for evidence of the widely reported phone calls, during which Manafort supposedly worked with the Russian government to hack the Democratic Party's emails, the Special Counsel's office replied that they had no such evidence.

"The special counsel has not produced any materials to the defense—no tapes, notes, transcripts or any other material evidencing surveillance or intercepts of communications between Mr. Manafort and Russian intelligence officials, Russian government officials [or any other foreign officials]," wrote Downing in his filing.[5] "The Office of Special Counsel has advised that there are no materials responsive to the request." So, the news reporting trumpeting such evidence is mass hysteria at best, deliberate lies at worst.

Sometimes mass hysteria morphs into sheer hypocritical stupidity. For example, the Trump administration has made it a priority to reinvigorate our moribund space program. In so doing, he saves us the $70 million we pay Russia each time they send one of our astronauts to the space station,[6] which is the only way we have of getting there since Obama killed the manned space shuttle. So you have President Trump depriving "malicious" Moscow of income it sorely needs, creating both American jobs and a sense of national purpose. Yet to the illiberal lunatics, he is still Russia's pawn and bad for America.

Sadly, even facts and reason cannot instantly tamp out mass hysteria. Like the reckless push to legalize a dangerous hallucinogenic drug, called marijuana, mass hysteria is stoned on its own fumes. Like the hateful, unfounded cries of "white privilege" that stain the lips of people looking to blame someone for their own failures, mass hysteria hears only the echoes of its own mind.

THE TRUTH ABOUT HUMAN NATURE

Shocking historical events have always brought out the best and worst in human beings. The

2001 World Trade Center attacks saw victims helping victims, strangers helping strangers, and first responders helping everyone. In the hours and days following 9/11, there was little mass hysteria. By that I mean the unhinged impulses that occur when a self-serving charlatan politicizes or monetizes an event and then rallies disciples blinded by manufactured outrage.

Unfortunately, the opportunists eventually poked their heads from the still-smoldering debris. There were the cries of the self-described "Truthers" that this was a government operation. The anti-Zionists declared "Israel knew!" and told Jewish workers to stay home. The warmongers used false evidence to launch a disastrous invasion of Iraq.

There was no social media then like we have now. It took time for the madness to catch fire among a wounded, susceptible populace looking for order in a suddenly disordered world.

Fifteen years later, another form of mass hysteria emerged: the widespread conviction that Donald J. Trump was the Antichrist. As I wrote in *Trump's War*, and discussed with candidate Trump many times on my radio program, no one at first took him seriously as a candidate. As he began to win primaries and knock off well-financed, machine-supported, veteran political rivals like Jeb Bush and Ted Cruz, half the nation slept soundly, comfortable in their belief the self-serving, corrupt, victim-harvesting, born-again progressive Hillary Clinton—with the full might of an equally corrupt Democrat machine—would send the upstart home to Trump Tower.

As we know, that did not happen. The pundits, the polls, the still-diapered Millennials, and, most of all, the agenda-driven factions on the left had a collective coronary from which they still have not recovered. Shock shaded to denial shaded to mass hysteria, vigorously and unrelentingly fanned by the twin evils of social media and the extreme left-wing, biased, mainstream media. According to these people—who are still suffering from postelection psychosis—there was and is nothing President Trump can do right.

Considering the generally respectful conservative opposition to the man who preceded him, a president who did very little right, this reaction is hysterically over the top.

The unthinkable mass shooting in Las Vegas on October 1, 2017, which left fifty-nine people dead and more than 520 wounded at an outdoor country music performance,[7] was another opportunity for the hysterics to deliver a body blow. Rational minds and compassionate souls immediately called for blood donations, offered free hotel rooms for the victims' families, and rallied to find missing persons. Law enforcement swiftly but methodically sought motives and possible accomplices.

The left's response was another story altogether. Before the blood had even dried, liberal politicians and hysterics were out in force. Within hours, Hillary Clinton went on a Twitter rampage against gun silencers, arguing that more people would likely have died had the murderer used a suppressor.[8] Ignoring the fact that a high-caliber automatic rifle cannot be silenced, the failed presidential candidate quickly turned that baseless allegation into a full-throated roar against the National Rifle Association.

Clinton was joined by a fellow Democrat, Senator Elizabeth Warren of Massachusetts, who said, "thoughts and prayers are not enough."[9] Translation: mass hysteria against everyone who does not think like you is the only possible response. Warren got her way when an attorney at CBS took a jackhammer to the cause of national unity by saying she was "not even sympathetic" to the victims because "country music fans often are Republican."

That attorney was fired from her post, and good riddance.

On October 3, that progressive mouthpiece the *New York Times* did its part to create divisiveness and hysteria when it recounted how, in 1966, shooter Charles Whitman defined the twisted phenomenon of mass sniping by shooting sixteen people during a rampage at the University of Texas at Austin.[10] The point of the article? Fear the male—implicitly, he is more dangerous than Radical Islam or AntiFA. The article neglects to mention that those latter two movements are driven by ideology, not sociopaths. Mass hysteria does not bother with fact or reason.

Part of the reason mass hysteria takes root more readily is that we no longer have a legitimate, responsible press to arrest it. Today the press skips from manufactured crisis to crisis, from Trump and groping to Trump and Russians to Trump and chaos on his staff to Trump and "white supremacy" to Trump and imagined racism. But unlike the proven crimes of Hillary Clinton, none of those issues are valid or sustainable. They are mass hysteria.

In addition to all things Trump, today's hysteria often revolves around the concept "fear the male," whether he is Christopher Columbus or movie mogul Harvey Weinstein. The abuse of women by that Hollywood mover and shaker and major Democrat donor—for whom former first daughter Malia Obama interned[11]—rocked the news media for weeks. Weinstein wasn't unique: Women have been victimized by filmmakers probably as far back as the days of the pioneering Lumière brothers of the late 1800s. The so-called casting couch is not a new phenomenon.

After the first wave of accusations against Bill Cosby and eventually some white men, the left acted on its alleged inclusionary nature to indict all men. Media personality Tavis Smiley, business mogul Russell Simmons, and sports figures Ike Taylor and Marshall Faulk have all either been suspended from their jobs or otherwise had their lives disrupted by accusations of sexual misconduct.[12] That's "accusations," not "convictions"—in other words, they are guilty until proven innocent (and maybe not even then). The left now asserts that any form of contact constitutes unwanted sexual contact. A self-hating male *New York Times* columnist wondered "how all women don't regard all men as monsters to be constantly feared."[13] Maybe it's because, unlike this observer , not all men view themselves as potential predators?

Rape and sexual assault are terrible actions, and those convicted of these crimes should be punished. You don't have to be a Supreme Court justice to grasp that. But the Social Justice Warriors aren't interested in justice and fairness. They are interested in smashing the patriarchy, as they define it. Social Justice Warriors don't even attempt to disguise the fact that a broad, deeply rooted hatred of men underpins what they are doing. One leading feminist man hater believes all men should whip themselves in public displays of penitence while declaring "how they have hurt women in ways great and small."[14] And a *Teen Vogue* writer revealed the left's agenda when she wrote, "If some innocent men's reputations have to take a hit in the process of undoing the patriarchy, that is a price I am absolutely willing to pay."[15]

This radical warrior is willing to pay the price of destroying innocent men's lives. How nice of her, especially since she herself won't suffer at all because of it. Of course, she doesn't believe there are any innocent men. As she also wrote, "false accusations VERY rarely happen, so even bringing it up borders on a derailment tactic."

This is how a new wave of femme-fascists inoculate themselves against any responsibility. In the eyes of the unvogue child writer, there are no innocents.

And her day job is writing for an impressionable teenage audience.

It shouldn't surprise anyone that madness is taking root in our education system. When the University of Rochester didn't immediately place one of its professors in stocks after allegations—allegations!—of "predatory and manipulative behavior," the university's board of trustees received a letter from more than four hundred unaffiliated educators saying they would discourage students from pursuing opportunities at the University of Rochester.[16]

The letter managed to be both hysterical and self-serving, which is more common than most people realize. In this case, if students are discouraged from going to the University of Rochester, they're that much more likely to stay where they are, which helps to keep professors at these institutions employed.

Is this latest movement mass hysteria? It absolutely is. Some Democrats are agreeing with me, as their own loudest left-wing voices—Al Franken, John Conyers, Garrison Keillor, Charlie Rose, the comedian Louis C.K., and many others[17]—are caught up in this madness. Matt Lauer, the darling of morning TV and women viewers nationwide, has proven to be one of the worst offenders. Some of those named, perhaps, will justifiably lose their positions, and perhaps their liberty. However, others may suffer the fate of the bystander in a mass panic.

I have no sympathy for them. Their accusers, the pundits and all who call for their heads, are their children, born out of their own insanity. The left has championed and profited from the victim culture for decades. Now that culture has turned against them.

It is astonishing that flawed, limping nations like Russia and China, like Spain and Greece, have survived for millennia while the United States may face extinction after less than three centuries. I am not a hysteric, and this is not—yet—a hysterical warning. It is a very strong caution. The strength of America is reflected in its great motto, *E pluribus unum,* "Out of many, one." Diversity as a divisive weapon, not as an add-on to the normal growth and development of our country, corrodes the "one." Progressivism masquerading as compassion weakens our ability to nurture the "one." We cannot correct past injustices like slavery, but becoming hysterical about the fact that it happened keeps us looking backward in a punitive way that fractures the "one"—especially when the very pillars of our nation, our brilliant Founding Fathers, are attacked simply because they were white, male, and flawed. No man or woman is perfect. Not even the great ones.

The abolitionist icon Harriet Tubman was a passionate Christian (what would today be called "the religious right") who suffered hallucinations due to an old head wound[18] and regarded them as visions from God. In 2012, the very industry that damns moral corruption presented a play, in Los Angeles, called *The Many Mistresses of Martin Luther King*.[19] The civil rights icon was a philanderer and he also liked his drink. Should we stop celebrating his birthday as a national holiday?

FROM *60 MINUTES* TO SIXTY HOOKERS

For those wondering why President Trump isn't bowing to this madness: I think it is because he, unlike the others, does not have a guilty conscience. Bill Clinton parsed the questions asked because he was guilty. Trump has flatly denied allegations because he isn't.

There have been numerous accusations leveled against Trump in social media, as well as lawsuits that were eventually withdrawn. As of December 2017, thirteen accusers had yet to withdraw their claims. If we are going to treat women the same as men, with names named before they are found guilty, we should let the accusers' names stand as part of the record: Kristin Anderson, Rachel Crooks, Jessica Drake, Jill Harth, Cathy Heller, Ninni Laaksonen, Jessica Leeds, Temple Taggart McDowell, Mindy McGillivray, Jennifer Murphy, Natasha Stoynoff, Karena Virginia, and Summer Zervos.[20]

Some of these accusers are reporters, and you know their feelings about the president. Several are models or actresses, and at least one is a porn star. Many describe the same situation over and over—Trump allegedly backed them against a wall and kissed them, sticking his tongue down their throats. One after another, that is what they say.

The sameness of their claims is made more ludicrous by a well-documented fact: Trump is a germaphobe.[21] He doesn't even like shaking strangers' hands.

People say some of these allegations were made before Trump's presidential aspirations were known—which, in several cases, isn't true, as he first mentioned running during the late 1990s. But regardless of when his political aspirations became apparent, his money and his celebrity were always well known. Trump had been a staple player in the *Forbes* list of richest Americans, as well as a fixture on the gossip pages, for decades. Anyone wanting a shot at instant fame—or Trump's money—would have been motivated to link herself with him.

The flash hysteria of people who are in positions of authority and responsibility is as dangerous, if not more so, than the kind that festers among a crowd and turns them into a mob. Soldiers or the police or any governing authority usually have the wherewithal to stop them. In the past, pamphlets and other media allowed people to become mobilized for good or, in the case of Occupy, for destruction. Now Twitter allows anyone with a raw nerve and a smartphone to hashtag their hysteria for the world to see. We see hysterics—some in positions of power—repeatedly threaten the president of the United States, as Missouri state senator Maria Chappelle-Nadal did when she posted on social media, "I hope Trump is assassinated."[22]

Anti-Trump rants of that caliber, like antipolice tweets from self-impressed college "professors," are the kind of hysteria that people would never hear if the media didn't trumpet them. The hypocrisy of these individuals is a new low in the annals of mass hysteria. It's like the old line, "Whatever he's for, I'm against." A kind of feral madness has consumed half the populace at the mere mention of the name Donald Trump. Ads for roommates specify that Trump-supporters need not apply—a discriminatory practice, the irony of which is lost on these people. If Donald Trump were to cure cancer tomorrow, the left would decry the female and minority doctors he is putting out of work.

There is a large degree of postelection psychosis attached to these reactions. Everyone expected Hillary Clinton to become president and continue the destructive policies of Barack Obama. When that didn't happen, these same people were shocked that, after eight years of a half-Kenyan person of color who aggressively supported the rights of gays, transgenders, smokers like himself, and Muslims, we now had another European-descended, white male in the Oval Office.

The convergence of this lunacy and anti-white-male hate created a perfect storm of mass hysteria that does not permit the application of rational thought. The progressives refused to hear, for example, that they were citing the same electoral process they had demanded the right uphold (when they expected Hillary to dominate it) as the basis for their futile effort to delegitimize the election of Donald Trump. If they couldn't draw that simple, A-to-B conclusion, you can see the problem with more complex reasoning. The left is stuck in the A–B disconnect.

With every passing day, the rhetoric becomes less rooted in rational thought, and today's ugly rhetoric has a way of becoming tomorrow's policy. We need to be on guard against this: just as some on the fringe, far right would suggest mass hysterectomies to control violent feminists, there are those crazies on the left who would deport all whites over the age of sixty to "end racism." No, I am not suggesting there will be mass sterilization of women or deportations of white Americans, but I caution against what would be placed against this extreme background and offered as a moderate position.

The verbal, text, and social media hate— lovingly promulgated by the left-dominated mainstream media—is not only vile, it's lawless. Protected speech does not include death threats against the president and his family—along with other members of government—with the speakers all given a free pass. Yet when Obama was hanged in effigy, once, on private property in Gainesville, Florida, in 2012,[23] the media descended like rats on the perpetrator. The act was condemned. When it comes to Trump, however, the rats hoist the perpetrators on their shoulders and parade them on social media platforms as heroes of free speech and bold thought.

Donald Trump may lack finesse, but these people are obscene. The mass hysteria of Trump hate should not require white men to recalibrate their values, be demonized for their skin color, or be forced to apologize for whatever perceived "privilege" they may possess. White males who are or have been in line with America-first and patriotism should stand as a warning to the rest of America that without a polestar—borders, language, culture—the voices of hate and hysteria will lead us to destruction.

The left-wing, agenda-driven so-called news media is complicit as well. These hysterics are not looking to inform the public. The once-distinguished news program *60 Minutes* contributed to this mania by giving a national forum to a porn star.[24] A broadcast in March 2018 generated viewing parties like we have for the Super Bowl—each of which was a hall of mirrors for anti-Trump hysteria.

For those who missed it, *60 Minutes* staged an unvetted side show, not out of concern for the health of our nation, but solely to enrich the bottom line of CBS. In doing so, they turned away from the crucial issues of our time—the ones where Trump is making a difference. Can you imagine if, during the Cuban Missile Crisis, a prime-time news outlet had chosen to interview John F. Kennedy's mistress Judith Exner, or do a major story called "JFK and RFK Killed Marilyn Monroe Two Months Ago!"? The result might have been nuclear war.

On June 14, 2018, Justice Department inspector general Michael Horowitz released the long-awaited findings on the conduct of the FBI and the Department of Justice regarding their investigation of Hillary Clinton during the 2016 presidential election. Former FBI director James Comey and other agency personnel were excoriated by lawmakers on both sides of the aisle for their zeal in protecting the former Secretary of State, for bias, and for whipping up anti-Trump hysteria. Republican representative Trey Gowdy of South Carolina called it "an alarming and destructive level of animus displayed by top officials at the FBI."[25]

The perpetrators of this unlawful favoritism may yet receive the punishment they deserve. But what about the wreck of a nation they leave behind? The same hysteria-as-distraction phenomenon hangs over us today. Military negotiations with North Korea and economic chess with China could fall by the wayside if the president is distracted or busy defending himself from the opportunists like a stripper. Think it's not possible? If not for Anthony Weiner sexting pictures to an underage girl,[26] the presence of classified emails on his unsecure computer might never have been known. We live in an era when a local pervert like the former congressman can shape a national election.

The historic summit between President Trump and North Korean leader Kim Jong-un has inspired some mass hysteria among both the president's political adversaries and his supporters. My view of this summit is that it was somewhere between Reagan and Chamberlain. Yes, this was a diplomatic breakthrough, but all history shows us is that we must remain vigilant.

Korea has made promises in the past and broken them repeatedly. Kim has signed documents before. In October 1994, Bill Clinton made a speech about a landmark nuclear agreement between the United States and North Korea saying, "This agreement is good for the United States, good for our allies, and good for the safety of the entire world."[27] So, what makes this different?

Well, the leaders are different. Kim Jong-un is not his father, and Donald Trump is not Bill Clinton. Perhaps that can make a difference.

The document they signed said it would work

toward complete denuclearization of the Korean Peninsula in exchange for security guarantees to Kim, including halting military exercises. But it said nothing about human rights abuses, nothing about the tens of thousands of people dying in death camps.

There was another document signed once upon a time by two men: Their names were Neville Chamberlain and Adolf Hitler. The document supposedly secured "peace for our time."[28] Then Hitler invaded Czechoslovakia, Bohemia, and Moravia on his way to taking over Europe.

Trump responded to NBC reporter about calling Kim "very talented," knowing that he's killed family members, citizens, and Otto Warmbier—the American student who tried to steal a poster from a North Korean hotel. Warmbier was arrested, beaten into a coma, and died shortly after his return to the United States[29] Trump said he "is very talented. Anybody that takes over a situation like he did at twenty-six years of age, and is able to run it and run it tough, I don't say it was nice or I don't say anything about it, he ran it—very few people at that age, you can take one out of ten thousand probably couldn't do it."[30]

We need to be careful not to gloss over the death

and starvation of millions of people. The old *New York Times* reporter Walter Duranty famously ignored and denounced reports of famine in Ukraine under Soviet control, and often explained away the brutality of Joseph Stalin, saying it was necessary to implement that system. Stalin loved the coverage he got from Duranty as he ruthlessly imprisoned and killed millions. Duranty even got a Pulitzer for his efforts.[31]

Yes, some reporters asked President Trump about these abuses, to their credit. But Trump's answers were lacking. You can say that's diplomacy, but President Ronald Reagan wasn't afraid to call the Soviet Union an evil empire or tell its then-leader Mikhail Gorbachev to tear down that wall in Berlin.

This is not an average business deal. This is tens of millions of lives on the line. So, while this is a decent first step, these crimes must be addressed, and we need proof that they will stop. We must be more Reagan and less Chamberlain.

Small distractions have a way of creating big results. The left knows this and is not above man-ufacturing little scandals to generate mass hysteria. The news jackals are so interested in showing profit and pushing their liberal agenda that they don't care if the nation falls along with the president. In contrast, China, Russia, Iran, and North Korea are focused on their own well-being.

Freedom of the press is a necessity in an open society. But lurid gossip from the mainstream media is a corruption of what our Founding Fathers intended with the First Amendment. The mainstream media has become not just the repository for fake news, it has turned into the flagship for agenda-driven, tabloid news.

Welcome to American mass hysteria, twenty-first century style.

Before we look back at the origins of mass hysteria in America, I want to discuss an event that took place right on the border of hysteria and legitimate fear. Employees at NASA refer to October 4, 1957, as "Sputnik Night." That was the day the Soviet Union launched Sputnik 1, the first artificial Earth satellite. As Roger D. Launius, a former chief historian at NASA, wrote, "The only appropriate characterization that begins to capture the mood on 5 October involves the use of the word hysteria."[32]

But is that really the only appropriate characterization? True mass hysteria, the kind we talk about in this book, involves an irrational, overwrought action to a false threat—whether, as we will see, it's an enemy who isn't really there, a situation that has been wildly inflated, or a desire for unwarranted attention.

In the case of Sputnik, there was a very real threat. Just a dozen years earlier, the Soviet Union and the United States had been uneasy allies during World War II. After the war, the Soviets began treating the world like it was the board game Risk, with global domination and freedom in the balance. Launching Sputnik, a spy eye in the sky, the Russians suddenly had a very real tactical advantage.

A year earlier, Soviet premier Nikita Khrushchev had told Western diplomats "We will bury you." After Sputnik, that same man boasted that "the United States now sleeps under a Soviet moon."[33] His implied threat was clear: The same missile that had launched Sputnik into orbit would be capable of delivering hydrogen bombs anywhere in the world. Up into space, down onto New York or London or Paris.

America reacted, but not with mass hysteria. We met the challenge head-on with science. Within a year we had replaced the National Advisory Committee for Aeronautics with NASA, the National Aeronautics and Space Administration.[34] Many triumphs in space, as well as technological advances that improved life on Earth, followed. Our reaction was not hysteria but resolve.

It is the same resolve, by the way, that you see now in President Trump's new, invigorated NASA. We are finally, swiftly resuming our role as the pre-eminent nation in space.

As we will see, true mass hysteria rarely has such positive consequences, and this is not the only instance in which the Establishment has falsely labeled legitimate fear of a real threat as mere "mass hysteria." When we discuss mass hysteria, we will often be talking about replacing freedom with an agenda—often a very dangerous one.

3.

MASS HYSTERIA
Anarchy's Secret Weapon

THE MORE THINGS CHANGE...

I have on my desk a copy of the *Connecticut Courant* newspaper from June 1, 1795. On page two is a report from Paris about chaos in the streets. The item was filed at a point during the French Revolution when royalist thugs were attacking revolutionaries. I'm certainly not siding with the revolutionaries, whose bloody, socialist Reign of Terror became the blueprint for violent, left-wing gangs like the Weather Underground in the 1970s and AntiFA today. Nonetheless, the *Courant* article includes this observation about roving gangs who were supporting the brief reign of Louis XVIII: "Is it not evident that they are paid by the villains who wish to overturn the reign of justice and of liberty?"

Plus ça change, plus c'est la même chose.

Fittingly, it was the French who coined that expression, which translates as, *The more things change, the more they stay the same.* More than two centuries later, those same words can be applied to the masked AntiFA marauders who terrorize decent American communities.

There haven't always been anarchists and agitators—but you have to go back to the dawn of human activity to avoid them. When primitive people lived in caves, they couldn't afford to whine about "privilege" or social classes. Everyone in the tribe pulled together, and with sharply defined responsibilities. The stronger young men were hunter-gatherers. The women nursed and cared for children. Identity politics and gender reassignment? I have been around the world and I haven't seen those topics in any cave paintings I've looked at. I *have* seen renderings of what appear to be gods in Paleolithic caves of Lascaux, France, at Ukhahlamba Drakensberg, South Africa, and at Tassili n'Ajjer, Algeria.[1] I doubt anyone objected to the presence of an almighty in their primitive communities.

Up to the dawn of the Bronze Age, circa 3000 B.C., there was no need for anyone to revolt, no call for anarchy. In fact, there wasn't even a word for the concept until the ancient Greeks coined *anarchia* and *anarchos* to describe the absence of rulers.[2] Historians agree the concept was first used in a political sense in the play *Seven Against Thebes* (467 B.C.) by Aeschylus.[3] In that drama, the character Antigone refuses to obey a political order not to bury her apparently traitorous brother Polynices: "I will bury him alone," she said. "Nor am I ashamed to act in defiant opposition to the rulers of the city."[4] Antigone acted with dignity and nobility; as the children of Oedipus, she and Polynices had learned to stand up for what was moral.

However, acting in the name of honor and ethics is rarely the case with anarchists.

The terrorist Guy Fawkes, whose likeness adorns the mask of modern-day anarchists, was a Catholic who helped mount the Gunpowder Plot in England in 1605. The plan was to blow up Parliament and assassinate the Protestant king James I, a scholar for whom the King James Bible was named. When the Catholic Lord Monteagle was advised to stay home that day, he became suspicious and alerted the monarch. King James had the cellars under Parliament searched. The gunpowder was found and the conspirators tracked down. Fawkes confessed under torture and was executed.[5]

Anarchists like Fawkes don't want discourse. They don't want to level the playing field, but rather they seek to destroy it—while hiding behind masks or in the shadows, of course, so they will survive. This is not to say that factions in any society do not have legitimate grievances. Quite often they do. Throughout the history of civilization there has been resentment and often struggle between the aristocracy—those who have had wealth and power handed to them without earning it—and those who by birth are denied even the opportunity to better themselves.

Socialists would eventually warp and pervert this idea into meaning that *everyone* should have the benefits of society handed to them. Thus was born the concept of "class conflict," popularized by Karl Marx in the nineteenth century. In some cases, when the issues involve human rights such as freedom, the conflict is just. One example is the Thracian slave and gladiator Spartacus, who led a revolt against the Roman oligarchy in the 70s B.C. The communists would later co-opt his noble struggle for freedom and dignity into anti-social-structure propaganda.[6]

Spartacus and Guy Fawkes represent the extremes of what are popularly perceived to be just and unjust movements. In America, we have seen those extremes play out within a single generation. Instead of the quest for true, inherent rights like liberty, private property, and the right to be represented in any government claiming jurisdiction over them, violent leftists, militant feminists, radical gays, and black liberationists are now claiming a privilege—the privilege to engage in antisocial behavior and immunity from prosecution for violent and destructive actions during "protests." They co-opted necessary social change and turned it into a power grab, a vendetta, demanding reparations and payback.

They did this by applying the proven technique of "mass hysteria," a tactic that has given us ancient wars and modern holocausts. As daily listeners of *The Savage Nation* know, it has reached a fine assassin's art as billionaire socialists like George Soros use social media and the corrupt, liberal mainstream media to infiltrate legitimate social activities with violent, salaried terrorists.

In this book, we will look at the past to understand how we got here—and where our nation, our world, is headed if we are not vigilant. Even now, we see the likes of New Jersey senator Cory Booker, Massachusetts senator Elizabeth Warren, and media mogul Oprah Winfrey warming up in the Democrat bull pen for 2020. Even Mark Zuckerberg of Facebook is reportedly considering a run, a Trojan horse if ever there was one.[7] His "interest" in protecting illegal immigrants is actually self-interest. Where I live, Bay Area employers are increasingly using the threat of reporting foreign workers who step out of line to immigration authorities. You better believe these employers want an unending stream of undocumented workers: they represent a captive, underpaid workforce for the Silicon Valley overlords, a collection of modern plantation owners.

And what are plantation owners without a future source of cheap labor? During the spring and summer of 2018, the hot-button issue for the left was another bogus one: the separation of children from their parents. Never mind that the entry into our country by *all* of these people was illegal. These rabid bleeding hearts would have us believe their interests were social and compassionate, not political and self-serving.

In my book *Trump's War*, I offered wisdom and warning for Donald Trump as he took on the role as president. I urged President Trump to "make sure GOP doesn't mean Grand Old Party, but Government of the People." Then I implored the president to be cautious of those who claimed to support him, those who alleged to represent the policies he set forth, calling upon the words of Shakespeare, "Et tu, Brute?"

Today, as Republicans join with Democrats to demand an end to separation of families as the illegals cross the border, we see the warning I put forth coming to fruition. Congressional Republicans as well as high-profile conservatives have caved to the emotional outcry championed by the leftist media. Oddly enough, their concern for these children has only come about under the Trump administration, as this practice was largely ignored in the Bush and Obama eras.

In fact, Democrats stalled attempts to stop this practice in 2014, when Senator John Cornyn of Texas introduced a bill to help the inundated Department of Homeland Security as a surge of illegal children reached the border.[8] From there, laws and courts have further complicated the policies for border detentions.

Not only has Congress rejected efforts to remediate these practices, but it has also failed to replace the largest immigrant family detention center, T. Don Hutto, in Taylor, Texas, which was closed in 2009.[9] Since that time, only one family facility has remained open, in Pennsylvania. Our lawmakers have neglected this issue for nearly ten years, and now, when it's politically expedient, they are exploiting these children at all costs.

Yet again, we witness the media, the Democrats,

and even Republicans being persuaded by madness. Public figures are attempting to influence the masses with outrageous statements and exaggerations. Most irresponsible came from former CIA director Michael Hayden as he compared this policy to Nazi Germany. On Twitter he wrote, "Other governments have separated mothers and children," along with a black-and-white photo of the Birkenau concentration camp and death camp in Poland.[10]

As one commenter pointed out, "There were no cafeterias and teachers and video games in the concentration camps of Germany! The kids in our amnesty detention facilities have all of this and more. This is nothing but leftists trying to avoid the real issue of a need for the Democrats to sign on to legislation that will address our immigration laws."[11]

Another found irony in their hypocrisy and wrote, "The National Socialist German Workers Party, AKA Nazi party murdered 6+ million innocent Jews who committed no crimes. The National Socialist American Non-worker AKA Democrat party has slaughtered 60 million innocent babies chopped them up their tiny bodies and sold the parts with the same zeal shown by their ancestors in the SS who pulled gold out of the teeth of their victims. For me the moral outrage from the common useful idiot on the left rings just a touch hollow."[12]

Rather than a logical debate on our nation's policies, we are once again dragged into an emotional hysteria that will undermine our nation's borders. Where we may have been able to deter the wave of illegals trespassing into our nation, our representatives would rather send a signal to the world that we are even more welcoming and inviting to these invaders.

I along with many other Americans would not choose for children to be separated from parents but, then again, we would all choose to live in a world where all parents were responsible, attentive, and caring to their children. Unfortunately, we do not live in such a place.

How is this different from the drug-addicted mother who is sent to rehab or the father sent to prison and whose children are removed by Child Protective Services?

Couldn't we argue that these people are so-called victims, too? Victims of the pharmaceutical companies, victims of their circumstances, and the list could go on from there. It does not override the fact that these parents have made a choice to commit a crime and the decision they have made has consequences for them as well as their children.

Now, some may say that those who are attempting to cross the border are simply doing so as "asylum seekers," but with a 27 percent jump in new applications in 2017 alone,[13] we would be foolish not to recognize that this is simply a ploy to avoid deportation.

It's always about the children. How many of them are being used as fronts for gangs? How many of these kids are bringing in drugs? How many of them are bringing in other contraband under the guise of family separation? Of course, the left ignores this and simply screams in chorus that we must let them all in and not separate children from their parents. Well, that sounds very compassionate on paper. However, we have millions of American people of all races who are poor, broken with nothing, without housing. We have homeless all over the streets of New York, San Francisco, and many other cities. Don't we have an obligation to take care of our homeless before we take care of the Third World's children? You might say, "well, we'll do it all." But we can't do it all. The solution to the border problem is the wall that we were promised.

We must not listen to the hysterics who are screaming that you can't separate children from their families. We must not allow the forces at work to entice us into an emotional compromise. We have to have the guts to stand up and say, "I'm sorry, but the lifeboat is full." We have to take care of our own poor first. When we detain people at the border with or without children, we must say, 'You're going home. We're giving you a care package. We'll give you clothing, but you can't come in the lifeboat; it's full." That's how you stop illegal immigration. That is how you support your national sovereignty and that is how you support your nation's identity.

Now take a step back and ask yourself, why don't the Democrats care about national sovereignty and integrity? Because the agenda of the Democrats and open-borders advocates is now to push to finish the job and make open borders the legal, as opposed to only the de facto, status quo. The reason is simple: millions more illegals means millions of additional reliable votes for Democrats in their plan to make the United States a one-party socialist country, such as what they have achieved in the state of California in less than two decades as the result of the invasion of illegals there, most of whom can now vote.

THE TRUTH WILL OUT

These tsunamis of special interests are already stoking the divide their predecessors created with opportunistic stands on child separations at the border, and with anti-Confederate and pro-drug legislation. It is just a short hop from firing up the base to burning up the Constitution and the rule of law.

If you are new to my books or *The Savage Nation*, understand that while I am a conservative, I am first and, above all, a patriot. And the son of immigrant parents. I was born in the Bronx. My father owned an antique shop and died of a heart attack at age fifty-seven. I put myself through college, became a biologist, a teacher, and then earned advanced degrees in botany and anthropology. I earned my PhD in nutritional ethnomedicine from the University of California. The earliest of my nearly four dozen books were about nutrition and human health.

I turned to radio in 1994 after my manuscript for a book about the correlation between illegal immigration and disease was unable to find a publisher. I was fundamentally a political independent until the increasing and increasingly vocal insanity from the left forced me to "pick a side," as it were. I have often said that liberalism is a mental disorder in that it rejects the essentials of borders, language, and culture as cornerstones of our America. As I did in my earlier works on physical disease, until that political sickness is cured, I will continue to speak out, as I have done for nearly a quarter century.

CROWD PSYCHOLOGY

Mass hysteria—or mass hypnosis—is insidious and stealthy. It falls into two categories. The first is "positive hallucinations or hysteria," when you believe something is real, absent evidence, just because someone says so or it fits your preconceived notions. The second is "negative hallucinations or hysteria,"[14] when you deny the existence of something real, despite overwhelming evidence that it exists. The media and governments exploit both—for example, selling the absurd notion that Russia cost Hillary Clinton the election or denying France and England are crumbling under the weight of Muslim immigration. One is demonstrably untrue, the other demonstrably true. Yet those in denial refuse to accept reality in either case.

You or people you know may be reasonable, sane, logical, and compassionate under most circumstances, but as the word implies, "hysteria" overcomes these qualities. Consider what occurred on October 30, 1938, when the radio anthology series *The Mercury Theatre on the Air* broadcast a dramatization of H. G. Wells's science fiction tale *The War of the Worlds*. The format of the one-hour broadcast was seductive: fake news bulletins inserted in a program of easy-listening music. The reports told about explosions seen on Mars, a spaceship landing in Grover's Mill, New Jersey, and extraterrestrials emerging with a death ray. The account went on to tell of similar landings across the country.

Panic ensued because many listeners believed these stories that were early examples of *fake news*. But it came from a reliable medium in a familiar format, spoken by familiar, trusted voices.[15]

Think about that for a moment. Listeners were driven to panic by a report about *Martians*. That was the stuff of science fiction magazines, of Flash Gordon and Buck Rogers comic strips, of the new Superman comic book stories. Now, people in the New York to Philadelphia corridor were relatively sophisticated in 1938. They read newspapers, subscribed to magazines, listened to the radio. How did this panic happen?

The reality, of course, is that Martians weren't the cause. How could they be? There weren't any. Instead, the panic was caused by otherwise rational people allowing their emotions to overcome their reasons. A century and a half earlier, Founding Father John Adams noted: "Facts are stubborn things; and whatever may be our wishes, our inclinations, or the dictates of our passions, they cannot alter the state of facts and evidence."[16]

Adams spoke those words while defending the soldiers accused of murder after the "bloody massacre," known today as "the Boston Massacre." Most of the soldiers charged were eventually acquitted, thanks to Adams's skillful defense. While undoubtedly a patriot, Adams refused to allow the mass hysteria resulting from the event—partially ginned up by his own cousin, Samuel Adams—to destroy the concept of justice, even if it meant defending King George's soldiers, whose presence in Boston he otherwise objected to.

John Adams was later appalled by the Boston Tea Party, a wanton destruction of private property, despite his political opposition to the way the tax on tea was used to try to control the colonial economy. Most Americans today don't know this, but the objection to the tax on tea was not primarily over lack of representation in Parliament, which the colonists did not even want. It was over the king exempting the East India Company and handpicked colonial importers from paying the tax, thus undercutting colonial smugglers of Dutch tea.[17] Adams agreed with the tea partiers, but not with their methods.

Those examples of colonial mass hysteria provide insight into how a fearful, easily manipulated audience often reacts to demagoguery or self-serving media—even when that media is innocuous. When the *War of the Worlds* broadcast aired, it was heard by an audience that had been primed for hysteria by the German annexations of Austria and parts of Czechoslovakia. Against this reality, there was just enough suspicion among this entertainment program's audience that they were prepared to think it was real. Sadly, with a little skepticism and a twist of the radio dial, they could have discovered there was no reason to panic. But they didn't. A necessary component of mass hysteria is the mob's desire to believe.

The impact of the *War of the Worlds* hysteria was ultimately limited—unlike earlier mass hysterias in our country, such as the Salem Witch Trials of the late 1600s. We'll be looking at these in greater detail, but in the supposedly enlightened colony of Massachusetts, dozens of people—mostly women— were killed during a panic of supposed morality. It was a mindless wave of fear in which anyone who attempted to inject a note of sanity into what the God-fearing public viewed as legal proceedings was viewed either as a witch or sympathetic to witches, and thus became a target for persecution, torture, imprisonment, and death.

The late 1930s and early 1940s were a banner time for these panics. Nathanael West was an American author who lived a tragically short life, dying in 1940 at age thirty-seven, the result of a car crash. A year before his death, West published the brilliant novel *The Day of the Locust*, which is set in and around Hollywood during the Great Depression. In an unforgettable climax, a crowd is gathered outside a Tinseltown movie premiere where a misbehaving boy throws a rock into the face of a simple man named Homer Simpson (yes, Homer Simpson). Homer lashes out at the boy, and the crowd, seeing only that, turns into a destructive mob, believing a pervert has attacked a child and ought to be "lynched." Witnessing all this is artist Tod Hackett, who ends up injured and carried away in an ambulance—unable to differentiate between the siren and his own scream.[18]

That crowd had been turned from reality by a misinterpretation of the truth of the scene. Mob violence—or as the psychiatrists like to whitewash it, "crowd psychology"—is a very short, incendiary step beyond mass hysteria.

Whether it's over witches, outsiders, or even government oppression—some of which is real, don't get me wrong—fear has, again and again, provided the fuel for mass hysteria.

THE SPARK OF HYSTERIA

How does mass hysteria begin?

It starts today with the likes of Sergey Brin and Larry Page of Google, who create algorithms that redirect young people to sites Google thinks they should see. Progressive sites that advance their agenda. The company that fired engineer James Damore for citing evidence that men and women have different aptitudes[19]—a controversial, not hateful idea—will obviously not be promoting balanced viewpoints.

This type of thought manipulation is how you begin to move centrists to the left and leftists to pure madness. Encouraged by Google, people start tuning into leftist television and film "comedians" and actors, many of whom have become Democratic Party jesters. When the seeds have been planted and the mind control begun, the ground is fertile to cultivate mass hysteria. That is how supposedly objective media like the *New York Times* and CNN work. Relying on, *preying* on, the public's short memory—John Q. Stupid forgot or never learned that the real danger is the masses' wishes, inclinations, and passions, as John Adams cautioned—the corrupt mainstream media encourages people to be afraid. Afraid of Trump. Afraid of Russia. Afraid of extreme weather. But they're never encouraged to fear Hillary or Pelosi or Warren or immigrant gangs, forces that serve the left's agenda, although they should.

The blitz from Wolf Blitzer and the rest causes a brutalized, frightened, susceptible public to buy papers, watch TV, and visit websites to see the latest developments in what they've been told they should be worried about. Here's just one example. On August 23, 2017, the Left Coast *Variety* ran this headline:

CEOs, Media Chiefs Aghast Over Trump's Reluctance to Denounce Neo-Nazi Violence[20]

What the liberal mouthpiece failed to mention is what the president said on August 14, which was covered live on C-Span: "We condemn in the strongest possible terms the KKK, neo-Nazis, white supremacists, and other hate groups that are repugnant to everything we hold dear as Americans."[21] In other words, a fake news headline was created, contrary to easily verifiable evidence. It was crafted both to inflame and to solidify a mean and disreputable point of view.

The brainwashing and mass hysteria machine purred on so that bleeding-heart Hollywood would click on that article, nod solemnly, and spread the word, absent any reality check, that President Donald Trump not only supports racism but is himself a white supremacist. Meanwhile, organizations such as the Southern Poverty Law Center exist primarily to label anyone—or any organization—who does not agree with the left's orthodoxy as a hate criminal or hate group. Those institutions of hate generate mass hysteria against those exercising their right to free, peaceful speech.

This steamrolling of facts, this false narrative, this hate-mongering is precisely the technique employed by Hitler and his minister of propaganda, Joseph Goebbels. From Hitler's election as chancellor in January 1933 to the anti-Jewish riot of Kristallnacht, or Night of the Broken Glass, in November 1938, they raised anti-Semitic rhetoric from moderate to fanatical.

Hitler used unwarranted fear to rally Germany

against the Jews. In a September 1942 speech to the Reichstag (the German parliament), he generated fear when he said—repeating a promise he had made in a prewar speech—"If world Jewry launches another war in order to destroy the Aryan nations of Europe, it will not be the Aryan nations that will be destroyed, but the Jews."[22]

Jews did not start World War I. Not even close. Jews weren't even present in many of the tinderboxes, such as the Austria-Hungary annexation of Bosnia and Herzegovina. The Serbian group the Black Hand was responsible for the assassination of Austria's Archduke Ferdinand, not Jews.[23] Hitler employed demonstrably fake news, even though he constantly decried the "lugenpresse" (lying press).[24] But the words came from a voice that was trusted by many Germans during a time of great economic need and suffering, and they were accepted as fact. The words enflamed many otherwise rational people and created hatred against a soft target. Mass hysteria allowed the execution of six million blameless souls.

To reap more latent hate, the Nazis threw Gypsies and homosexuals into the mix. Lest you think history does not repeat itself, Hitler employed the same tactics that were used against the Salem

"witches" in the seventeenth century. We'll be discussing that hysteria later; I mention it now because
in August 1992, at a ceremony commemorating the
three hundredth anniversary of the original "War
on Women," the Witch Trials Memorial in Salem
was fittingly dedicated by one of the most famous
survivors of the Nazi Holocaust, Nobel laureate
Elie Wiesel.[25]

Plus ça change, plus c'est la même chose.

Mass hysteria casts a long shadow of cognitive
dissonance, a state of mind that gives people the
ability to hold conflicting views without realizing
or acknowledging it. This hypocrisy was exem-
plified in the 1970s by lunatic liberals who were
fiercely pro-abortion but ferociously against the
death penalty. Today these same rabid loudmouths
who want to tear down the Confederate flag they
find so offensive proudly parade the gay pride flag,
which others find equally offensive.

These unhinged screamers also demand the
removal of nativity scenes in town squares—even
though they are American traditions—yet march
to defend the "religion of peace" in whose name
our citizens and homeland has been attacked over
and over since the first World Trade Center bombing in 1993. It goes back long before that, if you
count the Barbary Wars of the early 1800s, in

which Muslim pirates seized American merchant ships. The aggressively liberated women who participate in these marches conveniently ignore that in many of the nations dominated by this faith, women are shrouded, denied education, not permitted to drive or be in the company of men who are not their husbands, and are treated like second-class citizens. Gays are thrown off rooftops to their deaths in countries where this religion dominates.

More recently, you may recall an infamous communications professor, a rabble-rouser at the University of Missouri who, while participating in a racial protest—an issue of *rights*—was so caught up in her own tunnel vision, her own grandeur, her own hysteria, that when she was approached by a student journalist making a film, the only thing she could think to do was yell, "I need some muscle over here!"[26] She shut down his First Amendment rights while protesting for *other* rights.

There is a difference between what used to be a college education and what it is today, which is merely college attendance for the purpose of forming like-minded tribes. The danger in that is obvious, but I'll paraphrase the Benjamin Franklin character in the wonderful musical *1776,* anyway. He defended the legality of revolution by saying it's always legal in the first person, as in "our" revolution, but not in the third person, as in "their" revolution. The same is true of free speech on college campuses.

Cognitive dissonance is the lubricant that greases the gears of mass hysteria.

The mainstream media, the megaphones of the left, have embraced one of the basic precepts of brainwashing, articulated by Goebbels himself, who said, "A lie told once remains a lie, but a lie told a thousand times becomes the truth."[27]

Mass hysteria can be triggered by a mistaken interpretation of reality, as in West's novel. It can be launched by destructive design, like the terroristic Occupy movements of 2011. It can be opportunistic, like the looting that masqueraded as racial indignation after the August 2014 shooting of African American Michael Brown by white officer Darren Wilson in Ferguson, Missouri.[28] Or it can be driven entirely by paid hooligans, as was the case in Paris in 1795 and Charlottesville, Virginia, in August 2017, the latter incident perpetrated by AntiFA barbarians, financed by George Soros.[29]

No matter how mob violence comes about, it's an ugly aspect of the human condition. It is generally mindless and formless, failing to distinguish between legitimate enemies and incidental

victims—which differentiates it from the Boston
Tea Party of 1773, which we'll be talking about
more in the next chapter.

Many of you know I am a dog lover. In particular, I am devoted to my canine companion, Teddy,
who is with me in the studio, at dinner, in my car,
on my boat, when I'm shopping, on my regular
walks through my neighborhood—you get the picture. Teddy may nip at my sound engineer's sneak-
ers from time to time, but he is generally peaceful.
I'll say that another way: if all humans were as
even-tempered as Teddy, the world would be a very
serene, loving place.

But people are not like Teddy. This applies in
particular to mass hysteria. Animal behavior-
ists have identified a phenomenon called "terrier
frenzy." The phenomenon supposedly applies specifically to Boston terriers, but I have seen it in Jack
Russells and other terriers as well. In short, an outside stimulus causes the excitable breed to go a little nuts.

In time, the frenzy burns itself off. But if there
are two terriers, the actions of the first will trigger
a similar response in the second. The frenzy of the
second will reignite the first and typically send that
dog into an even greater frenzy. And so it goes until

the two of them have completely lost control. God help you if there are three terriers.

Mass hysteria is like that. It's like an old joke, updated: a hippie, a Millennial, and Hillary Clinton walk into a bar at Trump Tower...

I do not mention Hillary Clinton simply because she's a moderate who has been converted to progressivism, because she was a purveyor of Goebbels-level lies, or because despite those two "surefire" techniques the voters of America sanely rejected her as the forty-fifth president of the United States. The truth is—and the political correctness crowds better avert their eyes and close their minds a little tighter here—women are often prominent in news stories about what we call hysteria, whether perpetrators, victims, or both. The word *hysteria* itself derives from the Greek word for womb, *hysterikos*—whence also *hysterectomy*.[30]

Until World War I, hysteria as a psychoanalytical diagnosis was seen as a women's disorder. That changed when returning soldiers exhibited what was then called "war neurosis" and "shell shock."[31] These conditions resulted from the big artillery battles that hammered entrenched soldiers with unending concussive noise and instability of the ground and walls, resulting in the inability to sleep. Today we call the aftereffects of combat posttraumatic stress disorder (PTSD). The then all-male soldiery with this condition demonstrated overlapping symptoms with the hysteria exhibited predominantly by women.

History is littered with examples of exclusively female hysteria. During the Middle Ages, entire convents fell prey to hysteria, including a sixteenth-century outbreak of meowing nuns in France, and German sisters suddenly biting each other.[32] In 1894, sixty women at a Montreal seminary developed seizures.[33] In 2012, more than a dozen girls in Le Roy, New York, simultaneously began twitching, spasming, and exhibiting identical vocal tics.[34] The psychological waters got muddied when the environmental movement became involved, with activist Erin Brockovich blaming chemicals released during a 1970 train derailment for an increased incidence of cancer. After that, biology was no longer the cause of women's problems. It was evil capitalists in corporate America.

In the Brockovich matter, the truth was much simpler, as it usually is. Once neurologists examined the girls, they concluded that the outbreak was psychological, not physical. It wasn't the result of a toxic spill, but in fact mass hysteria.[35] The problem with that, of course, is that there's no one to blame but yourself. No one to sue.

No boogeyman to make you a victim.

A more recent example of female mass hysteria was the hundreds of thousands of women who felt compelled to march and stomp their feet just one day—one day!—after President Trump had been sworn into office. What were these useful idiots marching against? They couldn't have been marching against his policies...he hadn't enacted any!

No, they weren't marching against any real injustice. They were marching based upon their inclinations and the dictates of their passions. And they were dissonant, dare I say crazy inclinations and passions at that, since who in their right minds could protest what I have been saying for decades are the cornerstones of the American identity: borders, language, and culture? But these women were not in their right minds. They had been told Donald Trump would oppress them and they were primed and willing to believe everything they were told. They were wrong. As I write this, they are wrong. But they're still hammering the same fantasies.

This was modern-day mass hysteria. The number of women marching out of true conviction was minuscule. These women felt compelled by their peers, their coworkers, and their so-called friends to be part of the crowd, part of the mob, to—as the rock group Rush sings—"Be cool or be cast out."

We're going to be returning to this foundational idea of women and hysteria, because history shows that mass panic and groupthink can take root more easily among them. And before any of you says this is sexism, it isn't. It's biology. It's the unique capacity of a woman to mother and nurture.

Remember the day care scare of the 1980s, when every child care operation seemed to have a molester on staff? Who do you think was getting the kids to say they had been touched in a bad way? The fathers? No. As investigation after investigation proved, it was the mothers who needed their kids to be "special" in some way—even if that way was victimhood. Like the girls in Salem who needed attention and parental approval, their kids realized that mommy wouldn't love them unless they said they had been touched inappropriately. As a result, people lost their jobs and had horrible stains on their records. And most of them were innocent.

Again, I am not saying, as Freud once did, that mass hysteria is solely a female condition. He rooted that belief in *Verführungstheorie*, in seduction theory,[36] which suggested repressed memories of sexual abuse were responsible for hysteria. Obviously, women would be the recipients of those unwanted attentions.

However, hundreds of men in 1967 Singapore became convinced there had been an outbreak of *koro*, that their penises were withdrawing into their bodies. They flooded hospitals seeking help. Some even tied pieces of string around their genitals so they could constantly pull their penises back out should they so recede.[37]

It was just an instance of mind over matter, of mass hysteria in the form of hypochondria. This reflected the research conducted at the end of the nineteenth century by the great French neurologist Jean-Martin Charcot, who employed hypnosis to study hysteria in both men and women. He proved that thoughts alone could result in stigmata and other physical symptoms.[38] But at least the penis-challenged men weren't marching with penis hats. At least they weren't attacking cultural institutions. At least they weren't being manipulated by powers greater than themselves. Even the profit-minded hospitals in Singapore at the time weren't interested in starting a Great Koro Scare.

HYSTERIA, VICTIMHOOD, AND TRUE TRAUMA

Fiction, myth, and folklore similarly inform the history of hysteria in its earliest expressions, a mixture of rage and despair, resulting in irrational fits. The Sumerian saga *The Epic of Gilgamesh* dates to roughly 2500 B.C. and is widely considered to be mankind's earliest surviving work of fiction. In it, the titular hero, a great leader and demigod, loses his dear friend Enkidu to disease. Gilgamesh reacts by running wild, driven to mayhem by the thought of his own mortality. What we now call hysteria ensues.

In 1597, William Shakespeare described PTSD in *Romeo and Juliet,* act 1, scene 4, when Mercutio says, of soldiers, "[H]e starts and wakes, / And being thus frighted, swears a prayer or two, / And sleeps again." In Mary Shelley's 1817 novel, *Frankenstein*, the response of scientist Victor Frankenstein to the destructiveness of his monster is increasing hysteria. Victor himself calls his condition "enthusiastic madness," as if well-intentioned zeal can atone for a trail of death.

So, the etymology aside, women and men are both susceptible to mass hysteria. Today, in pursuit of "likes" for their cell phone videos posted on

the Internet, mass hysterics have added the terrorist tactics of fire and destruction to what were once
verbal protests, sit-ins, peaceful marches, and the
like. Unable to persuade with their flawed arguments, they seek to cause fear using flamethrowers,
tossing soda cans filled with concrete, hurling bottles of urine, and of course planting bombs and firing guns. The left is taking up arms, despite their
desire to curb the reach and power of the National
Rifle Association.

Mass hysteria has often changed the course of
history, rarely for the better. To understand the
danger it poses now, we must look back to see how
mass hysteria was spawned, the damage it caused,
and how it was eventually dissipated. Ultimately,
the American system is a masterpiece of self-
policing and self-correction. After the massacre at
My Lai in Vietnam in 1968 or the 1972 break-in
at the Watergate hotel and office complex, we did
not require an outside tribunal to come in and set
things right, as Germany did at the Nuremberg
Trials after World War II. We were able to rely
on our national conscience, enlightened by a free,
objective, and independent press.

That entire system—our system—is now at risk,
and the drift toward disaster must be corrected.

The mass hysteria of special interests, political correctness, Internet memes, and social media tropes must be identified as the partisan, anti-American force it is. It must be called out and stopped, if our republic is to survive.

Mass hysteria is not a new phenomenon. The PC-obsessed universities of today were actually born in the fifteenth century, when unpopular religious and political beliefs were often targeted. The impetus for Christopher Columbus's voyage in 1492 was in part the persecution he suffered for his religious beliefs. The New World he opened was equally hostile to outsiders. In seventeenth-century New England, rival religious factions vied for power by labeling powerless, often foreign women as pawns and then executing the "witches." Then they were burned at the stake. Today, victims are destroyed in Internet "flame wars."

4.

FROM PLYMOUTH ROCK
TO CITY HALL
The Seeds and Blossoms
of Mass Hysteria

Context matters. That's something the Social Justice Warriors (SJWs) who spread mass hysteria *for* this or *against* that either don't understand or choose to ignore. After all, if you admit that Confederates and their descendants are Americans with rights, you can't take it upon yourself to climb a flagpole and rip down the Stars and Bars because it offends *you*. Until the reign of Barack Obama, our nation did not work that way.

That's not even the most egregious example of misguided "justice." In July 2016, a Yale University maintenance worker decided to smash a stained-glass window with a broom handle. Exhibiting a frightening lack of self-control and an

equally frightening level of self-interest, he didn't
care whether anyone would be hurt by the falling
glass: he just was tired of looking at the window,
which depicted a scene of two slaves carrying bales
of cotton.

Yale rightly fired him and pressed charges...
and then rehired him and dropped the charges
after SJWs throughout the nation's college campuses protested.[1] And now this violent man is again
walking among students. That's context.

Before we talk about Christopher Columbus per
se—before anyone talks about any explorer or scientist, artist, or politician—we need to understand
the subject's motivation, background, and environment. Again, as a novelist, I can tell you that
one of the greatest jokes of modern sociopolitical
propaganda is that the kind of basic detail every
reader demands in *fiction*, such as "Why is that
sea captain chasing that white whale?" or "Why is
Dorothy so unhappy in Kansas?", somehow is not
required to be present in real life, in the memes
and tropes and mantras of the left and right. In
other words, fiction has to be more real than reality. That's not surprising: if the mainstream media
had looked carefully and objectively at the back-
story of Barack and Michelle Obama, the Obamas
never would have lived in the White House. If we

give Columbus the courtesy due any historical subject, it would not be possible to manipulate gullible SJWs into upending his statue—or that of Robert E. Lee or anyone else.

As anyone who went to school before the PC police started scrubbing the curricula of anything that some minority might find offensive would know, Columbus sailed from Spain. That nation has always been a hotbed of religious turmoil. In the eleventh century, more than half of Spain, the southern portion, was under Muslim rule and known as the Caliphate of Cordoba. Spain's national hero, Rodrigo Diaz de Vivar—popularly known as El Cid, "The Lord"—participated in the Reconquista, the military retaking of those regions under Muslim rule. The task took more than four hundred years but was completed at last in January 1492. Spain was once again a Catholic nation, both wholly and holy.[2]

In March 1492, six months before Columbus reached the New World, an event took place that was seemingly unrelated to the seaman but was clearly an offshoot of efforts to solidify the Reconquista. Spain's King Ferdinand and Queen Isabella decreed that within four months, all Jews had to leave Spain. Those who had converted to Catholicism, the *Converso*, could stay. The eight hundred thousand Jews who had not were out. Of course, an unknown number of the *Conversos* were attending mass but still secretly practicing Judaism. These people, these human beings, were known as *Marranos*—swine.[3]

There is good evidence that Columbus, whose Spanish name was Cristóbal Colón, was Jewish, possibly a *Marrano*. The evidence is found in the will he signed on March 19, 1506. In it he honored the Jewish custom of leaving a portion of his wealth to the needy. He specifically named a Lisbon Jew as the beneficiary of a portion of his estate. Columbus also earmarked part of his estate to go to a group that was charged with retaking Jerusalem from its Muslim occupiers. And finally, he signed the document with a triangle of marks that appeared on Jewish headstones. Those dots and characters were intended to represent the Kaddish, the Jewish prayer for the deceased.[4]

Though born in what was then the Republic of Genoa before it was part of Italy, Columbus went to sea at the age of ten and built a life for himself as a seaman and trader based in Portugal and Spain. He was married to the daughter of a Portuguese governor. He had two sons who lived in the region. He had local interests, both familial and professional, to protect. He also had a livelihood to expand, and trade with the Indies was a part of that. At that time, the traditional land route, the Silk Road, fell under the domination of the Ottoman Turks, who were intermittently at war with Europe. Merchants then came up with the sea route that was safer—though this so-called Cape Route (named after the Cape of Good Hope in modern-day South Africa) required a long and arduous journey around the African continent. Columbus—who was fluent in Latin—schooled himself in both the Bible and astronomy. His studies gave him the idea that there had to be a quicker way to get to the Indies and back, one that would give his adopted home a trading edge. It would also, perhaps, insulate him by both distance and accolades from Spain's rampant anti-Semitism.

This book is not the place to debate the modern-day furor surrounding Christopher Columbus and the voyage he undertook in 1492. The voices of political correctness won't even let us call it "the discovery of America" any longer, since uncivilized natives were here before the civilized Europeans arrived. Voices of mass hysteria want his statue removed from New York City's Columbus Park and his name removed from the October holiday that bears it—both actions I oppose, by the way. Whatever else may be said of him, Columbus had courage, sailing three tiny vessels west into waters that were uncharted and said to be populated by sea monsters, on a world that many uneducated souls still thought was flat. That alone should be celebrated. In its own way, he set a standard for the ideal of American exceptionalism in which I wholeheartedly believe.

Without ignoring the historic truth of the diseases his crew and those that followed introduced to the defenseless native population—among them, syphilis, measles, smallpox, and influenza—and also, of course, the horrors of slavery, Columbus's enterprise failed in its original goal yet succeeded on a scale he could never have imagined. Columbus's search for a trade route triggered the sixteenth-century colonization of the continent to the north of Hispaniola in the Caribbean, where he had landed.

Let me repeat what I said at the start of this chapter: context matters. The anti-Israeli rhetoric and passions of Barack Obama—a Muslim by virtue of his paternal descent and tradition—helped to fire new waves of anti-Semitism, the most open and vitriolic since the days of Goebbels and Hitler. Neither he nor the critics of Israel have a sense of history. They claim Jews have squatted on Palestinian land that was, in fact, Hebrew land since before the days of Moses. I mention this because the Jews of Spain today are faced with a situation almost identical to that faced by Columbus and the Jews of the fifteenth century. In August 2017, just days after a terror attack in Barcelona killed fourteen and injured more than one hundred others, the chief rabbi of that city gave an interview in which he warned that Spain had become a nexus for Islamic terror.

"I tell my congregants: Don't think we're here for good," Rabbi Meir Bar-Hen said, "and I encourage them to buy property in Israel. This place is lost. Don't repeat the mistake of Algerian Jews, of Venezuelan Jews. Europe is lost." He described the Muslim community in Europe as harboring radicals and terrorists and warned, "It's very difficult to get rid of them. They only get stronger."[5]

The voices who damn Israel, like the tobacco-smooth tones of our chain-smoking, forty-fourth president, Barack Obama, do so knowing that were it to fall, there would be no safe haven for Jews. Though Jews are accustomed to living in diaspora, spread among the nations of the world in communal pockets where tradition, education, and faith are peacefully preserved, it would be easy to find and target them in the modern era. No one wants to see injury caused to the people of Palestine, who are victims themselves—not of Israel but of their own greedy leaders and terrorist fringes. Many are content to work in the Jewish state, where they have always been welcome. But the voices raised against Israel are effectively proposing what I call a soft holocaust: the slow but methodical herding and destruction of the Jews.

Mass hysteria. What Ferdinand and Isabella did in 1492 actually fell short of that benchmark. They were purists, yes, but as monarchs they had the power to simply order Jews to convert, leave, or die. There was no need to win public support. Hitler was different. Hitler told lies in order to obtain a desired result.

There is not a nation on earth that was not founded in warfare and blood. The history of America, its Founding Fathers, its wars, is also not antiseptic. But to those of us who are patriots—no, let me proudly rewrite that as Patriots—the voices of mass hysteria will not discourage our love of country or silence both history and the truth.

IN THE NAME OF GOD...OR THE GODLESS

Religious persecution is often a form of mass hysteria. The war waged by the Third Reich against the Jews is the most extreme example of that. Islamophobia in contemporary America is sporadically that—but not entirely. In Great Britain, nine major cities, including London, have Muslim mayors. That was accomplished with just four million Muslims—a mere sixteenth of the voting population. There are three thousand mosques and more than 130 sharia courts in that nation.[6] At what point do they, or we, have a right to be concerned about what goes on inside mosques that are known to radicalize members? And mosques have an obligation to recognize that people of other faiths have a right to be concerned, since virtually all acts of terror are committed in the name of Islam. When loudspeakers blaring the call to prayer remind citizens in Germany that they are a conquered people—as one mosque has done— legitimate concerns have a way of hardening into mass hysteria.

America may have been opened for colonization as the result of religious persecution in Spain, but it was most definitely populated by people seeking to worship freely. Today, many Godless or—worse— God-hating people openly mock those of us who follow a Judeo-Christian faith. As if their narcissistic, sociopathic diatribes are going to change one single mind. When I was a boy, we began each school day with a standing, hand-over-heart salute to the American flag that was proudly displayed in every classroom. We stood that way as we recited the Pledge of Allegiance and its reference to "one nation, under God"—the kind of act that offends the ungrateful and graceless Colin Kaepernicks of this world, professional football players who are happy to collect huge paychecks courtesy of an American institution but think it's beneath them to stand for the national anthem.

Atheists and their allies in the American Civil Liberties Union (ACLU) seek to crush public displays of religion wherever it takes root, claiming that the Constitution provides for the separation of church and state. Unfortunately for them, the Constitution does no such thing. What the First Amendment actually says is "Congress shall make no law respecting an establishment of religion, or prohibiting the free exercise thereof...." In other words, the government is not permitted to interfere with worship or its doctrines. The Founding Fathers did not want to see the kind of internal and external conflict that occurred in Europe when churches were established and controlled by the government, such as the Church of England. There is nothing in the Constitution that says or even suggests that the Ten Commandments, some of the first laws ever devised to govern growing populations, could not be displayed in a court of law. The antireligious lunatics of the ACLU said that.

There are many millions who believe religion is the ultimate example of mass hysteria. Don't get me wrong. I believe in God. I wrote a book on the subject, *God, Faith, and Reason*. However, organized religion has corrupted the concept of the Almighty. Based on a mythical vision in the last of the ancient Israelites first Judaism, then Christianity and Islam emerged. For the Hindus, religion is expressed as fantastic idols, the Buddhists the image of a portly, naked man-baby. Yet to this day, millions of highly educated, highly conscious people continue to follow and practice the teachings of these and other ritual and personality-based religions.

Millions have died, and others have killed, in the name of one religion or another. Was the mass-murdering communist Karl Marx right when he said, "Religion is the opiate of the masses"?[7]

Which is not to say that religion without government is a good thing. Most Americans do not want to be governed by Muslim sharia law. If someone wants to practice it, among the willing, that is their business and their right. But they cannot—yet—force it upon any American.

We actually started down that path, once. And the result was a deadly fit of mass hysteria.

HYSTERIA AS BULLYING

Famously and historically, the permanent presence of European faiths on the shores of America was begun when a shipload of 102 English Pilgrims—along with thirty crew—departed England following a stop in the port of Plymouth, England. Reaching these shores, they anchored the *Mayflower* off the commemoratively named Plymouth Rock on November 11, 1620. These souls were refugees from England's Anglican Church who felt their religion had gotten too wrapped up in idolatry. The Pilgrims emigrated across the Atlantic, enduring the hardships of a voyage on an aging ship to potentially hostile shores for the sole purpose of establishing a settlement where they could freely practice their own brand of worship.[8]

But there is an interesting subtlety here, one that bred the seeds of future strife. Contrary to popular belief, the Pilgrims did not leave England because they sought religious *freedom*: They came to the New World to establish an order *under their own terms*, one in which anyone who didn't fit in, who defied their Calvinistic mores and morality, could be cast out—or worse. The foundation of their creed—the Bible—gave these fanatics all the guidance they needed to govern. They arrived with what was ultimately to be one of the most insidious ideas to take hold in the New World—that the Bible does not mention juries, and a truly divine society does not need them. Instead, with scripture as a guide, the Pilgrims were free to serve as judges and executioners. Men like William Bradford, a *Mayflower* passenger and Massachusetts governor, were among those who dispensed "justice."[9]

In such a setting, anyone who ran afoul of them didn't stand a chance. And by "running afoul," one can say that a primitive form of racial cleansing and class struggle was in effect: the victims were all misshapen, irreligious, or socially common.

The first recorded example of their unique brand of mass hysteria played out in 1642 in the matter of George Spencer. And it played out in the social media; not the Internet of today, but word of mouth. Mass hysteria on the village level. People discussed the matter in the town square, before and after church, in shops. You know how it is: all it takes is one person to be horrified for everyone to suddenly be equally horrified, afraid of being different or appearing sympathetic to the accused. In Spencer's case, his differences led to being charged with bestiality by a self-righteous populace, charges falsely substantiated by those who wished to ingratiate themselves to officials.[10]

Before any of this had happened, Spencer's very appearance—stooped, balding, with only one eye—made him an easy target for malicious taunting. It's what we'd call bullying today, and which until recently was accepted as a painful, inevitable result of simply being different. But the real root of the slander against him was his unwillingness to attend church, or to read the Bible unless compelled to do so. Twenty-two years previous, *The Mayflower Compact*, the original governing document of the land—which was written and signed by men only—laid out clearly what was expected of settlers. Christian advocacy and practice first and foremost, and the power to arbitrarily make new rules right below it:

> Having undertaken, for the Glory of God, and advancements of the Christian faith and honor of our King and Country, a voyage to plant the first colony in the northern parts of Virginia, do by these presents, solemnly and mutually, in the presence of God, and one another, covenant and combine ourselves together into a civil body politic; for our better ordering, and preservation

and furtherance of the ends aforesaid; and
by virtue hereof to enact, constitute, and
frame, such just and equal laws, ordinances,
acts, constitutions, and offices, from time to
time, as shall be thought most meet and convenient for the general good of the colony;
unto which we promise all due submission
and obedience.[11]

The reference to Virginia had to do with the
ship's original destination, which it was unable to
reach because of rough seas.

Spencer is said to have lived in or around Boston, where he had once been punished with a public flogging for being a thief. He thereafter moved
to the Connecticut colony of New Haven. It was
during his time as a servant to Henry Browning that a panic arose, fueled by those who were
inclined to mistrust or simply dislike Spencer
because of his *appearance*. Browning sold a sow to
John Wakeman, a farmer. The sow gave birth to a
litter of piglets, one of which was misshapen and
had large patches of soft, hairless skin. Most damning of all, the piglet was blind in one eye—and
the blind eye was gray and clouded, much like the
marble Spencer had placed in the socket of his own
missing eye.

That was all the evidence a society prepro-grammed to hate Spencer needed to become hys-terical and bring charges of bestiality against him—in other words, charges that he was the father of the piglet—with accompanying punishment being clearly laid out in Leviticus 20:15: "And if a man lie with a beast, he shall surely be put to death: and ye shall slay the beast."

Spencer was arrested, placed in prison, and told that if he confessed his sins his punishment would be tempered with mercy. This was a lie, of course, but the forty-two-year-old prisoner was no fool. He wanted to live. So he confessed to the charges, though he later denied the confession under oath at his trial, saying he had made it only to appease the magistrate.

At said trial, the skimpy puritanical legal code actually threw a roadblock into his potential con-viction. Under the code, a capital offense—one that would lead to a death sentence—required two witnesses. The accusers had none, the alleged crimes having been committed outside of anyone's view. But the Puritans were not ones to let their own restrictions come in the way of a preordained conviction, and the horrified and brainwashed pub-lic was not about to stand in their way. The Puri-tans decided that Spencer's own confession, though recanted under oath, made him the first witness.

For the second witness they presented the mute piglet itself, in all its hairless, misshapen, one-eyed misery.[12] The guilty verdict was like something out of a Monty Python film:

"How do you know she's a witch?" a magistrate asks the mob.

"She *looks like one*!" is the spirited reply, which is good enough.

Spencer was convicted and executed by hanging. As for the sinful sow, she was killed with a sword.

There were similar trials in New England, though 1642 was a particularly robust year. Perhaps the record holder for such "criminality" was one Thomas Granger, who was said to have had relations with a mare, a cow, two goats, two sheep, two calves, and a turkey. Overwhelmed by the sheer number and diversity of Granger's alleged bestiality, the offended public raised no objections and he was executed.[13]

Tragically, these were hardly isolated incidents of localized hysteria driving aesthetic and religious cleansing, in which the public was eager to be seen as being on the side of the angels—or at least on the side of the powerful clergy. They were so willing to serve *power* that they were willing to accept clearly unreasonable charges, without witnesses. In short, fake news.

Though records of the era are scarce, the New Haven Colony boasted at least one other similar trial in 1647, of another man whose only offense was being a lowly pig-tender for a well-to-do sea captain by the name of Lamberton. This farmworker's right eye protruded, and he suffered from a hernia which forced him to wear a posture-bending "steele trusse," according to court records. Perhaps the man's name made the charges inevitable: it was Thomas Hogg, and he was accused of bestiality by Captain Lamberton's wife, Margaret, because—according to the warrant—one of a sow's two piglets "had a faire & white skinne & head, as Thomas Hoggs is." Fortunately for Hogg, because he did not confess, the threshold for conviction was not met. And he passed a rather unscientific test, petting another sow who did not respond favorably to his touch.[14]

As it turned out, however, the Puritan bestiality trials were was just a warm-up.

We mentioned the Salem Witch Trials earlier, and we'll be returning to them shortly. But the witch hysteria of 1692 wasn't the beginning of the panic in New England. The roots of the New England witch hunt were planted when Alse Young, a forty-seven-year-old woman, was hanged in Hartford, Connecticut, on May 26, 1647.[15]

There is no record of the specific charges against her, or of the trial itself. Only the fact that she was executed as a witch. However, there are a few social and cultural facts that point us in a direction of borderline hysteria against women—possibly propagated by women.

Alse Young had a husband and a daughter but no son. Absent a male child, the woman would have been in line to receive her husband's inheritance should he predecease her. The idea of a woman obtaining property was abhorrent to many landholders. Certainly, neighbors would have been terrified, since Alse's holding land would have lowered the value of theirs. We saw this replicated three centuries later, when black Americans were forbidden to own property in white areas of the South and were discouraged from buying homes in upscale white neighborhoods elsewhere—even in liberal Hollywood. In 1948, superstar singer and jazz pianist Nat King Cole and his family found the word *nigger* burned into their lawn in the exclusive Hancock Park section of Los Angeles. Cole had already been cautioned by the property owners' association that the community did not want "undesirables" in their midst. His response? "Neither do I. And if I see anybody undesirable coming in here, I'll be the first to complain."[16]

Back to Alse Young. It is reasonable that one or two landowners wanted her gone—possibly even her husband—and a solution was obvious. That winter and spring, New England in general and the Connecticut town of Windsor specifically suffered through a severe bout of influenza. All that had to happen was for a rumor to be spread that Alse was a witch and responsible for the disease that killed a high percentage of children, and mass hysteria took root.

Though this charge was unprecedented in America, allegations of witchcraft were common in Europe and were on the rise in England thanks to the Witchcraft Act of 1604. Ostensibly a means of ferreting out witches, it was a way to discourage groups of women from congregating and exchanging ideas that might be injurious to men, such as the notion that a woman might own land. This means of striking fear into the populace was well known to the American Puritans of the time.

Whatever the cause or reasons, the public was roused against Alse Young and, in 1647, she was hanged as the first witch to be charged and executed in the New World. Talk about a nation being hatched with the mark of Cain: supposedly devout people, for reasons that were never supported by fact (since Alse was *not* a witch), allowed the base needs of a few to sway them to a murderous frenzy. But the civil crimes against the family did not end with her death. Thirty years later, Alse's daughter Alice Young Beamon—undoubtedly shadowed by her family's past—was also accused of witchcraft in Springfield, Massachusetts. There is no record of the charges, though we know that Alice escaped her mother's fate and died in 1708 at age sixty-eight.

But witch fever was rife among the populace of New England, the seventeenth-century equivalent of mass hysteria about Russians swaying the 2016 election or the hunt for Confederate statues consuming liberal lunatics in the summer of 2017. Through newspapers, through mails, through travelers, fear and hysteria spread with narcissistic enthusiasm. It was common, at the time, for articles to be reprinted from other newspapers, so witch hysteria offered a chance for a Connecticut journal to become known in Rhode Island. Out-of-colony newspapers might pay for the rights to reprint these stories. Merchants on the way from Hartford to Boston might get free food or lodging if they had a frightening tale to tell. Mail would have to be read aloud to the many who were illiterate, a chance for educated men and a few women to get attention. Make no mistake: The witch hunts were a socially fueled frenzy. The proof of this is that after Alse Young's death in 1647, another ten women throughout New England were randomly executed for witchcraft between 1647 and 1662.[17]

Then there was Ann Glover.[18]

It was 1688, eight years after Glover had come to Boston with her daughter, when she had an argument with Martha Goodwin, the thirteen-year-old daughter of well-to-do John Goodwin. Glover had worked for Goodwin as a washerwoman, and had a reputation for being confrontational with the family. After the dispute, Martha and several other of John Goodwin's six children began exhibiting a variety of unexplainable symptoms, including random pains in their necks and backs, distended tongues, spontaneous vocal outbursts, and occasional loss of control over their bodies. A physician was called in to cure the children. When he failed to do so, he pronounced the condition beyond his superb medical care because, said he, they were "bewitched."

Ann Glover became the scapegoat. She was charged with witchcraft and Boston went mad with hate for her—if not because she was a witch then because she was the next-best thing: a transplanted Catholic from Ireland whose husband had been executed for not renouncing his faith while the couple had been living on a sugar plantation in Barbados. Yes, this story happened in *Boston*. This hysteria continued as late as 1795. When the city's first Roman Catholic bishop arrived, only one percent of New Englanders were Catholic. In Boston, anti-Catholic feelings more than a century before the bishop's arrival were deep and unshakable.

Ann was of lowly birth and lacked any sort of education. Those citizens who would come to be known as the "bluenoses" of Boston (apparently named for a kind of potato)[19] needed no more than that to spread hate about Ann through the community. Before long, everyone *knew* she was guilty. During trial, Ann's lack of anything beyond basic English language skills, compounded by her panic at being arrested, caused her to answer questions with a frenzied gibberish—which was later determined to be her native Irish. By the time prosecutors realized their mistake and found a translator, mass hysteria had done its work. She had already developed an irreversible reputation for speaking in a demonic language. But that was outside the courtroom. Inside, the poor woman's inability to communicate with accusers at her trial was a form of self-incrimination. At one point, prosecutors asked her to recite the Lord's Prayer, which she did—in Latin from the masses of her youth, as well as in Irish. But not in English. No one understood her. Or if they did, they failed to come forward.

Then the big blow was struck. The infamous Cotton Mather, a minister at Boston's North Church, visited Ann during the trial and observed her chanting.[20] When he asked her what she was doing, she responded in her broken English that she was speaking to "spirits," which Mather interpreted, and later disseminated, as a confession that she was communing with the Devil. What Glover was actually doing, no doubt, was praying in Irish to the Catholic saints she remembered from her childhood. Praying for them to help her, since no one else would help her.

There was more such "evidence," of course. Two men who claimed to speak Irish said Ann had confessed in her native tongue, and their testimony was never challenged. A search of her residence turned up a collection of dolls—which would have been appropriate for a mother who had a daughter around the ages of the children of her employer. Obviously, she had used those to cast some voodoo-style enchantment over the Goodwin children.

As if the outcome were ever in doubt, Ann was found guilty and hanged on November 16, 1688.

Ann's legacy, however, extended well beyond the grave. Cotton Mather distributed his book *Memorable Providences Related to Witchcrafts and Possessions* in 1689. In it he used the case of Ann Glover to codify the guidelines that would characterize additional accusations, including those four years later in Salem, Massachusetts. When the state stopped killing witches, Mather turned to "curing" them, what one might describe as the "gay conversion therapy" of its day.

Mather's book was fake news at its destructive best, and, like the fake news of today, it had very serious consequences.

GROUPTHINK AND OUT-GROUPS

Psychiatrist Carl Jung believed that it takes a hysteric to cause hysteria. He wrote that, in both perpetrator and victim, "a constant tendency to make himself interesting and produce an impression is a basic feature of the hysteric. The corollary of this is his proverbial suggestibility, his proneness to another person's influence."

There is a subtle difference between that concept, hysteria, and the insidious practice of "groupthink." The idea was first named by author George Orwell in his prescient masterpiece *1984*. The term *groupthink* was co-opted by the psychological community in the early 1950s to describe a group for which the need for conformity and concord is so strong members will make decisions they know are wrong in order to achieve it. If you don't like a movie, but others do, you may very well say you do to avoid being seen as stupid, to avoid contentious debate. Others will do the same about different topics. For example, when ESPN decided that announcer Robert Lee should miss a broadcast because he had the same name as the suddenly toxic Civil War general,[21] they really weren't concerned about rioting if he did a play-by-play. No living human, not even the least educated among the Social Justice Warriors, would ever have mistaken that young man for someone who has been dead since 1870. What the network was doing, by this act, was "virtue signaling." They were participating in leftist groupthink by letting the viewers and the world know that they did not support the Confederacy or its die-hard supporters.

Under groupthink, personal opinions, essential points of view, even questions are no longer welcome. The result is a so-called in-group that feels it can do no wrong and is impervious to outside criticism. Moreover, it feels both justified and moral in attacking any "out-group."

The difference between groupthink and mass hysteria is time. The former takes awhile to congeal. The latter can happen overnight. Groupthink among the Nazi hierarchy produced a policy of anti-Semitism. Mass hysteria among the populace enabled the Holocaust.

More recently, groupthink allowed the press and nearly half the electorate to speak no ill of Barack Obama and to speak calumnies of out-group members like myself for pointing out his grave and divisive shortcomings. Groupthink has given free passes to countless figures in recent history, finding no flaws in everyone from the now-sainted Princess Diana to Muhammad Ali. It only takes a few highbrow art dealers or critics to elevate the ordinary to the extraordinary, such as the pour-and-dribble-paintings of a Jackson Pollock or the blown-up comic book panels of a Roy Lichtenstein. How many film critics did it take to elevate the box-office flop *Citizen Kane* to the greatest movie of all time? Essentially, one. *New Yorker* magazine film critic Pauline Kael achieved that with her 1971 book, *Raising Kane*,[22] and all the other critics followed suit. Just thirteen years before, at the Brussels World's Fair, critics agreed that the honor belonged to Sergei Eisenstein's silent Russian Revolution masterpiece *Battleship Potemkin*.[23] The movies hadn't changed. Only the groupthink did.

Groupthink and mass hysteria dominate college campuses where conservative or traditionalist voices are silenced by shrill professors, shouting mobs, and now violence. In August 2017, Berkeley, California, mayor Jesse Arreguin told my hometown newspaper, the *San Francisco Chronicle*, that he urged the University of California's flagship school to cancel a late-September free-speech forum by conservatives. His reason? "I'm very concerned about . . . right-wing speakers coming to the Berkeley campus," he told the paper, "because it's just a target for black bloc [*sic*] to come out and commit mayhem on the Berkeley campus and have that potentially spill out on the street."[24] Rather than protect the rights of the out-group students who invited them, Arreguin would rather gut our Constitution.

Incidentally, Orwell also coined the term "newspeak" in *1984* to indicate a form of controlled speech designed to inhibit thought. That's been on the rise, too, especially in the corrupt mass media. As I write this, the Associated Press, a once-reliable news source, has shifted from using the phrase "illegal aliens" to the flatly incorrect "undocumented citizens." By no law of the land, by no possible progressive distortion of reality, are illegal aliens "citizens." This is the level of idiocy that clear-headed men and women must deal with.

Whether it was Cotton Mather on witches,

Hitler on Jews, or Barack Obama on American exceptionalism—remember his "You didn't build that" speech in July 2012?—mass hysterics do one thing more that Jung did not mention. They frequently use hysteria for one of two ends: to turn attention from their too-slow or utterly failed policies, or to pave the way for an even greater atrocity. For example, anti-Semitism was the catalyst that Hitler used to rouse German nationalism and force-feed war down the throats of a people for whom World War I was still a painful memory. Obama crafted racial tension to turn attention from catastrophic economic policies, inept and disastrous foreign policy, and to open the door to placating social engineering policies such as Obamacare and gay marriage.

Pertinent to the history we have examined thus far, we presently have a hysteric serving as the mayor of New York City. With more homeless than ever living in the streets of the city; with disgusted police literally turning their backs on His Honor-less after being shackled by mayoral distaste for law and order that protects the status quo; with open contempt for parades that honor traditional European values—for instance, St. Patrick's Day and Columbus Day—the raging communist Bill De Blasio has fully embraced the tactics of hysteria.

Rather than fix problems or repair broken relationships, in August 2017 he formed a task force to root out statues and street names that might be offensive to a minority of New York City citizens. (I wonder when this lunatic will decide to curtail the city's annual 9/11 commemoration since some Muslims may find it insensitive. Mark my words, that's coming.)

On his list of targets was the statue of Christopher Columbus in Columbus Circle at the foot of Central Park, an icon gifted to the city in 1890 by *legal* Italian immigrants,[25] and Grant's Tomb. What was the crime committed by General Ulysses S. Grant, the man who defeated General Robert E. Lee whose statues offend so many, the Union leader who *won* the Civil War against the slaveholding Confederates? Grant had condemned Southern Jews who were smuggling cotton to the North during the Civil War. Grant later regretted his statements.[26]

No one would agree that this statement is true now. Today, America is a country of white men, white women, black men, black women, Hispanic men, Hispanic women, Asian men, Asian women— you get the picture. But 150 years ago, the United States *was* still a country run by white men. That's a historic fact. Hence the 1868 Democrat Party slogan "Let white men rule."[27] Politicians play to their base or they become ex-politicians. De Blasio did not complain when either of the Obamas slammed whites. Remember when Barack Obama made the incendiary comment, "If I had a son, he'd look like Trayvon,"[28] referring to the black teenager shot in 2012 during a confrontation with neighborhood watch volunteer George Zimmerman—who was later acquitted of second-degree murder? Remember when Michelle Obama said, during the ascendency of her incompetent husband during the 2008 presidential race, "For the first time in my adult life, I am really proud of my country"?[29] De Blasio didn't bat an eye.

De Blasio probably believes the utter nonsense he's spewing, but in defacing or entirely rewriting history—following in the footsteps of the Nazis, Stalin, and the Iranian ayatollahs, to name just a few—he displays his own hysterical nature while fueling mass hysteria in others. It is fair to say that many New York youths know nothing about Columbus or Grant other than what may—*may*—be mentioned in the schools controlled by bitter, contemptuous liberals, which is that these two older Caucasian men were both ruthless conquerors and white supremacists. That is a moronic simplification and distortion of the facts. But remember what Goebbels said: Facts don't matter. All that matters is the lie, repeated over and over.

My observations here are not solely political. They do not just reflect my natural distaste for anti-American rhetoric and the politicians who opportunistically wield it to whip up, but not help, the underprivileged or suffering members of their base. If anything, I should be grateful to these ham-fisted officials for simultaneously alienating a large swath of the electorate, like Italian Americans who revere Columbus or older whites who do not happen to be former hippies and who *do* understand the world in which Ulysses S. Grant lived. The De Blasios of the nation, of the world, go out of their way to try to make those of us who are not "of color" hate ourselves and be ashamed of our past. It is a new application of mass hysteria, not focused on the "other," like witches or Jews, but on the "self." Do you know the name Sherrod Brown, Democratic senator from Ohio? How about David Howard, former staff member to Washington, D.C., mayor Anthony Williams? Maybe Stephanie Bell, a fourth-grade teacher in Wilmington, North Carolina? Each of these people was chastised—or, in the case of Howard, asked to resign—for using the English word *niggardly*, which means "stingy," and which comes from the Old Norse word *hnøggr*,[30] and has nothing at all to do with the word that blacks find offensive, other than when they use it among themselves as a term of endearment or fraternity. The hysteria foisted by the uneducated upon the educated is upon us and is proliferating.

Modern De Blasio–style mass hysteria actually embraces a return to the discredited fourteenth-century concept of self-flagellation, which was practiced by extremists in the Catholic Church. Monks, priests, and other adherents would whip themselves in order to beat to death whatever sin was within them. The church eventually banned this practice, preferring the more genteel fasting as a form of atonement and purification. Don't expect politicians to do the same. Aging white baby boomers still vote, still give campaign donations, and, as they watch their grandkids struggle in the aftermath of the Obama-sustained recession, they can be guilted into accepting blame for the nation and the race that supposedly spawned this crisis. While writing this section, I saw a photo online of the seventy-seven-year-old actor Sir Patrick Stewart—a British citizen who made his fortune in America, in the *Star Trek: The Next Generation* TV series and films—holding a sign that said, "People will not listen unless you are an old white man, so I'm an old white man and I will use that to help people who need it."[31] After Donald Trump's election as president, Sir Patrick also applied for U.S. citizenship to "fight" him. That was his word, mind you. *"Fight."* A combative, violence-inducing word chosen to roil those who haven't the wit to distinguish him from the benign, high-minded captain he played in *Star Trek*. I also saw a photograph of the two white stars of *The X-Files* "taking a knee" in support of NFL protesters.[32] If "the truth is out there," as the show says, don't count on these two self-important stars to find it.

Causing mass hysteria in the name of a fictional hero. Maybe Sir Patrick read *Ripley's Believe it or Not*, too. We have a modern-day Daniel de Bouchet, donning the armor of St. George to cause hysteria—not among the opposition but among his followers. Like De Blasio, he is not sowing frenzy among the enemy but among his slavish fans.

It will come as absolutely no surprise that Sir Patrick lives in a borough of De Blasio's city. And both of them should be careful what they wish for. One hundred years hence, when white people are a minority and no longer welcomed at all in history books, both of those men will disappear, just like the towering figures they seek to erase.

In the summer of 2017, I coined a phrase, "Enemies without Enmity." The origin of that phrase was in a story I heard about a German tank commander who obliterated a British position during World War II. Finding just one Allied survivor, the Axis officer took him aboard and delivered him from the battlefield. Though the two forces were at war, these two men were not. The hysteric cannot afford to embrace that quality. President Trump invokes the idea when he talks about America being for all Americans, even those with whom he disagrees. He is sending a signal from the top that we should all try to be "Enemies without Enmity." This acknowledgment of differences was something Barack Obama never even attempted.

The journey in America from mass hysteria toward a group to mass hysteria directed at oneself was an evolution, one that was centuries in the making. And the first stirrings of this occurred in an event I mentioned in the introduction—the abomination that has come to be known as the Salem Witch Trials.

Today's youth are the targets and cause of campus progressives. Children have always been victims of manipulation. The testimony of children was used against the supposed witches in Salem, Massachusetts. Children are the ones whose minds are being anesthetized and destroyed by drugs, including pot. Throughout history, those who perpetrated hysteria are immune from the consequences. The essential question our nation has been forced to ask, over and over, is: Who is pulling the strings and why?

5.

FROM SALEM TO CNN
How Hysteria Taught us to Anesthetize Ourselves

We are at risk of returning to this medieval state as we allow the corrupted mainstream press and agenda-driven agitators to gain control of sections of the population. How is the nation's best interest served when the self-serving, New York race-baiter Al Sharpton calls for federal defunding of the Jefferson Memorial? He complained on TV that his tax dollars should not have to pay for a man with "that kind of background." This from a man whose background includes vocal visible support for fifteen-year-old Tawana Brawley from Wappingers Falls, New York, who in 1987 lied and claimed she was raped by several white men, police officers among them.[1] Sharpton was joined by those other pillars of the black community, the racist Nation of Islam head Louis Farrakhan, and that famed booster of women's rights, Bill Cosby. Together with a complicit media, they whipped up blind frenzy, mass hysteria—all of it based on a lie. Brawley later converted to Islam, changed her name, became a nurse, and moved to Virginia. Though Sharpton lost all credibility for his rush to judgment, he continues to do now what he did then: spread mass hysteria that elevates him in the eyes of his community. Like the inhabitants of seventeenth-century villages, people hear him speak with authority about subjects in which he has absolutely no objectivity...yet they cheer and follow and call for blood. Today it's mass hysteria raised against one of the towering figures of American history.

Do I have to school anyone on the background of Thomas Jefferson—a flawed man, yes; a slaveholder, yes; but the author of the Declaration of Independence and a man who, at great personal risk, helped to found this nation, a nation in which Sharpton lives quite comfortably? The idea that we should erase large swaths of our history because the men and women who made it weren't completely devoid of flaws is one of the more insane examples of mass hysteria I've even come across. Nothing and nobody is perfect: not Thomas Jefferson and

certainly not Al Sharpton. And no political platform will ever please 100 percent of the population.

I don't like that my tax dollars are continuing
to fund a land war in Afghanistan. A lot of people who read my books, who call into my radio
show, don't like the fact that our tax dollars pay to
help the members of Rev. Sharpton's congregation.
They didn't like the fact that Barack Obama was
okay with allowing tax dollars to fund the surgery
of transgender individuals serving in the military,
a policy reversed by President Trump. But they're
not calling for Sharpton's or Obama's memory to
be erased from the history books.

This is why primaries and elections are held,
because this nation isn't about just *us*, whoever that
"us" happens to be. I would add that it's a good
thing our nominating and election process takes so
long. In most cases, mass hysteria burns off under
the scrutiny of leaders with moral character and
a responsible press. An honorable grand jury and
legitimate journalists were the ones who exposed
Tawana Brawley as a fraud—not Al Sharpton.

This nation is about everyone living legally
within our borders, a lesson Sharpton apparently
never learned. Apparently, during those dozens
of visits he made to the Obama White House to
"counsel" the president on race relations, no one

ever tapped Rev. Sharpton on the shoulder and reminded him that this is a nation of "all," not of "Al."

Unity is not a word in the vocabulary of the Al Sharptons of this nation. It is not a message the mainstream media wishes to promote. In 1776, when the so-called "free" colonies forged a nation with the "slave" colonies, they knew they were making a pact with a devilish practice. John Adams, Benjamin Franklin, Continental Congress president John Hancock, and the other members of the Continental Congress were not stupid. They understood the hypocrisy of the words in their Declaration, that "all men are created equal." Many recognized that slavery and second-class citizenship for women could not be reconciled under that document. But if they were ever to be free of the tyranny of Great Britain, they understood the need for compromise. Perhaps independence-advocate Adams grasped that better than most, since he left his farm in Braintree, Massachusetts, in the care of his wife, Abigail. Their unbroken correspondence gave Adams the courage he needed to continue his uphill battle to persuade his fellow members of Congress. In fact, though she later scaled back her own rhetoric, the future second first lady of the United States may have set the tone for today's civil disobedience when she cautioned her husband in one letter, "If particular care and attention is not paid to the Ladies we are determined to foment a Rebellion, and will not hold ourselves bound by any Laws in which we have no voice, or Representation."[2] The difference, of course, is that Abigail was an educated, traveled woman, one who stood up for the rights of *all* people. Personally enrolling a young black boy in a local school, she crushed the objections of some by stating, "merely because his Face is Black, is he to be denied instruction? How is he to be qualified to procure a livelihood?"[3] No further complaints were heard.

There was no hysteria in Braintree and there was never any mass hysteria to the south in Philadelphia, in Congress—not then. There was heartfelt debate, reason, and compromise. That is how progress is made. It is a skill we have lost, a concept on which the media and the demagogues and their constituents have willfully turned their backs, and we are poorer for it. As a result of them putting self-interest ahead of the national good, cities like Ferguson and Charlottesville burn—just as women did when subjected to mass hysteria in the seventeenth century.

The art and craft of the mass hysteric has been refined to a high degree. The approach is to exploit an existing weakness or predisposition among the target group. If blacks feel oppressed by whites, fan those flames. If whites feel threatened by people of color, stoke those resentments. If progressives feel threatened by any religion except the one they *should* fear, then rally round the mosque. If gays feel a bias against them, highlight that insecurity by picking on a single bakery that won't make a wedding cake instead of the countless others that will.

It is a noxious tactic that refutes the wishes of the American citizen. In the late summer 2017, a Rasmussen Reports national telephone and online survey found that fully 85 percent of American adults believed honoring the constitutional right of free speech was more important than protecting the snowflakes who might be offended by what is being said. A slender 8 percent believed it was more important not to give offense.[4] No sane American can disagree with those sentiments.

THE DEVIL IN THE NEW WORLD

It's fascinating to me that a culture that once feared witches enough to put them to death has done a 180-degree turn. Over the last hundred years, they are best known as figures of entertainment in movies such as *The Wizard of Oz* and the television series *Bewitched.* Zombies and ghosts appear far too frequently in today's entertainment. But witches have been rehabilitated by a name change: The ladies who were once executed as witches are now respected as practitioners of Wicca, pagan witchcraft. They embrace both atheistic and pantheistic beliefs and work their magic through various rituals and tools such as candles, knives, incense—basically, all the things you'd expect to see in a pagan pantry. It's harmless at worst, a fascinating anthropological study at best. On the road to earning my PhD I earned my first master's degree in anthropology in 1972. In my scientific investigations I encountered many religious and quasi-religious practices around the world that were based on minerals, flora, and other earth-related elements. The practitioners were generally quite dedicated to their beliefs, and I never found any of it either classically threatening or as broad and comical as in the movies or on TV. I think one of the most vocal proponents of witchcraft in the mid-twentieth century, Sybil Leek, was right when she said, "All human beings have magic in them."

It is more than just our relatively enlightened times that allow us to embrace the different faces of witchcraft. Most people are still afraid of the dark, and under the right circumstances even a highly educated person would be afraid to walk alone through a graveyard. The difference between the seventeenth century and today is that power was invested in a handful of centralized voices, typically the clergy or magistrates. Those figures spoke for God and governors.

Salem Witch Trials is the name given to events that occurred in a string of New England towns from February 1692 to May 1693.[5] The cases were all tried in a Salem town court created by Governor William Phips.

Why was a special court necessary?

For decades, the Puritan colonies were effectively a theocracy. The Bible was law, and the interpretation of Scripture was controlled by a few men. We have seen in our own time how such systems can be triggered and corrupted by greed and/or sex. One need only look at ISIS to see how dogma was used to acquire oil profit, sex slaves, and also to murder and maim nonbelievers. Wherever the ISIS barbarians went, videos chronicled their abuses to spread fear and mass hysteria: conform or die, horribly. When you create a situation of mass hysteria, and people cannot get away—as we saw with ISIS—the result is utter submission. Against all reason, the citizenry will do what you tell them. The terrorists flourished, not just abroad but on our shores in the person of lone-wolf killers. And if that situation seems to pose an obvious response—stop the monsters—think about how little was done against ISIS during the Obama administration. Even the media was complicit in Obama's Islamophilia, providing scant reporting on the ISIS atrocities, the mass rapes of innocent Christian girls, for example.

Now try to imagine yourself a hardworking, God-fearing New Englander of that era, one who had lived his entire life in a single community. Life was a constant misery since you and your family were frequently ill, not only with minor maladies but with diphtheria, dysentery, yellow fever, smallpox, and polio. In response, your church taught that the fitness of the soul was more important than the health of the body. You were most likely illiterate: according to estimates, only 30 percent of the population could read, with the figures slightly lower for women than for men. Outside religions were a mystery and a terror. The only Jew known to be living in the entire northern region of the continent during that time was Solomon Franco from Holland. He came to Boston in 1649, but his stay was brief: there was a dispute over monies owed to the merchant he represented, and Franco was booted out. Quakers, Anabaptists, and other Christians were generally not tolerated, and I have not been able to find any Muslims on these shores during that period.

Given a very cloistered life of constant hardship, how quickly would local villagers toe the line when men of learning and power spoke to them with authority, especially when that authority came not from a king but from God?

Now flip the coin. Among those leaders, it is impossible to know how many colonial leaders actually believed in the faith-based guidelines they professed to their congregations...and under which they committed their atrocities. I suspect that for many there were very strong core beliefs that drove them to seek out witches. Keep in mind, to many of these people the Devil and his minions were every bit as real as God and his Heavenly Host. Indeed, it would be counterintuitive to believe in one without giving some credence to the other. But it is also clear that many behaved the way they did...though the impending loss of power and local property issues no doubt factored into the trials, just as they did in Connecticut.

A REAL WAR AGAINST WOMEN

In 1692, the foremost Social Justice Warrior of the era was someone I mentioned earlier, Cotton Mather, who had a hand in the earlier witch trials. By modern standards, the well-educated Mather was surprisingly young to have gained the prominence and wield the influence he did. At the time of the first Salem Witch Trials, he was not yet thirty. But Cotton Mather had been ahead of his peers for most of his life: He graduated from Harvard College in 1678, at the age of fifteen. By the time he was twenty-three, he had been named pastor of Boston's North Church.[6]

Mather was a gifted and charismatic orator, combining a measured vocal tone with vivid rhetoric and fantastic images of corruption and damnation. Had he merely stayed with the North Church as its minister, he would be remembered today as a relatively enlightened church leader. But when the Salem Witch Trials began, Mather moved from being the peripheral voice he had been in Boston to a highly influential figure in Salem.

The hysteria against witches in the Salem region was fomented in an environment of economic and sociopolitical turmoil. Three years earlier, the English monarchs William and Mary had begun a war against France in America. It was known as King William's War, and for nine years it was waged largely in upstate New York, Nova Scotia, and Quebec.[7] The conflict sent countless refugees south, many of them to Salem Village. The needs of these outsiders were many and their resources were few, and they exacerbated preexisting tensions between the port city's wealthy merchants and the less affluent farmers. The Puritans had a simple explanation for all the strife: It was the work of the Devil. And the Devil had a favorite target.

The minister of Salem Village was the strict, pious Rev. Samuel Parris, who had a son, Thomas, and two daughters, ages eleven and nine. In January 1692, the girls began having tantrums—"fits," as they were called at the time. They threw objects, screamed, made strange noises, and twisted themselves into bizarre positions. As with John Goodwin's children in Connecticut, a doctor was summoned. And once again unable to cure the girls, the physician pronounced the ailment to be demonic in nature. When another local girl, eleven-year-old Ann Putnam, began behaving in a similar fashion, a pair of magistrates demanded that the young ladies name the source of their bewitchment. On February 29, under pressure, the girls identified three women: Sarah Osbourn (also Osborne), an elderly woman living in poverty; Sarah Good, a pregnant beggar woman; and the Parrises' Caribbean slave, Tituba. Conveniently and predictably, two of them were among the rabble that authorities did not want in their town. Good and Osbourn professed their innocence to no avail, and so did Tituba at first. Though slaves were rare in the region, she had been with Rev. Parris for fourteen years and she loved the Parris children, for whom she was largely responsible. But Parris whipped her into confessing, promising to secure her release if she did. The poor woman admitted to the magistrates that "[t]he Devil came to me and bid me serve him," and added that she was not the only local witch wanting to harm the Puritans. She also informed them that she had in fact baked a "witch cake" from rye and urine with which she gave the family dog, just in case the pet was a "familiar" or helper of a local witch.

The three women were imprisoned the next day; despite his promise, Parris bowed to political expediency and allowed the slave to remain behind bars. It would be late spring before the governor finally convened the Special Court of Oyer and Terminer.

As soon as the women were imprisoned, the Salem authorities undertook a program we know all too well: the art of distraction. If there were problems between the merchants and farmers, if there were challenges to the local theocracy, then leaders must create a diversion, an event that would dominate what passed for a news cycle in 1692— and that was witches, right in their midst. Tituba

had said there were others; the word was spread
that they had to be found. Using the tactics of mass
hysteria and paranoia, Europe had purged itself of
tens of thousands of undesirables that way. Salem
and its environs had to do the same.

As with so many things, one can hold the media
partly responsible for the hysteria. In this case, one
of the sources of fake news of the time was Cotton Mather's 1689 book, *Memorable Providences,
Relating to Witchcrafts and Possessions*.[8] The events
described in Mather's book charted the course for
the Salem Witch Trials. Many of the shocking cases
cited in that book began with children's behavior.
In 1692, much like today, a lurid fake story was
destined to be passed around far more quickly
than a calmly reasoned, and less sensational, factual discourse. Once the idea had been set in the
public's mind, there was no shaking it. A book by
the respected clergyman, and the odd behavior of
the three local children, were a match quite literally
made in heaven.

As news of the arrests and of the children's
behavior spread through the town of some six hundred citizens, parents may have realized they had
an opportunity to settle old scores under the guise
of witchcraft accusations.

While the hysteria gathered force throughout

the early spring, the numbers of those accused continued to grow. By the end of May, more than sixty people were jailed and awaiting trial. That was when the governor was finally forced to establish his Special Court of Oyer and Terminer.

On June 10, that institution hanged its first victim, Bridget Bishop—a brassy widow whose late husband had run an inn. She was apparently accused of no crime in particular other than that she was a soft target. The woman was known for playing shuffleboard and wearing red clothing, which was considered to signify sexual yearning and prowess.[9]

Meanwhile, Mather wasn't done writing. His words continued to fan hysteria. After Bishop's death, the court was temporarily suspended and a group of Boston ministers were asked for guidance. Mather, who drafted the group's response, had an opportunity to inject some coolheadedness into the proceedings.

He didn't. Instead, putting his agenda ahead of justice, he crafted the equivalent of fake news and contributed his own call to arms to the court, writing, "we cannot but humbly recommend unto the government, the speedy and vigorous prosecution of such as have rendered themselves obnoxious, according to the direction given in the laws of God, and the wholesome Statutes of the English nation, for the detection of witchcrafts."[10]

At the peak of the hysteria, few citizens, regardless of their standing, were immune from accusation. Martha Corey, a member in good standing of Salem Village's church, came under suspicion when she bravely voiced concerns about the truth of the young girls' accusations. At Corey's trial, some of her accusers began mimicking her actions and claiming they were under her control. She was found guilty and hanged on September 22. Her husband, Giles, who had sought to defend her against the allegations, had been crushed to death under a pile of stones three days earlier.[11]

Dorothy (also Dorcas) Good was another early defendant: the testimony of the four-year-old implicated both herself and her mother (a non-churchgoer whom Dorothy swore she had seen interacting with the Devil). Dorothy was released from prison on December 10, 1692, without being charged. Her mother, however, had been hanged five months earlier, on July 29.[12]

Taking a moral stance against the hysteria was dangerous. Dudley Bradstreet, nearby Andover's justice of the peace, issued thirty warrants related to witchcraft between July 15 and September 7. After writing out eighteen on a single day, he refused to grant any more arrest warrants—and was promptly accused of killing nine people through witchcraft himself. Bradstreet took the charges so seriously he fled the region.[13]

Ironically but fittingly, the end of the hysteria was inadvertently brought about by Cotton Mather. In September 1692, he requested records from approximately a dozen trials of individuals condemned for witchcraft. He incorporated these into his book, *Wonders of the Invisible World*, which he presented to Governor William Phips. Distracted by the responsibilities of his office and wrongly trusting in those judges he had named to the court, Phips recognized the dangers the trials presented. He ordered an immediate halt to the proceedings. While the courts themselves remained convened until late April 1693, Phips's order marked the end of any executions based off witch trials in Salem. It also, not so coincidentally, crushed for all time the power of the Puritan church in the region.[14]

By the time Phips intervened, nineteen blameless souls had been executed, one had died of torture, and four had perished in prison.

What of the three women whose arrest had begun the short reign of terror?

Poor Sara Osbourn died in prison. Sarah Good was found guilty and executed. As for Tituba, she recanted her testimony and for reasons unknown the court decided to be lenient. Though she was not indicted, the woman stayed in prison until the following year, when someone purchased her for the price of her bail.[15]

IMAGINED THREATS VERSUS REAL DANGER

At the time of the trials, the combined population of Salem and the surrounding "witch" towns was roughly two thousand.[16] The number of accusers, the people who used the trials as a way to eliminate local rivals or distract the public from the refugee problem or even bring closure to unhappy love affairs, was relatively few. The perpetrators of this kind of mass hysteria are generally not members of the populace. Rather, the perpetrators manipulate the population into a state of mass hysteria to serve their own ends. Those among the populace who dare protest may be accused themselves. Or, worse, they may be led to believe their souls will be damned. Those who don't necessarily get caught up in the hysteria are driven to silence.

It's important to make a distinction here, one that we face today: the difference between mass hysteria and justified concern. If, for example, the public had risen up against Mather and his cohorts, that would not have been hysteria. In 2018, this is something the mainstream media do not understand. If you look back through history—history, not agenda masquerading as history, which is all you get from the media today—you would learn the following: For the last 1,400 years, Radical Islam has been at war with the world. That isn't Islamophobia, as the mainstream media would have us believe. It is fact. It is history, and I urge you to read this without the bias I mentioned earlier in the book—indoctrination versus truth. Let's go back only forty years for just a partial listing of the atrocities:

1979: The U.S. embassy in Iran—American soil—was taken over by Muslim males.[17]

1983: The Beirut barracks of the U.S. Marines was blown up by Muslim males.[18]

1985: TWA Flight 847 was hijacked in Athens and Robert Stethem, a U.S. Navy diver who was attempting to rescue captives, was murdered by Muslim males.[19]

1988: Pan Am Flight 103 was blown up by Muslim males near Lockerbie, Scotland.[20]

1993: The World Trade Center was bombed by Muslim males who packed explosives into a van and drove into the underground parking lot, killing six. Their goal had been to destabilize the North Tower and crash it into the South Tower.[21]

1996: Nineteen U.S. Air Force personnel and one Saudi national died in Saudi Arabia when a housing complex was bombed by Muslim males.[22]

1998: The U.S. embassies in Kenya and Tanzania were attacked by Muslim males.[23]

2000: Seventeen sailors died when the destroyer USS *Cole* was bombed in Yemen by Muslim males.[24]

2001: Four airliners were hijacked. Two were flown into the twin towers of the World Trade Center. One struck the Pentagon and the other was brought down in a field in Pennsylvania. Thousands died on that day and more, later, from having selflessly served as first responders in the toxic pile created by those homicidal and suicidal Muslim males.[25]

2001: The United States undertook a war in Afghanistan against Muslim males.[26]

2002: *Wall Street Journal* reporter Daniel Pearl was kidnapped in Pakistan. A video of his execution and subsequent beheading was released by his captives—Muslim males.[27]

2002: More than two hundred people died when a nightclub in Bali, Indonesia, was blown up by Muslim males.[28]

2003: Twenty five people died when two synagogues in Istanbul, Turkey, were car bombed by Muslim males.[29]

2004: Helping to rebuild Iraq, radio tower repairman Nick Berg was kidnapped and beheaded by Muslim males. A video of his grotesque execution was released, initiating a new phase of terror perpetrated by Muslim males.[30]

2013: Three people were killed—including a child—and 264 others were injured in the Boston Marathon bombing perpetrated by Muslim males.[31]

2015: Twelve employees at *Charlie Hebdo*, a French satire magazine, were shot and killed after the magazine published drawings of the Prophet Muhammad. The two shooters were Muslim males.[32]

Notice that I said history; fact, not opinion. This is not an indictment of an entire people, though anyone who harbors terrorists is complicit. It is a fact that the mainstream media has not presented any criticism of Radical Islam as bias, as hate. The goal of their knee-jerk progressivism is a relatively recent phenomenon—that of mass amnesia. Like the vile Goebbels, media executives believe that if they obscure the truth long enough and hard enough, it will be overlooked.

Why would they do that? Part of it is profits: their revenue goes up each time there is a terrorist attack and people tune in, click on, and drop what they're doing to watch. But part of it is also this insane liberal dream of a *pax humana*, a human race of blended skin color in a world without borders. Of course, these blindered lunatics ignore their own cognitive dissonance. If they achieve their goal, with Radical Islam in the mix, protected by mass amnesia, there will be no gays, no Jews, no Christians, no Buddhists, no Hindus. There will be no law, other than sharia. Women will have no rights, no education. The only women's faces you will ever see is that of your wife, in private, or one of your sex slaves.

That, too, is fact.

IT'S ALL GOING TO POT

Mass amnesia is not a myth. It is a conspiracy of sorts, a vaguely defined plan to undermine the nation. Its perpetrators know that a malleable populace is a necessary tool to achieve an agenda, and as Bernie Sanders discovered with his pie-in-the-sky promises during the 2016 presidential campaign. And if you cannot seduce them with promises of free "things" and mass hysteria about "the other guy," you have to take another tack. You have to dull their wits but tell them that the means is okay. It's harmless. It's fine. Youth is especially vulnerable as they have always been susceptible to overconfidence. I was watching Turner Classic Movies the other night and I saw a silent film from 1921, *Enchantment.* The opening title card set the tone for the movie and defined a generation: "What is more amusing or more charming than a girl at the flapper age? That egotistical youth so gloriously confident of never being conquered...so all-wise...so tolerant of the last dull generation of grownups[.]"[33]

There is never a last dull generation of grownups because someone has to bail out the untrained, unfocused youth. The youth who have been told, against all evidence, that Muslim males would never harm you. Youth who have been fed affordable, available marijuana. Those are the two pillars of mass amnesia. As Aldous Huxley warned in his masterpiece *Brave New World*, a stupidly drugged population is a happy population. A happy population is one that can be easily controlled.

This was not new to Huxley or to the United States, by the way, and there is a cautionary tale there. This was how the Roman Empire began its decline. In 123 B.C., the government began controlling its citizenry with welfare in the form of heavily subsidized grain.[34] After that, according to the poet Juvenal writing approximately two hundred years later, around 100 A.D., "Tyrants would distribute largess, a bushel of wheat, a gallon of wine, and a sesterce; and everyone would shamelessly cry, 'Long live the King.'"[35] The politician and orator Cicero commented, "The evil was...in the willingness of the people to sell their rights as free men for full bellies and the excitement of games."[36] Bribed, doped, the Romans suffered short-term memory loss. They forgot their real problems, fell into complacency, and couldn't be bothered to remove ineffective or tyrannical leaders.

When I talk about amnesia, I don't mean the movie trope of being hit on the head, forgetting your name, and spending ninety minutes looking for clues. I am talking about the relaxation of inhibitions, morals, and basic decency. The mind control masters in the media lie and tell us that this is a *good* thing. They say, for example, that relaxed scrutiny of Muslim men who were entering our nation under Obama as "refugees" was an act of mercy.

What that contemptuous lie did, of course, was all but guarantee some kind of horrific attack in the future to fill several news cycles...and enrich media coffers.

That's why politicians on the left and the mainstream media are pushing the legalization of marijuana. Of course, I think it's a waste of time to prosecute overzealously for pot—this is not *Les Misérables*, and I don't want to ruin someone's life over a crust of bread. And I know there are alkaloids in cannabis that have medicinal properties without the recreational high. But the left thinks we should let taxi drivers, airline pilots, and surgeons light up when they want a buzz. They're wrong, and the impulse to allow people to impair themselves whenever and however they want is wrong, too.

Back in the 1920s, the flappers and jazz babies didn't want to depend solely on the music for their fix, for their night of relaxation and forgetfulness. They drank, but when that legal high was denied by Prohibition, they were compelled to find another.

It wasn't that marijuana and opioids were freely available in the Jazz Age. The opium dens of the nineteenth century were out of fashion, as authorities had become increasingly concerned about addiction, and in 1906 the Pure Food and Drug Act took the first steps toward regulating that drug, requiring that all medicines be labeled with their contents.[37] So, the young people looking for a wild time turned to another, more readily available high—marijuana, which had swept up from New Orleans along with black jazz musicians in the nineteenth and early twentieth century. As pot moved into the cities of Detroit, Chicago, New York, and elsewhere, the sons and daughters of white families increasingly had access to it, and authorities began to take notice.

The great pot party—and the arrogance of youth referred to in that quote from the movie *Enchantment*—ended on October 29, 1929, with the stock market crash. America needed its youth—needed all of its citizens—sober, alert, and skeptical of the demagogues who sprang up to take advantage of the country's crippled economic state. Despite the economic free fall, the underlying strengths of the United States still made it a desirable target for subversion, whether from outside forces such as Stalin's communists, or inside agitators such as Louisiana governor and presidential candidate Huey Long, whose proposed Share Our Wealth program would have been the closest thing to socialism this country would see until Barack Obama.[38]

From a legal standpoint, the U.S. war on pot gained significant momentum during the Great Depression. Desperate people have always been more susceptible to the allure of crime. Add marijuana to the mix, with its effect of numbing the pain of poverty, lowering inhibitions, and erasing ethical boundaries, and the problem became pervasive. The government couldn't do much about the poor and homeless but individual states began to wage war against pot. In 1930, the United States created the Federal Bureau of Narcotics, and by the following year, twenty-nine states had outlawed marijuana completely.[39]

Marijuana was demonized in the media as way of trying to counterbalance the natural allure of escape. The most prominent example was the campy 1936 film *Reefer Madness*, about a man and woman who live together and sell pot, and the psychosexual and homicidal effects it has on others.[40] There were more serious works about the psychoses caused by the narcotic, like the 1941 novella *Marihuana*, by Cornell Woolrich (author of *Rear Window*), writing under the pseudonym William Irish.[41] But that didn't solve the problem. The problem was the modern world. The Depression gave way to World War II, which gave us the nuclear age, which rolled into the Cold War and Vietnam and Watergate. For many, especially the young, the name of the game was "anesthetize." People drank bootleg liquor until Prohibition was repealed in 1933, and then they drank legal liquor. They still smoked marijuana. In 1948, actor Robert Mitchum and friends were famously jailed for smoking pot in a private home.[42] But the addictive nature of pot's effects is not the only problem. Threats do not go away simply because we have numbed ourselves to them. That being the case, people just continue to smoke.

I have a doctorate in ethnobotany and I can tell you that crops have dramatically shaped civilization, whether through ensuring an adequate supply of food that allows people to settle in an area, or the cultivation of cash crops that open up commercial possibilities, or in the introduction of invasive species of plants that can destroy an ecosystem. In fact, there is evidence that past societies have used this idea as an early form of "special ops" warfare.

What marijuana has done is more insidious. This invasive crop has destroyed us, our alertness, our resolve. Take sex and sexual mores. As much as the birth control pill, marijuana had a direct impact on the launch of the sexual revolution in this country. Its role was not an accident. It was the direct result of men who sought to create youth hysteria for their own profit. During the

1930s and 1940s, marijuana-fueled jazz and bebop music spread throughout the urban centers of our country. Enter record producer Sam Phillips, who in 1952 founded Sun Records in Memphis, Tennessee.[43] In the 1950s, white parents didn't want their children going crazy over black men onstage. Phillips knew this, and in 1954 he found his white boy, a slim, swivel-hipped truck driver named Elvis Presley. And with Elvis came the perfect storm that led into the sexual revolution, because now white girls were going wilder than their parents ever did for Frank Sinatra. The rock-and-roll era had dawned, and all it took was one more event to utterly shatter the relative innocence of prosperous, baby-booming, postwar 1950s white America: the assassination of President John F. Kennedy in November 1963. Hope and a patriotic youth were destroyed in an instant, followed and replaced by the shaggy-haired Beatles, confrontational and frequently deadly civil rights actions in the South, war in Vietnam—which was brought to American homes in living color on the nightly news—and of course the use of drugs to escape these onslaughts. Marijuana was back serving the same function as before: dulling the fear of the young.

The hippies of the 1960s merged all of these phenomena into the tradition of "sex, drugs, and rock and roll." That was sold to the eager, youthful masses by the gateway concept of "flower power."[44] The American Beat poet Allen Ginsberg created that concept in 1965 as a form of antiwar protest. The idea was, you dress in floral-design clothes, hand out flowers, keep everything bright and colorful and dance, and you could turn what were frequently illegal demonstrations into a happy, mindless celebration of all things natural and good...like drugs, except that the popular hallucinogenic lysergic acid diethylamide—LSD—was not natural and frequently resulted in death, as did the "organic" cocaine and heroin. Pot was quickly foisted on the so-called flower children as a part of that, used to get everyone in the mood for glassy-eyed celebration. Once that was accomplished, once pot had spread beyond the ability of law enforcement to effectively contain it, everything from concerts to protests to sex were "helped along" by pot. The psychedelic clothes, posters, graffiti, became as important as the reason for the gathering. Soon there no longer had to be a reason. Like zombies, the drugged masses gathered. In my own city, the Haight-Ashbury intersection famously became the beating heart of the hippie movement, the counterculture—a heartbeat driven to dangerously accelerated levels by drugs.

At least back then marijuana was ghettoized. The current rush to poor judgment would have it legally spread across an entire state, and from there across the nation. In January 2018, Attorney General Jeff Sessions announced the reversal of the reckless 2013 Obama-era policy that protected certain legal marijuana programs in select states from federal intervention.[45] Sessions was entirely right to do so. The pro-pot hysteria is embraced, on the consumer end, by frightened and entitled youth who have been raised not to accept responsibility and, when they do accept it, to believe that oblivion is their fitting reward for a day's work. On the supplier end, it is a thinly disguised effort to create a new generation of cocooned, fuzzy-thinking, inert Americans who will become state-dependent Democrat voters. If you think Millennials are dull-witted now—not all, but enough of them to elicit deep concern—Heritage Foundation chief of staff Charles Stimson wrote in a 2010 report, "Using marijuana creates losers. At a time when we're concerned about our lack of academic achievement relative to other countries, legalizing marijuana would be disastrous."

The rationalizations for legalizing it aren't rational. The pro-pot lobbyists equate marijuana's use with alcohol, forgetting in their haze that most people can drink alcohol without it being habit-forming. Pot, on the other hand, requires ever-increasing amounts or strengths for the same high. Additionally, alcohol can be used in moderation for relaxation without becoming impaired: with pot, the entire *point* is to become impaired. And tangentially, to overeat—causing health problems that require further dependency on state-sponsored solutions like Obamacare.

Not that anybody knows what the legal standard of "under the influence" with marijuana is. There is no established level of THC, pot's psycho-active ingredient, that would indicate someone is incapable of acting responsibly, whether driving—or potentially worse, piloting—a vehicle, or acting correctly in other critical situations.[46] The only way, currently, to determine whether someone has become incapacitated from marijuana use is to wait for that person to be involved in a tragedy, and then determine whether or not pot was being used. There is no federally accepted "safe" level.

What we do know is that, unlike responsible alcohol use, long-term marijuana consumption is unsafe. It dulls memory, weakens the bronchial system's immune response, contributes to cardiac and cerebral damage and likelihood of strokes, and creates artificial mood swings. It can also cause birth defects. I wonder if the women who were so quick to abandon alcohol and cigarettes during pregnancy will do the same with pot. Or will they rationalize continued use by citing uneducated, common "wisdom" that it isn't the same? Assuming, of course, that women can get pregnant at all if their partners are busy smoking pot. It not only lowers a man's sex drive, it reduces testosterone and sperm count.

Thomas Lifson, the editor and publisher of *American Thinker*, summed up the stupidity of the "Prohibition worsened alcohol's impact on society, so let's legalize pot" argument. As Lifson put it, "The other side on legalization always claims the experience of Prohibition proves their point. But if you look at it the way a true conservative does—always being skeptical of rapid radical changes from tradition—the experience of Prohibition tells us to beware of change driven by social movements, like the decriminalization movement. Prohibition and legalization both used the power of the state, driven by political movements, to change abruptly the legal rules regarding intoxicants.

"At least, that's one way of looking at it.

"We'll see how it works out. We're guinea pigs, or maybe we're the petri dish."[47]

To my mind, Lifson is being kind to the cynical progressives who are rushing ahead with reckless disregard for physical and mental health, and the hysterics who are whining for "more, more, more." What Lifson is comparing to the modern-day "Great Social Experiment" of Prohibition—legalizing pot—is actually a rush to social destruction we cannot imagine. Legalization advocates say that a tax on marijuana will produce economic benefits. What they fail to tell you is how much pot will have to be consumed in order to see those great tax windfalls. Which means the pro-pot lobby is banking on increasing use of this dangerous substance.[48]

The legal-pot forces have begun to bring marketing to bear on their products. In addition to pot in its purest form—a smokable tobacco-like substance—it is being combined with flavorings so it can be "vaped" through smokeless cigarette systems, and even packaged in such a way that it looks like, and often contains, candy and other enticements. Those enticements, those packaging efforts, are geared toward children, toward a whole new generation of consumers, who will be exposed to toxins both inherent in pot as well as added to it during the growing process.

Furthermore, states permissive enough to allow legal marijuana are going to turn blinder eyes on how it is cultivated. Within ten years, we will start seeing reports on how the chemicals used by semiregulated pot growers are seeping into the water supply, or contaminating the earth, and eventually into all of our bodies, whether or not we've chosen to ingest pot itself.

Legalized pot's damage goes beyond how it affects people physiologically. Count on street violence to rise in areas where legalized pot competes with criminals. How will government-run marijuana shops stay in business? They will need to have increased security measures paid for using the tax revenue they say is going to benefit all of us.

Pot was the perfect drug for the near-ruination of a generation during the 1960s and it's back to wreak destruction with ferociously greater potency on far more people. The irony is, that was just the tip of the marijuana iceberg; pot has been a part of mass amnesia and mass hysteria for centuries.

THE WAR ON VITAMINS

Just as much of the public suffers one type of mass hysteria regarding marijuana—denial of a real threat—it suffers under the opposite type when it comes to vitamins. Thanks to the deep pockets and insidious political influence of the pharmaceutical industry, vitamin supplements are in danger of being treated the way marijuana should be by legislators and regulators.

It's no secret the pharmaceutical industry wants to destroy the vitamin supplement industry, nor is it a mystery why they wish to do so. Every person who avoids an illness due to better nutrition is a lost customer for drug sellers. And they're willing to attack an industry that helps keep people well, so they can profit from more people being sick.

Back in 2015, they were going after fish oil supplements, a good source of omega-3 fatty acids, which naturally help reduce cholesterol. They don't want people reducing their cholesterol with natural, side-effect-free natural supplements because then those people won't buy statin drugs. Big Pharma's lobbyists were so effective they had the corrupted National Institutes of Health saying fish oil supplements were useless on one page of their website and likely effective in preventing heart disease on another. That shows you the negative NIH findings were purely bought and paid for.[49]

This is a topic I know a little something about, having earned my PhD in nutritional ethnomedicine from the University of California. I've been a leader in this field for more than forty years. I can tell you firsthand that, despite their full-throated support for complete legalization of marijuana, it's the Democrats who will help the pharmaceutical companies shut down the vitamin supplement industry. They believe in top-down government regulation, often imposed under the pretense of public safety. They'd like nothing better than to impose a 1950s-style Food and Drug Administration, which would help prosecute Big Pharma's War on Vitamins.

The free market approach of the Republican Party is the complementary medicine industry's best friend. There is a difference between liberty and licentiousness. On this issue, the Republicans support the former and the Democrats the latter. Unlike the licentious, unqualified legalization of marijuana, the liberty to use vitamin supplements improves public health. It is vital that liberty be defended.

The scourge of fake news and mind control began with an eleventh-century Arabic religious leader whose techniques are still used today by liberals. The combination of alcohol, pot, and outright lies were present on these shores during the dawn of the American Revolution. Misinformation, fake news, and mob rage destabilized families and institutions, and their repercussions lasted long after the actual hostilities of the American Revolution ceased—to the Occupy movement of 2011, and beyond.

6.

FROM ASSASSINS
TO GENERALS
Mass Amnesia and Lunacy
of Marijuana Advocacy

Just as today's pro-pot lobby would use marijuana to curb the moral inhibitions of its foot soldiers, historically people have used marijuana, hashish, and its ilk to control their followers. People like the eleventh-century Arab missionary Hassan-i Sabbah.

As a young man, Hassan traveled throughout the Arab countries, learning and preaching. His view of the all-important line of succession of the imams was not always well received and he was forced to seek protection in the mountains of Persia. There he came across a fortress of the ruling Seljuqs—Sunni Muslims. It was from this fortress that the Seljuqs maintained control over the

Ismailis—Hassan's clan. Hassan believed this fortress would be a perfect base for his missionary work. How he took the fortress—with a minimum of bloodshed—should terrify any right-thinking reader.

Capturing the fortress through a direct attack was impossible: From the date of its completion in 602 until Hassan arrived in 1088, it had never been taken. To do so would have required, quite literally, an impossible uphill battle.

As Muslim warriors have demonstrated over the millennia, their two greatest weapons are patience and stealth. The fortress drew its manpower from the villages that surrounded it. Over the course of two years, Hassan's emissaries went into the villages and slowly brought many people into their fold. By 1090, Hassan had converted enough adherents that any summons for manpower would inevitably admit significant numbers of Hassan's agents. That is precisely what happened.

It was at this fortress that members of Hassan's community became known as *Hashshashin*—or, as they have become better known, Assassins. Chalk up another gift to the world from the religion of peace.[1]

While the term *assassin* was originally applied specifically to members of Hassan's community, it was soon broadly applied to other minions known as the Fedayeen—an Arabic word meaning "those who sacrifice themselves." Which brings us to mind control.

Nearly all organisms share a common trait: the desire for self-perpetuation. Even plants, which don't think, will send tendrils toward water, or turn toward sunlight. I have watched these slender fingers wrap themselves around other upright plants to keep their flowers to the sunlight. How, therefore, was Hassan able to create a cadre of men willing to risk themselves in opposition to this basic instinct?

According to the writings of the Venetian merchant Marco Polo, who reportedly witnessed the process, the answer was the promise of Paradise— and drugs. At some point in the training of these young men, they would be given a drugged drink. The exact mixture is lost to antiquity, but knowing what was available then and there, chances are it was a flower-based mixture of a relaxant, an opioid, and an intoxicant. The specific plant was apparently named for those who took it: the *Hashshashin* were fed *hashish*. After ingesting it, the young men would fall asleep, at which point they would be carried to an enclosed section within the valley and left to wake on their own.

When they awoke, they were surrounded by dense gardens populated with fruit-bearing trees. Small channels flowed with honey, milk, and wine—constructed at Hassan's demand in accordance with the descriptions of Paradise. And yes, upon waking these young men were greeted by beautiful women—women with whom they were encouraged to sample every manner of earthly delight.

After several hours of bliss, the young men would be given another drugged drink. This time, when they awoke, they were in Hassan's court. Their benefactor would ask each young man where they had come from. In their drugged state, combined with the teachings of their faith, the youths truly believed that they had visited Paradise.

It was at this moment that Hassan's psychological control came into full force. He knew the young man before him would do anything to return to that Paradise and he also knew that the other men in the fortress, those who hadn't yet been to Hassan's prefabricated Paradise, would similarly desire entry. The price, of course, was simple: Kill an enemy of the sect and Paradise could be yours. And if they died in the assassination attempt, the angels would nonetheless bear them to Paradise. The roots of mass amnesia can be found in those who never experienced Hassan's fake paradise garden. Think about it: would-be assassins, those who came to be eager killers for Hassan, freely accepted the words of drugged-out assassins! How is that different from today, when stoned protesters are interviewed on the news and spout nonsense they heard from other stoned protesters—or even modern-day Hassans? Why was Hassan's version of Islam more appealing than that of some other acolyte?

That's not for us to say. Hassan continued to study, reportedly never leaving the fortress he had conquered for three decades, apparently secure in the righteousness of his vision. What we *can* state is that he succeeded because he used his name and fortress as a base from which to promote his views. He did that in much the way that the mass media today uses once-valued brands like the *New York Times* and CNN to push their fanciful agendas from secure fortresses.

We all know the terrible effects of people being able to send hateful messages on social media, protected in their own anonymous fortresses. The truth is that many of the people who send me hate emails, who post vitriol on my social media sites, who actually protest outside my radio network, have never bothered to read one of my books or listen to my show. It's like that game "Telephone," where phrases became increasingly distorted as they are whispered from player to player. Only in this case, stupidity is the passed-along commodity. There's a test you can do to prove this. The next time someone is protesting "climate change" or "the religious right" (as if that's a homogenous bloc) or even Donald Trump, ask them to articulate their concerns deeper than a thought or two. They can't. That's because they have been brainwashed by the *Hashshashin* of the left, driven to mass hysteria by trusted voices, dulled above the neck by marijuana. And the effect, by the way, isn't only to the brain, where increased dopamine release can cause impaired judgment or memory loss. The mouth may burn, the lungs will become irritated, phlegmy, and subject to increased cancer risk, the heart rate accelerates, the immune system will be suppressed, and overeating—people joke about "the munchies"—can cause its own health issues. Who on the left and among progressive politicians have you heard warning the public about these serious health issues?

How seriously should we take this issue of pharmaceutical influence on our minds and our nation? Very.

In June 2018, we saw the tragic suicides of two celebrities who seemingly had it all. Kate Spade, the iconic fashion designer, took her own life by hanging in her Park Avenue home. Later, chef and travel host Anthony Bourdain took his own life while shooting on location in France.

Both deaths struck a chord with Americans as they brought to light the escalating crisis of suicide, reported by the U.S. Centers for Disease Control and Prevention (CDC) to have increased by nearly 25 percent in recent decades. While no reports established whether or not Spade or Bourdain sought drug treatment for their mental health, their shocking loss sparked a national dialogue on suicide, depression, and the prescriptions so closely associated with psychiatric treatment.

I assure you the mainstream media will not report the relationship between antidepressant drugs and suicide although the correlation was first noted in 1990 and has been generally accepted since 2002. In a 2016 study published in the *British Medical Journal*, researchers at the Nordic Cochrane Center in Copenhagen revealed that pharmaceutical companies were not offering the full impact of these medications in reports. Their research concluded that suicidal thoughts and aggressive behavior doubled in children and adolescents who used medications such as selective serotonin reuptake inhibitors (SSRI) and serotonin and norepinephrine reuptake inhibitors (SNRI).[2]

Even more concerning from their findings was that they determined that antidepressants do not offer their prescribed results in children. Nordic Cochrane Centre professor Peter Gøtzsche said: "Antidepressants don't work in children, that is pretty clear, in the randomised trials children say that they don't work for them, but they increase their risk of suicide."

In response to this study, a spokesman for Eli Lilly told the *Telegraph*, "No regulatory authority has ever determined that Lilly withheld or improperly disclosed any data related to these medications."[3]

Experts said the reviews findings were startling and deeply worrying, stating that people in the United Kingdom are consuming more than four times as many antidepressants that they did two decades ago.[4]

Now what about the United States? America is no stranger to the antidepressants, either, as our nation increased its use of them by 65 percent in fifteen years.[5] I'm sure you know a number of people who run on antidepressants like M&Ms. But this is no laughing matter, rather an alarming moment indeed for our nation as a growing number of us are beset by depression.

If we examine the school shootings in America,

in almost every case the deranged child was on antidepressant medications but inevitably it is swept away by the drug companies before we can recognize these perils.

My concerns were only solidified as the media once again pushed the use of antidepressants in reaction to these high-profile suicides. Instead of recognizing the risks associated with antidepressants, a Reuters article called for pharmaceutical companies to introduce new antidepressants to the market: "A spike in suicide rates in the United States has cast fresh light on the need for more effective treatments for major depression, with researchers saying it is a tricky development area that has largely been abandoned by big pharmaceutical companies."[6]

With more research pointing to the dangers of these medications, we would expect news outlets to warn the masses about these worrisome outcomes, but unfortunately, they won't. As I have maintained for years, we must consider the board of directors of major media companies and then check out the interlocking corporate directorships.

Ultimately, antidepressant medication is a bad immediate solution and not the long-term solution.

Hassan's techniques of deception, mind control, infiltration, and false narrative have been and continue to be aggressively employed by those seeking profit and power against an entrenched individual or system—whether or not that person or institution is corrupt.

Not all mind-control techniques rely on drugs and the promise of unearthly delights. In some cases, moral corruption or a paycheck can be used to build a protest army. There is also a third path. Sometimes a strong sense of real injustice is enough to turn rational people into criminals. The decade leading up to the American Revolution saw several examples of ways to build and deploy a destructive mob.

PROTESTING AND PATRIOTISM

Whatever else the Stamp Act of 1765 was, it was legal. Britain ruled the colonies, the British Parliament passed the act, and it became the law of our land.

However, individuals may decide what is just and unjust and take appropriate steps—steps that, ideally, are legal, peaceful, and no threat to other people.

Colonists in New York and Boston in 1765 acknowledged none of these limitations. The Stamp Act, under which the British taxed almost all forms of paper, such as pamphlets, legal documents, government documents, newspapers, and even playing cards, was a profound insult to the colonists. Not only did it take money from their pockets, not only was this tax created without the colonists having representation in the British Parliament, but the proceeds were used to offset the expense of maintaining British troops on these shores.[7]

The act became law on March 22, 1765, and was supposed to go into effect on November 1, but within the colonies, those facing the additional taxes didn't wait for it to be implemented. In the early morning of August 14, a newly formed group from Boston, calling itself the Sons of Liberty,[8] hung an effigy of tax official Andrew Oliver from the Liberty Tree, an elm that stood in Hanover Square. They made clear to any loyalists or officials approaching the effigy with the intent of removing it that doing so would put their lives at risk. The effigy stayed—but only until that night. By then a form of mass hysteria had settled in, triggering long-held resentment of the Crown. Not long after dark, members of the merchant class who were sympathetic to the Sons of Liberty took the effigy down and carried it to an unfinished building owned by Oliver.

The rumor was that Oliver planned to use this

building as an office to distribute tax stamps. Mob logic held that if there were no building, there might not be a tax, so the marchers quickly tore the building apart. Then they carried the lumber from the destroyed office, along with the effigy, to Oliver's home, where they beheaded the effigy and threw rocks through Oliver's windows. The official and his family wisely fled to the home of a friend. But the mob wasn't finished. They toted the wood and the effigy up Fort Hill, where the timbers were used to fuel a massive bonfire. Oliver's effigy was burned there as well. Once the fires burned down, participants danced in the ashes.

Yet even this was not enough for the mob, which stormed back to Oliver's home, beat down the doors, and ransacked the place. The mob was gearing up to do a house-to-house search for Oliver—a search that would have almost certainly ended with Oliver receiving the same treatment as his effigy—when someone speculated that he was likely holed up in the well-fortified Castle William, within Boston Harbor. That took the wind from the rabble and Oliver was allowed to survive. No fool, he swiftly resigned his position as the Stamp Act's overseer, despite the fact that the act hadn't gone into effect and that he hadn't taken a single official action under it.

There is significant difference between mass hysteria to *achieve* an outcome and mass hysteria to *change* an outcome. The witch burnings were the former. Fueled by fear and prejudice, the fervor of the populace was renewed every time a new victim was arrested and brought to trial. The Sons of Liberty and their supporters were different. They felt abused by a governing body across the ocean and wanted the misconduct stopped. Before you ask, "How is that different from AntiFA, Black Lives Matter, and other far left groups?" remember that the colonials acted at great personal risk for principles of liberty and property that today's hooded clowns of the left haven't the brains or will to understand, nor the sense of personal honor and responsibility to respect. In both the witch trials and in AntiFA, there was little chance of punishment for participating in hysteria: denouncing witches became status quo, and AntiFA anarchists are lionized by the liberal left. The colonists standing up against the Crown may have been prone to hysteria at times, but they all knew that if they had been captured and made to account for their actions, they would be hung.

Furthermore, as the American Revolution would demonstrate, the hysteria mostly passed after the outcome—independence—was achieved. Cooler heads, especially among some of the Founding Fathers, would eventually impose the rule of law and the protection of private property within the colony, although as we will see, British sympathizers weren't exactly welcomed back into the fold.

The successful action against Oliver empowered the Sons of Liberty and those who supported them. On August 26, protesters ransacked the homes of two British officials: William Story, who was responsible for hearing trade law cases in court, and Benjamin Hallowell, Boston's comptroller of customs. The mob then made its way to the residence of Governor Thomas Hutchinson, demanding that he disown the Stamp Act. When Hutchinson refused, the protesters burst into his home, stole what they could, and gutted the structure. Hutchinson and his family barely escaped with their lives.

These incidents showcased the extent to which the authorities had lost control of Boston. A call went out for members of the sheriff's office to step in but, as with Hassan's followers, authorities discovered that many within the office were already part of the mob. However, as frightening as it may be, even the reach of a hysterical mob can only go so far. As we saw with Cotton Mather's printed accounts, real influence comes from the media.

The Sons of Liberty had evolved from a smaller, earlier group called the Loyal Nine. It is no accident that the Loyal Nine regularly convened in the offices of the *Boston Gazette*, a news publication Massachusetts governor Francis Bernard once called "the most fractious paper in America." Benjamin Edes, the paper's printer, was a member of the Loyal Nine,[9] and both the symbolic and chilling significance of the group meeting at a media outlet, a place where opinions are shaped—and reputations could be destroyed through unfavorable press—cannot be overlooked.

Massachusetts wasn't the only colony in which a newspaper played a prominent role in the Stamp Act revolt. In May 1765, twenty-nine-year-old Patrick Henry, a member of the Virginia House of Burgesses—a colonial legislative body—helped pass four "resolves"—statements of opposition to the Stamp Act. A fifth resolve boldly stated that the Virginia Assembly had "the only and exclusive Right and Power to lay Taxes and Impositions upon the inhabitants of this Colony[.]" That one was struck down as being too radical.[10]

That fifth resolve, however, was not too radical to be published in the *Newport Mercury* newspaper, out of Newport, Rhode Island, which printed all five without noting that the last hadn't been passed.

The *Mercury's* account also included a sixth resolve, the authorship of which has never been conclusively determined. That resolve stated that inhabitants of the Virginia Colony were not required to comply with any taxes not passed by the colony. Not to be outdone, the *Maryland Gazette* account of the resolves printed all six, plus another that stated that any individual outside the General Assembly who attempted to levy a tax on Virginians "shall be deemed, AN ENEMY TO THIS HIS MAJESTY'S COLONY."

Most historians attribute the last two "fake news" resolves to Patrick Henry.

He was angry that the *Virginia Gazette* had refused to print *any* news of the resolves, including the four the House of Burgesses had actually passed, so Henry and his associates distributed the full list of seven to news outlets throughout the colonies, representing all of them as having passed.

One can understand newspapers' willingness to help foment unrest against the Stamp Act. The paper tax alone would have been onerous, but there was also a clause in the act that demanded an additional two-shilling tax on every advertisement that appeared in its pages.

Without the help of the media, the August 26 events in Boston would have been isolated incidents of mob fury. But when word got out about the successful intimidation tactics the Bostonians had used, agitators in other cities were quick to pick up on their methods. The next day, in neighboring Rhode Island, a merchant mob erected a gallows in the town square and hung effigies of three stamp distributors. In New York, stamp distributor James McEvers resigned his position four days after the August 26 Boston riots. In his resignation letter, McEvers made specific reference to the damages realized by the Boston distributors, writing, "I have a large store of goods and seldom less than twenty-thousand pounds currency value in it with which the populace would make sad havoc."[11]

At this point, any chance of the Stamp Act actually being enforced was effectively over. McEvers's resignation was quickly followed by those from stamp distributors in New Hampshire, New Jersey, North Carolina, and Patrick Henry's Virginia. The distributor for Delaware and Pennsylvania announced he would not enforce the Stamp Act unless the other colonies did so.

Officially, the Stamp Act went into effect on November 1, 1765. But by then the only stamp distributor left in the colonies was Georgia's George Angus, who did his job for a fortnight before fleeing.

Knowing when to stop. That's the quality that made the Sons of Liberty unique, effective, and most of all credible. Knowing how to apply pressure in the media without actually corrupting the media, influencing others with your actions instead of brainwashing them, creating support without hysteria. They were picking appropriate targets, not lashing out with blind, brutal tactics the way ISIS or the anarchists on Soros's payroll do. Those savages are only looking to destroy. You can't build a nation on the aftermath of terror, you can only tear one down.

These are the qualities that distinguish the revolutionary era from the present. They are the qualities that marked George Washington for command of a seemingly impossible mission: to secure American independence.

Like many of the upper class of his time, George Washington was a farmer and a businessman. He was also a candidate for perpetual pain management: What few teeth he had were rotting away. As a farmer, Washington had several options for treating pain available to him, and one of them involved a plant we do not automatically think of in connection with an illustrious Founding Father.

Washington's diaries are full of details on sowing

and harvesting hemp—marijuana—and then sep-
arating the male and female specimens. As potheads know, the female buds are more potent for
both pain relief and as intoxicants. In 1796, Washington discussed raising "India Hemp"—*indica*—
in a letter to his foreman:

> What was done with the Seed saved from the
> India Hemp last summer? It ought, all of it,
> to have been sown again; *that not only a stock*
> *of seed sufficient for my own purposes might*
> *have been raised*, but to have disseminated
> the seed to others; as it is more valuable than
> the common Hemp. (emphasis added)[12]

Washington's claim that *indica* was valuable is
curious. At the time, wheat was a much better cash
crop, and the fibers from *indica* are not as suitable
for industrial use as the more common *sativa* variety
of cannabis. Washington raised a number of strains
at his farm and he would have been familiar with
their wide-ranging uses.

If, as seems apparent, Washington was using
medicinal cannabis—a possibility that may give
pause to those who ridiculously want plaques commemorating our first POTUS removed because,
like all southern farmers of his time, he was also a

slaveholder—Washington knew how to balance his medicinal needs with his responsibilities. Washington was a general whose troops and equipment were of far poorer quality than those fielded by the British army. Yet by the time the war ended, the thinking of the commander in chief had evolved to encompass strategic retreats as well as cutting enemy supply lines, which had the added benefit of helping to replenish his own ill-equipped troops.

There's a moral in this obscure bit of history. As with so many basically good concepts, the left has taken the idea of medical marijuana and, like intractable children, decided they want pot all the time, for any purpose. That's like alcoholics demanding that we let them stay impaired while they work, drive a car, interact socially, and slavishly protest Donald Trump. Not only is pot itself becoming a major business, but a cottage industry of questionable medical practices has sprung up for the purpose of authorizing marijuana's use by the general public. Again, a drugged public, an easily coerced electorate, is the left's best friend. And normalization means we're all going to be exposed to it. Anyone who has walked down the street and smelled cigarette smoke knows this—people will light up freely, and the rest of us, those of us who want our mental facilities to remain unimpaired, are going to be subject to contact highs, headaches, and all the other unwanted effects and side effects of pot use.

We've already seen how the Assassins used pot and hashish to entice or trick young men into doing things they normally wouldn't do, things that were morally repugnant. Make pot freely accessible and what few restraints the left has will be gone. Remove inhibitions and violence will come easier, the threat of arrest being an abstraction. In our current day, if left-wing rioters lose the fear of arrest for beatings, violence, unlawful gatherings, they'll be further emboldened to disrupt legal, peaceful expressions of thought they don't like. Soon the only voices will be those of the progressive left puppet masters urging their doped lackeys on.

I'll make one prediction. It's not going to be the beautiful world that leftists imagine in their pot-fueled haze. As we've seen, when one voice, unchallenged, is allowed to create mass hysteria and group amnesia, the results are destructive for their frequently innocent targets.

And the worst was yet to come.

In a way, the colonial victory in the Revolution spurred the kind of outburst we see after a home team wins the big game and the celebration gets out of hand. Americans had every reason to be proud and euphoric. But mass hysteria settled into some parts of the new United States and the victors became vengeful against those who had supported the Crown. Abraham Lincoln would learn the hard lessons of this hysteria. A few weeks before assured victory, in his Second Inaugural Address, he cautioned the North to treat the South "with malice toward none; with charity for all[.]"

But that speech was still the better part of a century away. And the better part of our natures had not yet emerged.

LIBERTY, LOYALISTS, AND LIBERAL LIES

During the Revolutionary War, the Patriots' attitude toward the Loyalists, or Tories, was malicious. For the duration, mass hysteria and lawlessness toward Loyalists was rampant. In New York, for example, Patriots destroyed printing presses that had churned out pamphlets against the revolt and stole cattle and other personal property.[13] There were also physical assaults. Patriots relied on tarring and feathering, a form of public humiliation that was both shame-inducing and painful. Sticky pine root tar and occasionally more adhesive and maiming coal tar heated to a point where it can be poured can cause painful blistering and burns. And removing the chicken feathers one by one took skin with it.

Tarring and feathering was initially a tool of the mobs, but in December 1776, less than five months after the Patriots had declared the colonies an independent country, the Provisional Congress of New York ordered the Committee of Safety—a shadow legislative body that governed when the Provisional Congress was not in session—to take possession of enough tar and pitch "necessary for the public use and safety."[14] They weren't using it to patch holes in ships.

One can understand how the Patriots might have felt emboldened. After July 4, 1776, the colonists had declared themselves a separate country and believed that allegiance to the Crown was treason. The Loyalists, however, did not recognize the legitimacy of the newly declared country and considered the Patriots to be traitors. Leadership on the side of the Patriots was itself frequently in conflict. During the war, American general Israel Putnam came across members of the Sons of Liberty strapping Loyalists to sharp-edged rails, their legs hanging on either side, and parading around with them. This is where the phrase "riding the rails" apparently originated, since the victims were carried on the shoulders of the Sons of Liberty so that other

Patriots could abuse them.[15] The mob had no legal authority to carry out such sentences, and Putnam interceded. When Putnam's commanding officer, George Washington, heard about his actions, he reprimanded the officer: "To discourage such proceedings was to injure the cause of liberty in which they were engaged, and that nobody would attempt it but an enemy of his country."[16]

Perhaps Washington understood what Putnam did not: These bold acts of aggression gave others the will and confidence to speak up. In abusing the Loyalists, Patriots effectively came out of the closet. Like fire, these pockets of conviction had a way of uniting and spreading into a form of mass hysteria. This is also what happened later, in France and Russia. People, once roused, are a terrible force. But there is a difference between these three examples and, say, ISIS or the far left of today. The cause must have a just core. Repressive sharia law or anarchists plunging nails into the flanks of police horses is not that. Enough people know it and, in time, the barbarians are crushed.

While these extreme but somewhat understandable abuses were initially expressed by lawless mob actions, some were eventually codified into statute while others were tacitly approved by authorities. State by state, the colonies enacted a series of anti-Tory laws that demanded Loyalists sign "test oaths"—statements in which the signer rejected English rule, swore not to provide aid to enemies, and pledged loyalty to the Patriots. The punishments for refusing to sign these oaths varied, but they ranged from depriving men from holding office, to fines and additional taxation, to losing the right to keep weapons, to being jailed. In a few cases, Loyalists lost legal protections, such as the right to sue or collect debts.[17] After the war, many Tories had their estates confiscated.

The morality of these statutes is immaterial: once they were put into place, they were the law of the land. The question is whether they legitimized mob actions, whether economic or physical. And they did. In this case, the hysterical reactions against the Loyalists were the result of both fear of subversive activity and anger about opposing viewpoints—even if those viewpoints did not come with any threat to our budding nation. While I certainly agree the cause of independence from Great Britain was just, it could have been achieved without the injustice, born of mass hysteria, done to the Loyalists. Depriving anyone of liberty and due process does not reflect the ideal values of America... and as we will see, hysteria does not contribute to America at its best.

In theory, the Treaty of Paris, which officially ended the Revolutionary War in 1783, should have ended hostility toward the Loyalists. Instead, property seizure continued without much interference from the federal government or the courts. Loyalist landowners were considered lucky if they were permitted to sell their holdings at bargain prices. Somewhere between 15 and 20 percent of the Tories—around 70,000–75,000 people—gave up trying to establish lives in the new country and emigrated to Canada, Great Britain, or the British colonies in the Caribbean.[18]

The Loyalists' flight created economic vacuums that were soon filled by Patriots—for example, in shipping. England was not as loyal to the Tories as the Tories were to the motherland; Britain was happy to be able to sell goods to the former colonies once more. The departure of Loyalists also enabled working-class Patriots to move into the upper class—but their rise was seen as the result of their efforts as opposed to their birthright, strangling the last vestiges of the British class system. American capitalism was born.

Lost in the loud din of anarchy perpetrated by the progressives in particular and the left in general is the idea that this nation was built on two ideas:

that this nation was founded by immigrants; and that many of those immigrants, and those who came after, made the journey to better their lives through freedom—of speech and religion primarily, but also to own property, to start businesses, to begin anew.

Laws and processes were established to make that possible, in the Constitution and then the Bill of Rights to start, and via the legislative and executive branches of government after that. As the Israelites in the desert understood during the time of Moses, without the law there can be no freedom.

In September 2011, the Occupy protesters pitched their tents in Zuccotti Park in lower Manhattan. Make no mistake: These people were socialists who did not want to compete within the American system of hard work resulting in financial gain. They had contempt for finance, period. And they expressed that by wearing a mask of Guy Fawkes—the man who tried to blow up the British Parliament—based on a design from the movie *V for Vendetta*, which was based on the comic book of the same name. We've come a long way in the wrong direction from the comic-style illustration by Benjamin Franklin that became a symbol of the Revolution: the dismembered snake under the legend *Join or Die*. But the Guy Fawkes allusion they made

with the mask was accurate, at least. These savages
did not want to modify a system, they wanted to
destroy the bedrock of the American way.

The short-lived movement began, so the organizers said, to call attention to global economic inequality. For two months, in the park and around the
world, angry kids, graying hippies, a few movie and
TV stars who thrive on attention, and the complicit
news media all pretended that the illegal squatting
in public places was somehow legal and somehow
noble. In New York, a world center of media, reporters gained personal attention, the newspapers gained
circulation, and the networks gained ratings with
coverage that portrayed the barbarians as activists,
the underdogs as heroes. A good friend of mine lives
around the corner from Zuccotti Park. What he
witnessed in and around the tent city that arose in
the 33,000-square-foot public space—from which,
by the way, the bulk of the public was barred from
entering due to police barricades that separated tax-
paying citizens from unemployed, out-of-town, and
troublemaking Occupiers—was a far cry from what
most Americans saw on the nightly news:

- Rapes and drug use were real and reported, but
  not widely reported. Members of TV crews
  did, however, ask Occupiers with guitars to

play folk songs, with others gathering around, so they could broadcast heartwarming—if manufactured—*greeting card* moments.

- Condoms were tossed at Catholic schoolgirls on their way to class.
- More than three thousand dollars in intentional damage was done to the lavatory of a restaurant adjoining the park because the Occupiers were not permitted to line up inside, without making a purchase, and use the restroom.
- The owner of a nearby framing shop was assaulted by Occupiers for politely declining to put up one of their "We Support the 99%" posters, a reference to the alleged 1 percent who control all the wealth in America. Different Occupiers then came by and offered to protect his shop—for a price. He told them, "You know who else does that? The Mafia." It was this assault, reported by a responsible journalist for the *New York Post*, that finally drove then-mayor Michael Bloomberg to oust the rabble, ending the media outpost and effectively stopping the movement.[19]

The point of this is not to take a swipe at Occupy, though they deserve it. It's to point out the difference between a worthy movement and an unworthy one. The former—the establishing of the United States of America and its system of merit-based capitalism—took root quickly and firmly because no American was barred from participating. Over the years, inequalities in the original system were addressed within the system as women and blacks became participants in the process. Not always at the speed they desired, but it happened. Working in unison, peaceful protest, articulate voices, genuinely concerned politicians, and a fair press triumphed. The American system was firm but flexible enough to accommodate these shifts.

We've been "instructed" by the know-it-all progressives that corporations aren't people, that they don't have inalienable rights. Let's grant that, but add that they *are* a form of artificial intelligence. Businesses and governments both have the instinct and/or charters to adjust and change. Were that not the case there would be no mergers, no maternity leave, no compensation "packages" instead of just wages, and the minimum wage would still be about a dollar, as it was when I was a kid. What that process requires from the public is for all participants, all citizens, to follow the rules lest the system topple on everyone; and it requires patience to climb a ladder or build a franchise business; and/or it needs a good idea, like an Apple Computer.

The American Revolution lasted seven years. That's about the time it takes for someone to get a PhD today. That is more time than it takes for a legal immigrant to become a permanent resident and then a United States citizen. What is implicit in those three examples are two qualities: diligence and some patience. They are precisely the attributes that progressives lack. And it is exactly the reason why rabid liberals have failed, continue to fail, and will always fail. It is why all tyrants fail.

Whether it's burning witches or tarring and feathering Tories, the ephemeral nature of mass hysteria cannot sustain. The foundation is not weight bearing, as we will see.

Without an external enemy, American mass hysteria turned to internal antagonists. Catholic, Jewish, and Chinese immigrants felt the wrath of the economically downtrodden. Mormonism, a homegrown religion, faced not only persecution but full-out military attacks from the U.S. government. The agricultural South expressed its discontent with the industrial North using rebellion—and while war fever did not sweep the North, hate did. The hate for the Confederate flag continues to this day. Is the South to blame or has the country always fallen prey to hysterical factionalism?

7.

FROM WAR TO PEACE
The Enemy Without
Becomes the Enemy Within

Financial panics have a great deal in common with mass hysteria. Runs on the bank and stock sell-offs are definitely "mass" and they are certainly "panic." But there are two big differences. The first is that the precipitating event of a financial crisis tends to be one thing, such as the failure of a financial institution or the collapse of a stock. That may be the result of a slow-building financial bubble, but it's still a singular, memorable occurrence that ends up having a day named "Black" after it. Hatred and paranoia tend to build more slowly. The other significant distinction is in their aims. Mass hysteria operates under the illusion that the mob is working for the public good. Financial panic is not a collective act about the collective. It's a collective act about thousands or tens of thousands of individuals looking out for their own self-interest.

There was just one exception.

The first financial crisis we suffered in America, as Americans, was the Panic of 1785.[1] It lasted roughly four years and came about because businesses took on too much debt after the Revolution, overexpanding without considering using better, and often cheaper goods coming from England; and a lack of trade *between* the states, which was caused in part by currency that varied from region to region. The panic itself was triggered in the financial institutions and among the well-to-do by imminent defaults on debts. The end result was that states and institutions realized we needed a stronger federal government and got together to make that happen. It was done for the good of these states and institutions, of course, but had the added benefit of serving the young nation.

After the economy stabilized in 1788, we ran right into the Copper Panic of 1789,[2] so called because the counterfeiting of copper coins literally caused a halt to commerce until paper currency could be introduced. That overlapped the Panic of 1792, which was caused—again, and not for the last time—by banks extending too much credit and having to be saved by the federal government. The Panic of 1796–97 wasn't even our fault: the Bank of England faced a solvency crisis due to the chaos across the Channel during the French Revolution. That impacted American banks, and it was primarily the sound financial footing of the southern states that kept the nation afloat. I have not heard this fact mentioned in any of the protests against the Confederacy. It is by no means a justification for slavery, but it is nonetheless a critical moment in our nation's history that cannot be ignored.

There were other ebbs and flows in the American economy, including the Recession of 1802–1804, the Depression of 1807, the Recession of 1812 . . . and then a big one.

If the previous financial crises were the expected ups and downs of a new nation, the Panic of 1819 was an unexpected tailspin.[3] In short, the country's economy crashed. As with any war or financial setback, the collapse was a result of several converging events.[4]

The United States had barely recovered from the Revolution before it was thrust into the War of 1812 with England. As a result of the Napoleonic Wars that engulfed Europe, Britain established a naval blockade to prevent trade with the French. That dramatically affected the American economy and, along with the impressment of American sailors into British service, triggered a three-year conflict. The war made a hero of future-president Andrew Jackson, then a general; made a legend of First Lady Dolley Madison, who saved White House art when the mansion was burned; and gave us "The Star-Spangled Banner" as Francis Scott Key witnessed the bombardment of Fort McHenry in Baltimore Harbor.

The four years between the end of the war and economic disaster was marked by banks once again being obligated to support speculation in business, farming, and land. Obviously, their solvency depended on the cash coming in being more than the cash going out. The nation did as it often does to fuel the financial engine: It printed money. A lot of it. But when people demanded metal money, considered true tender, the banks could not oblige. By 1818 the economy began to fail from west to east. American farmers, especially those who had already pushed west of the Appalachians, saw a dramatic drop in exports as the European economy—liberated from war for nearly three years, and of having to feed soldiers—was free to turn to agriculture. As struggling banks called in loans, the farmers could not meet the demands. Farms and banks both failed. The shock waves rippled through the nation as farm suppliers and then shippers struggled for survival, banks stopped lending money, and unemployment rose.

For the first time in American history, there was a nationwide panic as every citizen saw how a weakness in one or two areas could drag everything down. When "what-ifs" start to grip a population, no rabble-rouser, no Cotton Mather is required to spread mass hysteria. In 1819, people of all classes, in all professions, panicked over what they read in the newspapers and saw in their own towns. There was widespread doubt in our very system of capitalism. On the state and federal level, politicians went to the people with a wide variety of ideas—none of which had been tested and all of which spurred local debate and hostility, feeding the panic.

It took two years for Congress and our fifth president, James Monroe, to put solutions into place—again, all previously untried for a new kind of capitalism.

The three major acts were ones that modern politicians continue to resurrect in one form or another: debt forgiveness, bank regulation—they had to keep a minimum amount of capital on hand at all times—and protective tariffs. In that last were planted seeds for the Civil War: the South vigorously objected to these taxes since their economy was driven by exports.

Each of these actions met with varying degrees of success, but they all succeeded in doing one thing. They killed the hysteria. Sometimes all an agitated population requires for calm to be restored is to see their government taking action. However much different regions were negatively impacted by some polices, they were helped by others. People in New England griped that debt forgiveness on land purchased from the government helped the expansionists in the West more than it did merchants in Boston. However much cotton growers protested tariffs, manufacturers in New York and Pennsylvania liked the fact that it was cheaper for our citizens to "buy American" than to purchase European goods.

This single issue led to the Nullification Crisis of 1832, during the administration of President Jackson, when South Carolina refused to respect the tariff laws imposed by Washington.[5] A negotiated settlement was released, but as Jackson presciently wrote in 1833, "the tariff was only a pretext, and disunion and southern confederacy the real object. The next pretext will be the negro, or slavery question."[6]

Still, back then, with the Revolution in memory yet green, American citizens understood that when the nation as a whole prospers, the individual prospers. Yes, a necessary federal bureaucracy rose to help those who fell through the cracks. But we were still a country composed largely of men and women who believed that if they worked hard, the existing system would allow them to succeed.

Before we leave this era, Andrew Jackson is the heroic and visionary leader that the unchallenged voices of diversity want to chase from our twenty-dollar bill. Abolitionist and U.S. military spy Harriet Tubman was heroic and absolutely deserves a place of institutional recognition. But an African American woman should not be used to "beat up" an old white man simply so one party can claim a political victory. When Trump administration Treasury secretary Steven Mnuchin said that the change was far from a priority, petulant children on the left began writing Tubman's name across Jackson's face on our currency and using that as profile pictures on social media[7] ... as if that mini-hysteria were going to win allies rather than alienate moderates. A new denomination should be created in her honor rather than an old institution supplanted to appease the SJWs. There is room for all, as the survivors of the Panic of 1819 understood. When we carelessly, appeasingly swap one for another, that's when we fall.

TIPPING POINTS

During the nineteenth century, America would face more challenges than a charitable God would have allowed to settle on a new nation. One idea many Americans could agree on was the concept of protectionism, keeping foreign companies and foreign goods from these shores when it impacted American manufacturers and farmers. The nation had expanded considerably since the days of the Revolution. President Jefferson had made the Louisiana Purchase in 1803, greatly expanding our holdings in the West. It was a shrewd move. Though the price tag was a considerable $11,250,000, more than half went to paying down the American debt to France— which we owed anyway. By 1840, the nation had grown in other ways. From the thirteen original colonies of Delaware, Pennsylvania, New Jersey, Georgia, Connecticut, Massachusetts, Maryland, South Carolina, New Hampshire, Virginia, New

York, North Carolina, and Rhode Island, we were now twenty-six states. Vermont joined the new nation in 1791, followed by Kentucky, Tennessee, Ohio, Louisiana, Indiana, Mississippi, Illinois, Alabama, Maine, Missouri, Arkansas, and Michigan.

I chose 1840 because it was a watershed year in terms of mass hysteria. To populate the West, to man the factories, to expand and operate the growing transportation systems, immigration was essentially unrestricted. Quotas and bans did not exist until 1862, when Congress passed a law barring American ships from carrying Chinese immigrants.[8] Which isn't to say that there were no laws against foreign people and faiths: during the seventeenth and eighteenth centuries, laws were passed in many colonies that forbade Catholics from voting or becoming lawyers or teachers. It was an early form of separation of church and state, except that the only church being separated was Catholic.[9]

Prior to 1840, there had been sporadic violence against Catholics—mostly against property, since the angry Protestants still believed in the biblical commandments. For example, in 1834, a hysterical mob burned the Ursuline Convent in Charlestown,

Massachusetts, outside of Boston. The thinking was that if you burned the nests, the birds would fly. Often, they did—but just to another state.

By the end of the 1830s, the bubbling resentment of unchecked immigration exploded into full-blown mass hysteria with "idol-worshipping" Catholics as the target. A slew of local and even national political parties were formed and began winning elections. The broad platforms were simple: no more Catholic immigration. But the oppression went deeper than just religious differences: The Germans and Irish were singled out for special hate. For the Germans, there was lingering resentment over the imported German soldiers, the Hessians, who fought alongside the British during the Revolutionary War. Never mind that most German colonists tended to side with the Patriots;[10] mass hysteria doesn't bother with reality. The Germans who came from Catholic regions faced extra discrimination. Lutherans could be tolerated in certain circumstances; Papists could not. The Irish, on the other hand, were resented not just because of their faith but because of their numbers. Irish immigration levels had been rising steadily during the early 1800s due to terrible conditions at home, which would culminate in the Irish Potato Blight of 1845.[11]

The twin prongs of Catholic immigration gave rise to conspiracy theories, such as the idea that Pope Pius IX was an antiprogress theocrat[12] bent on subverting the United States by flooding it with a new voting bloc more loyal to Rome than to Washington, D.C.[13] Irish immigrants, especially, were also portrayed as undereducated, lower-class drains on state welfare systems and were accused of being responsible for a jump in crime rates nationwide.

From 1840 onward, anti-Catholic hysteria, based on absolutely no facts, just supposition, became an operating system throughout the general population and their state and national legislatures. Like slavery, it was legal, institutionalized fear and loathing. All those mythical qualities of tolerance and acceptance that the left goes on about simply did not exist. They never did. And the panic only got worse as immigration increased.

As for the Chinese, in fairness to American citizens, the press was filled with accounts of the Opium War of 1840, which came as a result of England smuggling large amounts of opium into China in exchange for Chinese silver and treasures, which caused economic chaos in that nation.[14] That resulted in the Treaty of Nanjing in 1842, which humiliated the ancient nation by turning it into a colonial empire divided among Britain, France,

Russia, Japan—and the United States. Many Americans believed that Chinese immigrants came here seeking revenge and also to spread the deadly scourge of opium. Again: mass hysteria requires only fear, no facts.

Throughout 1854, political candidates who opposed immigration secured victories throughout New England, as well as mayoral seats in Philadelphia, San Francisco, and Washington, D.C. Anti-immigration extremist candidate positions included barring immigrants from taking jobs, prohibiting—in San Francisco, of all places—Chinese immigrants from testifying against whites in legal proceedings, and requiring public schools to conduct daily readings from Protestant Bibles. Meanwhile, anti-Catholic fervor continued to grow until it was so great that when Jesuit priest John Bapst of Ellsworth, Maine, protested the use of Protestant Bibles, he was tarred and feathered.[15]

In 1855, a new political party sprang up that provided a national umbrella for what had previously been disparate anti-immigrant, anti-Catholic parties. The party was formally known as the American Party, but since members, when queried about its activities (a mix of secret meetings, secret passwords, and knocking codes) and its agenda were instructed to reply "I know nothing," followers quickly became known as the Know-Nothings.

Confrontation between Know-Nothing mobs and Irish and German immigrants came to a head during summer elections in Louisville, Kentucky. Louisville was a stronghold for the Know-Nothings since the population was around one-third immigrants, significantly larger than nearby locations.

One of the city's newspapers, the *Louisville Daily Journal*, was instrumental in boosting the Know-Nothings' cause. Editor George D. Prentice's editorials clanged with inflammatory statements, such as "Another anti-American candidate proclaimed that the Germans and Irish shall vote even at the cost of a fight half a mile long,"[16] and "Until the light of Protestantism shone in the world there was no religious freedom."[17] And finally, on the morning of the summer elections, "Let the foreigners keep their elbows to themselves today at the polls. There's no place for them in the ribs of natives."[18]

On Monday, August 6, 1855, Louisville citizens went to the polls to elect a governor, a congressman, and a variety of judicial positions. The day started out ugly as pockets of Know-Nothing supporters gathered. When former congressman William Thomasson confronted one of the mobs, seeking calm, he was attacked from behind and brutally beaten. The day devolved into further chaos in the afternoon, when an unknown assailant fired shots into a crowd, killing a policeman and at least one civilian.

In the early evening, rioters set a brewery on fire, as well as several houses occupied by Irish tenants. Anyone attempting to flee was shot. As night fell, the shootings, burnings, and beatings escalated. It was only the intervention of Mayor John Barbee, a Know-Nothing himself, that prevented a German church from being destroyed.

By the time Mayor Barbee got the streets under control, at least twenty-two people had been killed, more than one hundred businesses had been vandalized or looted, and an entire block of Irish homes had been burned. While police arrested a handful of rioters, ultimately nobody was convicted in connection with the events of August 6, a day that would become known as "Bloody Monday."

As I mentioned earlier, mass hysteria cannot sustain itself if the movement is based on fear rather than reality. The colonies had legitimate grievances against England. The war was fought and won, and the nation had a good basic foundation. The anti-immigration extremists had only paranoia.

Now, before you jump to the obvious progressive

talking point, the difference between immigration then and now is that the people who came to our shores *wanted* to become Americans. They did not want to establish a wing of the Vatican in Washington, they did not seek to put opium dens on every street corner. While there were enclaves of immigrants, they wanted their children to learn English, to become Americans. That is not the case today, even among many leftist Americans who prefer diversity over unity. In these times, fearing onslaughts from the left wanting to erase our borders, language, and culture is not paranoia. It's survival.

By 1860, the Know-Nothings had ceased to exist as a party, but they had established a working framework for mass hysteria, a beachhead in the American psyche that morphed with devastating effect.

SWELLING THE RANKS

As elections tend to do, the voting in 1856 brought up deep divisions within the Know-Nothing party—and thus, the nation—regarding regional attitudes toward slavery. With the demise of the Know-Nothings, the antislavery factions joined the Republican Party—yes, you read that

correctly—while the proslavery supporters aligned
themselves with southern Democrats. This shift
occurred just one year before the Civil War, and
the rift was almost immediate. Republican Abraham Lincoln was elected in 1860 and flung down
the gauntlet when he said, "Government cannot endure permanently half slave, half free...."[19]
Despite his victory, Lincoln was not even close to
being a majority president: he had won just 40 percent of the popular vote, and only 180 of a possible
303 electoral votes. Just six weeks later, South Carolina showed a rare instance of agreeing with Lincoln and left the Union. Within two months they
were followed by Mississippi, Florida, Alabama,
Georgia, Louisiana, and Texas.

One does not have to wonder what the Internet
would have made of an instantly "failed" presidency.
Anti-Lincoln hysteria was all over the press, spoken of in the streets and in homes. Before secession,
the South already considered Lincoln's party "Black
Republicans," and they weren't alone in their open
hatred of the new president. In addition to the Deep
South, there was antagonism in many of the border
states, especially among Democrats and conservatives. Then there was the full-on enmity from the
Democratic Party of the North and the antislavery
radicals within the Republican Party. Europe was

split but the English press was genuinely united in bashing the sixteenth president from the left and the right. In 1862, even after Lincoln issued the Emancipation Proclamation, which would become effective on the first day of 1863, the *Times* of London found cause to be cynical: "Mr. Lincoln proposes that every slave in a rebel State shall be ever after free, and he promises that neither he, nor his army, nor his navy will do anything to repress any efforts, which the Negroes in such rebel states may make for the recovery of their freedom. *This means, of course, that Mr. Lincoln will, on the 1st of January next do his best to excite a servile war in the states he cannot occupy with his army*" (emphasis added).[20]

The *New York Herald* was more blunt. That newspaper was known for its pro-Know-Nothing, anti-black, anti-Catholic, anti-Republican screeds, such as an 1860 Election Day editorial that warned, "If Lincoln is elected to-day, you will have to compete with the labor of four million emancipated negros [*sic*].... The North will be flooded with free negroes, and the labor of the white man will be depreciated and degraded."[21]

Lincoln was inaugurated in March 1861. Nearly a month before, the Confederate States of America had been formed, with West Point graduate Jefferson Davis as its president. The inevitable Civil War began swiftly, on March 4, when Southern general Pierre Beauregard opened fire on Union forces at Fort Sumter in Charleston, South Carolina.

Both sides needed soldiers. In the South, men young and old could not volunteer fast enough. In the North, it was a different story. In New York in particular, the antiwar sentiment was strong.

It's difficult to imagine that 157 years ago, what is now the maddeningly "progressive" city of New York did not view the Civil War as a civil rights cause. The city relied on southern cotton for its textile industry, and its ports were a major hub for cotton exports. The scourge of slavery was a remote concern.

As in Louisville, Catholic laborers from Germany and Ireland had been pouring into the city for nearly half a century. These workers competed with free blacks for the lowest-end jobs the city had to offer. Then as now, Democrats at the time saw an opportunity: immigrant laborers, especially the Irish, would swell their voting ranks if offered something of value. During the period leading up to the Civil War, that something was running protectionism up the flagpole. For an Irish worker, the choice was clear: vote Democrat and protect your job from going to blacks—or, as some New York publications portrayed them, a subhuman whose criminality was bred in his bones.

From 1861 through the following year, resentment and opposition to the war grew to a point just shy of mass hysteria... and then the tipping point was reached. The Conscription Act of 1863 declared that every male citizen between twenty and forty-five was eligible to be drafted into the Union army. As the New York Irish viewed this, they were being asked to fight on behalf of the very threats to their jobs. Making matters worse, since blacks were not considered citizens, they were exempt from military service. That would soon end, however, when the pool of white males dropped precipitously and there was a large black population eager to serve.

There was also another group exempt from military service, and this fired up slow-burning resentment among poor immigrant citizens in regard to the upper classes. Any man who could pay a three-hundred-dollar fee could purchase a deferment.

On July 12, 1863, the draft board selected the first round of names without incident, primarily because the selection process was done quietly. Draft officials believed there would be less opposition if men learned of their conscription results through newspaper accounts as opposed to hearing their names in a town square or hall. Officials selected 1,200 men that day.

In New York, when firefighters learned how many of their brothers would be going to war, they were furious. Many of their number had already volunteered for service when the first call for men went out on April 15, 1861. But service had never been compulsory. Not only would public safety be compromised, but their own lives would be at risk due to thinned ranks being replenished with inexperienced and unfit men. At dawn on July 13, hundreds of firefighters assembled in city streets. At the head of this mob were firefighters of the "Black Joke," a volunteer fire department named after a warship from the War of 1812. I talked earlier about the cognitive dissonance of mass hysteria. I doubt the men were aware of the irony that they were the namesakes of one war about to violently protest another.

The mob of around five hundred men stormed the draft headquarters on Third Avenue and Forty-Seventh Street, smashing the drum that contained potential draftee names, destroying the records of those already selected, and—in another ironic touch—burning down the draft building. When other firefighters arrived, the mob did not let them combat the main blaze but did allow them to keep it from spreading.

Perhaps it was the fire, perhaps it was the sheer numbers, but the mob had gone from anger to hysteria and would not be mollified. There was also encouragement from outsiders. The rioters were goaded by female supporters, whom one observer characterized as "low Irish women, stalwart young vixens and withered old hags egging their men on to mischief." Police superintendent John Kennedy arrived and attempted to restore order. The mob beat him mercilessly. The armed police officers Kennedy had brought with him found themselves outmanned and overwhelmed. What would have passed for "mission accomplished" in the days of the Sons of Liberty now could not be contained. Almost immediately, the rioters sabotaged telegraph lines, cutting off communication. Not only did that confuse efforts to contain them, it allowed rumors to flourish. The primary media was the noise of the mobs and smoke rising from the fires it set. Hysteria spread among the general citizenry.

During the next two days, gangs roamed the

streets, targeting what they saw as a cause of the war. They beat and killed black citizens as well as whites sympathetic to the abolitionist cause. The Colored Orphan Asylum was set on fire by crowds screaming "Burn the niggers' nest!"[22] Mercifully, all 237 children inside escaped. The media, which had played its own role in stirring the pot against Lincoln, against the war, and against the draft, was not spared. Henry Raymond, who owned the pro-immigration, pro-abolitionist *New York Times*, personally manned one of three Gatling guns the paper had set up as the riots broke out. The guns' presence turned aside the mob, which was angry but not suicidal. The *New York Tribune*, however, which held similar political views, stupidly created barricades using bales of newspaper, which the mob set ablaze. Luckily, those fires were extinguished before they could get out of control.

After these institutions had been destroyed, new if marginally related targets were needed. The Brooks Brothers clothing store served several symbolic purposes. Not only did it cater to wealthy patrons—the sort who could buy their way out of military service—but it was also a supplier of Union army uniforms. On the second day of rioting, the company's store on Broadway and Grand Street was ransacked. (As a sidebar to show

how things change: After the World Trade Center attacks in 2001, the Brooks Brothers tower across the street refused to fall. Fire fighters expected it to, but they kept working in the pit, searching for survivors, knowing that at any moment that big black building could fall on them. It did not. Reviled a century and a half ago, it is now part of the symbol of our national resilience. Things change.)

As the rioting continued through the second day and into the third, the mob chose targets less for political reasons and more for punitive ones. In much the same way that Occupy would one day trash restaurants that wouldn't let them use the bathrooms, bars were attacked for refusing to serve liquor to rioters already drunk with power and portable supplies of liquor. Businesses suspected of employing blacks were vandalized. A pharmacy once owned by black abolitionist James McCune Smith—the first man of his race to own such a business in the United States—was destroyed.[23]

On the third day of rioting, orders came from the headquarters of the United States Army in Washington to postpone the draft. While that deflated the hysteria to some degree, enough rioters remained on the streets to require further action. New York mayor George Opdyke requested federal troops and Secretary of War Edwin Stanton moved four thousand men from the Gettysburg battlefield to the streets of New York.

The city's death count from the riots was around one hundred. But that figure is likely low, reflecting the difficulty of tracking blacks who had been murdered, as well as the army's unwillingness to give an accurate count of the rioters (and possibly onlookers) its soldiers had shot. Property damage was pegged at between $1 million and $5 million.

The *New York Times*, which even then was promulgating fake news, immediately published editorials claiming that sinister forces, possibly in league with the Confederacy, were behind the riots. There was absolutely no evidence of that, just supposition and hearsay. The truth was simpler. The Social Justice Warriors of the day had regarded blue-collar whites as dispensable and without rights. That oppressed class, which was willing to work, resented a process of social engineering built on their labor and sweat. As the original American Dreamers, they did not hate the upper class they hoped one day to join. But they did not appreciate privileges being bestowed upon the upper class after the fashion of the aristocrats in Europe. That was the world they had left.

Naturally, the cause the mob had embraced was quickly lost. The government needed soldiers. With armed soldiers in place now, less than a month later the New York draft was reinstated without incident. However, the real war was effectively won by tamping down the underlying racial trigger. Over the next two years, New York's black population dropped by 20 percent from its 1860 level. The truly insidious result was the mentality of "us vs. them." We were no longer a population of Americans but pockets of multicultural interests. Like a cancer, this has given rise to the social tumors of today among minorities: a growing sense of entitlement, a desire for separatism, and a willingness to participate in the hysteria of self-serving victimization.

HYSTERICS VERSUS HEROES

It is fair to say, and not just with hindsight, that the Confederacy was doomed from the start. In terms of population, the North had a massive advantage of 22 million to 9 million. And of those, 3.5 million people in the South were slaves, potential allies for the North. In terms of supply lines and troop transport, the North had twenty-two thousand miles of railroads, the South less than half that.

The North enjoyed a manufacturing economy that was roughly nine times greater than anything the South had to offer. Add to that a whopping disparity in essential raw materials: the North had 94 percent more iron and 97 percent more coal.

The South also fought a primarily defensive war. As soon as Union General Ulysses S. Grant found vulnerable spots in the Confederate lines, he poured men and arms through, crushing the enemy from west to east. After a little more than two years of fighting, the Union army was just six miles from the Confederate capital of Richmond, Virginia. For this reason alone, not a single plaque or statue of General Robert E. Lee should be touched. And I'm not alone in this belief. Recently, jazz great Wynton Marsalis took heat from his peers and from the left for his brilliantly astute comment that rap music has been "more damaging than a statue of Robert E. Lee"[24] to the African American community.

With the sheer numbers and resources of the North piled against him, he still managed to deny Grant victory for a stunning two *more* years. Lee was not a political ideologue. He was an American patriot, the son of Revolutionary War hero and former Virginia governor "Light Horse" Harry Lee.

The younger Lee was a top graduate from and former superintendent of the United States Military Academy at West Point. His heart ached at the very thought of a divided nation but he was unable to take up arms against his beloved Virginia.

FROM THE BIBLE BELT TO THE LIBEL BELT

It's maddening that there is so little subtlety to thought, so little room for nuance, that a towering figure *who was not perfect* can be demonized by the left. Somehow those same critics can elevate to near-legendary status a president who sat on his hands through eight years of war, masterminded the lowest economic growth in our nation's history, did nothing while record numbers of citizens went on food stamps, permitted homegrown terrorists to thrive while inviting millions more to these shores, created an unparalleled rise in health insurance costs, oversaw a new high for the national debt, did nothing to relieve the highest level of poverty in our history, supported the most devastating rioting since the Civil Rights era, said nothing as we saw an unprecedented hatred of police, ordered the shameful end of the American manned space program, allowed the rise of ISIS, and so much more.

If leftists could erect statues of Barack Obama to replace those of Robert E. Lee, they would do so. Maybe the big tobacco-growing states of Virginia, Kentucky, and North Carolina would go along with that if Obama smoking a cigarette were incorporated in the design. Maybe the statue of the Wall Street bull, which was drenched with blue paint in September 2017, to protest the U.S. pulling out of the climate change accord,[25] would find a happier home relocated to beef country, where vegans could stick to their old, hackneyed protest of splashing it with red paint. If the deaf and insanely vengeful left could rename parks and squares after Michelle, Sasha, and Malia Obama, they would do so—just as in 2017, hate-filled, self-impressed, smugly dismissive "Americans" celebrated Malia's birthday on July 4 *instead of,* not alongside, Independence Day. As Obama buys his expensive estate in Martha's Vineyard, and takes scarce lakeside land for his pharaonic "library" on Chicago's lakeshore, I wonder if our forty-fourth president, the former community organizer, would ever contemplate doing what General Lee did for this nation, accepting with quiet dignity the federal usurpation of his lands for transformation into Arlington National Cemetery.

THE (IMAGINED) ENEMY WITHIN

One of the stranger fits of mass hysteria in the United States ran parallel to the events discussed above. I say it's stranger because it emerged suddenly in the 1830s, not from a long-festering resentment or a fear of a race that was different from WASPs. It was homegrown.

The early Mormons, members of the Church of Jesus Christ of Latter-day Saints (LDS), were homegrown aliens and the country had no idea what to make of them. The faith was a hybrid of ideas that had no precedent. They were communal before communism was even a thought, preceding by almost twenty years Marx and Engels's *Communist Manifesto* and more than a century Israeli kibbutzim and hippie communes. They were theocratic like the discredited Puritans, expansionist like Europeans, exclusionary like many religious sects, and eventually polyamorous. And most troubling to others, they were American citizens.

Actually, that wasn't most troubling of all. That was problematic. I love the Bible, both books of it, and toward the end of the New Testament, in Revelation 22:18, there is a passage: "For I testify to every man that hears the words of the prophecy of this book, if any man shall add to these things, God shall add to him the plagues that are written in this book." Mormons not only added to the Bible, they held that the words of their prophet, Joseph Smith, superseded those that had come before. Understandably, other Christians took this as a provocation.

In 1830, shortly after the founding of the Church of Jesus Christ of Latter-day Saints and publication of *The Book of Mormon*, Smith was arrested in New York State and charged with "being a disorderly person."[26] He wasn't; that was just what panicked and influential church leaders said since he represented a threat to their hegemony. When Smith was acquitted, he received instructions from God to relocate his church from western New York State to Ohio.

That was an ill-advised move. The Mormons' growing numbers gave him increasing political power and caused panic that blossomed into hysteria. In 1832, the locals of Kirtland, Ohio, beat, then tarred and feathered Smith. Still, he didn't leave that state until a bank he had established failed in the financial panic of 1837. Smith relocated to a Mormon settlement in Missouri, where the faith was no more welcome than it had been in Ohio. Even before Smith's arrival, Missouri vigilantes had opened fire on Mormon homes, set crops ablaze, and smashed a Mormon printing press after the newspaper published an antislavery article.

Throughout the summer and fall of 1838, LDS Church members fought intermittently with mobs. Members of a Missouri militia sent to quell the violence ended up joining the mobs, and a late October battle resulted in four Mormon deaths. Shortly after, Missouri governor Lilburn Boggs authorized a 2,500-man force to deal with the Mormons. Think about that: A state governor sent an army after a bona fide religion of peace. Never mind the Constitution. Boggs issued an official statement that read in part, "The Mormons must be treated as enemies, and must be exterminated or driven from the State if necessary for the public peace[.]"[27]

A few days after Boggs's decree, a two-hundred-man mob slaughtered seventeen Mormons in Haun's Mill, Missouri, and Joseph Smith and some fifty LDS Church leaders were arrested. While most were released after a few weeks, Smith was indicted for treason. He escaped while being transferred and fled with the rest of the Mormon community to Illinois.

The Mormons purchased the Illinois city of Commerce and renamed it Nauvoo. It was here that Smith's hubris became his undoing. He announced a new set of revelations, including that Mormons would engage in celestial marriage—or, as it was known in layman's terms, polygamy. By 1842 he was openly declaring his plans to create a world-wide theocratic kingdom. At this point, any shred of welcome offered by Illinois was gone. When an unknown shooter wounded Missouri governor Boggs, rumors circulated it had been at Smith's behest. For the next two years, Smith battled extradition efforts.

In 1844, Smith announced he would run for U.S. president. When a non-Mormon newspaper in Nauvoo ran articles criticizing Mormons' polygamist practices, Smith ordered the newspaper shut and its press destroyed, much as a mob had done to *his* press seven years earlier. Unease turned into outright hostility, and newspapers urged non-Mormons to rise up against the community. Smith was arrested and charged with inciting a riot, but was never tried: on June 27, a mob stormed the prison and shot him to death. Illinois revoked Nauvoo's city charter and the Mormons, under new leader Brigham Young, moved west. Eventually they reached the Salt Lake Valley, which at that point was part of Mexico. That changed after the Mexican-American War of 1846–48. The region was made a territory in 1850 with Young as its governor.

Young proved almost as incalcitrant as Smith. He refused to step aside as governor at the end

of his term, and the ongoing practice of polygamy rankled many in Washington...and across
the nation. The idea that Mormons were not only
strange and dangerous but also un-American had
had more than a quarter century to settle in the
American consciousness. The result, once again,
was an intemperate flash of hysteria. In 1857, U.S.
president James Buchanan declared Utah to be in
a state of rebellion and sent 2,500 federal troops to
install a new governor.

Young prepared his followers for war. His tactic
was simple. He wouldn't attack armies but would
disrupt supply lines. Unfortunately, a wagon train
consisting of settlers crossed into the territory,
and Mormon troops brutally murdered 120 people. While the Mormons initially tried to blame
the Indians, they eventually admitted guilt. Young
agreed to implicate one of the militia leaders and
to recognize federal authority over Utah. In return,
President Buchanan withdrew federal troops to outside Salt Lake City and pardoned all other leaders.

For the most part, this ended armed conflict
between Mormons and federal troops. Questions
about the church's practices remained, however,
and it wasn't until 1890 that the Mormons formally renounced polygamy. That paved the way
for Utah statehood in 1896.

Personally, I would have loved to see what today's Social Justice Warriors would have done to help the Mormons. In fact, I wonder why none of them has taken up the question of polyamorous couples marrying. The "cause" is no more or less moral than any sociosexual relationship. The number of polyamorous people in America is between 1.2 and 2.4 million, so it *should* be on their radar.

And it would be, if SJWs relied on study, reading, and actual communication for the sake of understanding, instead of blindly following the will of people in power and people with money, and ranting hysterics on Twitter and Facebook telling them what to do.

WE MUST PROTECT THIS HOUSE

I have always said our nation's future depends upon three qualities: borders, language, culture. Look at any nation or empire throughout history, from ancient Rome to the Ottoman Empire to colonial Great Britain. Once any of those have been compromised, the entity cannot be sustained. Appropriately, as Lincoln said, quoting Jesus Christ in that 1858 speech against slavery, "A house divided against itself cannot stand."

The concepts of American unity have been lost to the progressive mainstream media and social media,

and to the screeching vultures on the left—the sow-
ers of mass hysteria like Obama, Bill De Blasio, the
clinging Clintons, Nancy Pelosi, and financial bakers of social unrest such as the infamous George "the
disrupter" Soros—who have stopped listening to
any voices but their own and have willfully divided
this house. Like ISIS blowing up historic sites in the
Middle East in an effort to erase history that does
not perfectly conform to or align with their myo-
pic worldview, SJWs will not rest until they have
destroyed America, taken its territory, and instituted
laws that favor only their point of view.

I would trade a thousand such leaders for one
Robert E. Lee.

Even after the Civil War, hysteria continued within these Disunited States. In the South, antiblack, anti-North rage among vanquished Confederates led to the rise of the Ku Klux Klan. Other southerners found themselves joining mob movements in support of northern Democrats, who remained proslavery. Chaos reigned, and greedy politicians used their influence—and the military—to crush the culture of a proud, vanquished people. Today, for the first time in a century and a half, the oppressed conservatives are fighting back, fighting progressive hysteria with righteous indignation and action.

8.

FROM PEACE TO WAR
Hysteria Creates Seismic Shifts in America

ic semper tyrannis. Latin for "Thus ever to tyrants."

Some sources credit the phrase to Brutus as he plunged his knife into Julius Caesar. Certainly John Wilkes Booth thought so. Those were the infamous words the ham actor-turned-assassin shouted when he leaped from the president's box to the stage of Ford's Theatre. Before moving on to the mass hysteria spawned by the president's policy of Reconstruction, this question of Lincoln's tyranny is one that needs answering. And that answer is "yes."

Lincoln assumed unconstitutional "war powers" to deal with the rebellious South. The first military draft in American history was one of those. Suspending rights regarding illegal imprisonment—the

so-called writ of habeas corpus, literally that prosecutors "present the body" to a court of law for
judgment—was another. Unsure of the loyalty of
courts in the border states, Lincoln insisted on cases
there being tried by military courts. Whatever the
morality of the Emancipation Proclamation, as an
attorney, Lincoln knew it was possibly unconstitutional. He issued it anyway.

The executive branch grew in size and power
during the war, and there is no way of knowing
whether Lincoln would have rolled that back with
the cessation of hostilities. Certainly Reconstruction was going to be a difficult thing for the South
to swallow, and it is likely the sixteenth president
would have assumed even greater powers to deal
with that. His main objective was to rebuild the
union, not to punish the South. Abolitionists and
Lincoln's own left-leaning Republican Party might
not have been pleased with a general amnesty.
Repairing the ruined infrastructure would have
been a top priority. That would have meant north-
erners traveling to the South . . . with both panic and
resentment among the proud but defeated locals,
and punitive measures from the victors. A massive
military presence would have been required to preserve the peace. Enfranchising the freed slaves would
have been another challenge, especially concerning

voting rights. As a first step, Lincoln may have had to contort the Constitution to accept the right of only literate males to cast ballots.

We cannot know how that would have played out. What we do know is that Reconstruction was a disaster. Under Lincoln's successor, Andrew Johnson—a Democrat and by most accounts a racist—old hatreds combined with mass hysteria to produce chaos...and impeachment.

Some of the national chaos was intentional and politically motivated. There was massive debt on both sides after the war. No one had expected it to last as long as it did, and there were no debt management policies in place. Though there was never any danger the United States would default, that notion was floated to persuade creditors to reduce the monies they were owed and to allow the government to hike taxes. Republicans and Democrats both played the fear card—for example, the Republicans spreading rumors that Democrats would forgive the debt, harming manufacturers, and Democrats arguing that specie (coin) made of negotiable, valuable metals was reliable and paper currency was not. These arguments ensured that people would pay attention to their platforms and vote. The hysteria died in 1870 when it became clear that the republic would survive, that debts were being honored, that war bonds reaching maturity were being paid, that the prices for crops were steady and rising…and the fake news subject was dropped by politicians and newspapers.

But the horrors in the South were real, the panic was not without cause, and the solution was radical.

DEMOCRATS: THE PARTY OF "COMPASSION"

The "New South" of 1865 was a breeding ground for everything unwholesome in human nature. We've all seen video of the devastation caused by superstorms like Katrina, Sandy, Harvey, and Irma. Now imagine if that carnage spread across towns and cities covering a third of a continent, and instead of water, the means of destruction were fire, artillery, and gunfire. Add to that not dozens dead but more than one quarter of the military-age men who would have made up its working class. The proud, once-thriving farms had been either underworked or abandoned during the war, and a significant portion of the Confederacy's livestock, including workhorses, mules, and food animals, had been killed. Much of the farm implements needed for the South's agrarian economy were ruined. The railroad and riverboat equipment required to bring southern goods to market had been destroyed, and what remained of these had been taken from commercial and agricultural areas to military locations during the war where it was useless during peacetime and too expensive to move back.

Imagine an entire society where what we now call posttraumatic stress disorder affected not only soldiers but every member of the civilian population, young and old. Add to that the freed slaves who were largely without education or guidance, who were either scrounging for food—like everyone else—or searching for family members from whom they had been forcibly separated. Top off that mix with the fact that the southern states were under domination by a vanquishing army. Even the most compassionate, wise, and politically astute president would have had difficulty managing that miasma in a land where even the basic means of communication—newspapers and telegraphs—had been severely compromised. Abraham Lincoln, stupidly murdered by an assassin—an actor foolishly working from his own script—would have been that. Andrew Johnson was not.

Against this unthinkable background, white resentment did not just simmer. It was placed in a pressure cooker where it turned, understandably, into explosive hysteria.

Given that even Lincoln would have required the northern army to occupy the South, Reconstruction would have come under the military's purview, and therefore was the responsibility of Secretary of War Edwin Stanton. Stanton was a Radical Republican, a faction that sought immediate, sweeping, and punitive oversight of the South's reentry into the union. President Johnson feared the antiwhite, problack excesses his stewardship might bring. In August 1867, Johnson overstepped his authority, a mild overreach compared to Lincoln: He suspended Stanton and installed a new secretary of war. In response, Johnson was impeached. He managed to avoid removal by a single vote.

One can imagine defeated, starving, and disease-plagued southerners becoming even more desperate and emboldened as they watched the chaos within their occupiers' government. In Pulaski, Tennessee, what began in 1865 as a Christmas Eve gathering to honor six Confederate army officers soon turned into an outlet for resentment over the region's defeat, anger toward newly freed blacks, and a forum for empowerment. This organization, which took its name from a bastardization of the Greek word for circle, created hooded white "uniforms" and was soon terrorizing and murdering enemies of the Old South as the Ku Klux Klan.[1]

As word spread of this vigilante force, similar groups formed throughout the South. There was no central organization and no formal agenda other than mayhem and intimidation. The hoods they wore and the guns they carried enabled them to create mass hysteria by scaring or lynching blacks, intimidating voters, attacking "Yankee" troops, committing felonies, and settling old scores, regardless of the race of the victim. There was, of course, an underlying theme of white supremacy and the reclamation of twisted honor, but that wasn't codified until early in the next century as the result of a motion picture. More on that later.

The lack of central command may have worked to the Klan's benefit. While individual cells were identified and intermittently persecuted by northern soldiers, the KKK as an entity did not come under federal clampdown until 1870—well after the impact of its voter suppression terrorism had been felt in Georgia, Florida, and especially Louisiana, where in the weeks leading up to the 1868 elections more than two thousand people were assaulted or killed.[2]

The Klan didn't have a monopoly on creating violent hysteria. In Louisiana, a single rumor—which, like the Salem Witch Trials, was originally sourced from children—ended in hundreds of deaths.

Emerson Bentley was a teacher in Opelousas, Louisiana. His students were blacks and Creoles. Bentley was also the editor of the *Landry Progress* and in his spare time he registered blacks to vote. He actively supported the problack Republican Party, which met in a building adjacent to the *Landry Progress* office.

During the summer of 1868, rumors spread that Radical Republicans were quietly provoking blacks to riot. By fall, hysteria among southern whites was growing and two shipments of arms arrived for the purpose of arming Democrats. It was said that a large Republican gathering planned for Washington, a village north of Opelousas, was a cover for black plans to pillage.

The gathering, at least, was real—and peaceful, if uneasy. Word spread—most likely untrue—that hundreds of armed white men were hiding in nearby woods. At one point a white supremacist leader pointed a gun at Bentley's head. Speeches were curtailed and the gathering broke up without significant violence. Less than a week later, Bentley wrote about the Washington gathering in the *Landry Progress*. In the piece, he called out the Democrats for their tactics.

On the morning of September 28, indignation and anger was transformed into mass hysteria— but mass hysteria with the will, the mandate, and the tools to set things "right." Mass hysteria that didn't burn off with the settling of a single score.

Three Democrats visited the school where Bentley taught and expressed their displeasure over the article. As Bentley's students fled, the three men beat him and pointed a pistol at him, although they did not kill him. Bentley hid overnight and, the next day, fled Opelousas. But the children he was teaching did not see him survive his beating. Their last image of their teacher was of three white men beating him, and holding a gun to his head.

The panic of the children, their fear of returning to school, rippled through the region. Yet it wasn't the problack Republicans who became afraid, it was the pro-white Democrats who feared retaliation for Bentley's beating. They armed themselves as rumors of white people being killed began to circulate. Driven to hysterical resolve, these armed Democrats began searching for blacks—armed, unarmed, involved, or otherwise.

The afternoon of September 28 saw the first fatal conflict between Democrats and Republicans—or, more specifically, whites and blacks. A handful of Democrats got word of armed black men at a plantation just south of Opelousas. When the whites arrived, they indeed found two dozen armed black men. Faced with armed whites, the blacks refused to lay down their weapons and, instead, fired upon the Democrats. The subsequent firefight left one black man dead. Eight others were taken into custody and imprisoned.

Hysteria may not have been the goal, but it was the

result. By the next day, most blacks in Washington village had fled. White Democrat militias kept an active search for blacks, however, and at the end of the day an estimated twenty-nine blacks had been sent to the jail in Opelousas, and scores more were likely killed: the Democrats weren't keeping detailed records.

The blacks in the Opelousas jail may have thought themselves lucky. They weren't. That night, a crowd broke into the jail, removed the prisoners from their cells, separated them into small groups, brought them into the woods, and systematically shot them. While this was happening, the offices of the *Landry Progress* were destroyed and its printing presses were burned in the streets. The building next to the *Landry Progress*'s offices was looted, and the Democrats used the Republican party records contained therein to hunt down potential "insurgents"—white or black. Many were shown the same level of justice and compassion given to the twenty-nine prisoners in the woods.

This intimidation of Republicans and the lawless killings went on for weeks. Anyone who was not known to be a Democrat was a target. Outsiders representing law and order attempted to ascertain what had happen in the region. They were met by intimidated, silent blacks and recalcitrant whites. The randomness of the killings prevented those authorities from determining the number of deaths. Democrats put it at around a score, while a Union army officer who visited the area in early October estimated there had been more than two hundred. Whatever the number, few Democrats were ever held responsible.

The effectiveness of the Democrat tactics can, however, be measured. On November 3, 1868, the United States held a presidential election between Republican candidate Ulysses S. Grant and Democratic candidate Horatio Seymour. Of the 4,787 votes cast in St. Landry Parish, which incorporates Opelousas and Washington, not a single vote went to Grant.[3]

The 1868 elections were profoundly discouraging for huge areas of the South. But they also emboldened the first incarnation of the Klan. More and more white supremacists were relying on hoods and robes to keep their crimes anonymous, and even southerners who might have been sympathetic to these groups raised concerns that their activities were justification for northern authorities to further dictate southern affairs. By 1871, several southern states had passed anti-Klan legislation. Additionally, the U.S. Congress passed the Civil Rights Act of 1871, which, among other provisions, authorized President Grant to suspend habeas corpus when dealing with white supremacy organizations.

Unlike Abraham Lincoln before him, and Franklin Roosevelt after him, when Grant did this the United States was not at war.

DRAMATIZING THE SINS OF THE FATHER

The right to be heard, whatever the topic, is generally guaranteed by the Constitution. The need to be heard is baked into the American psyche. Generations after the peaceful marches of the civil rights era, that has been corrupted by the modern Democrats the same way it was corrupted by their forebears, the mid-nineteenth-century Republicans. And using the same techniques: loud speech to spread mass hysteria… with violence as the predictable result.

The degree to which the already-defeated white population of the South resented this suppression became evident in 1915 with the release of the film *The Birth of a Nation.* By many accounts, adjusted for inflation, it remains the most successful film in history. It was also groundbreaking in that it was a feature-length film in an era dominated by short subjects, and it employed many modern techniques of filmmaking, such as close-ups and moving cameras—rare in an era when movies were more often than not static, filmed stage plays. The movie was directed by D. W. Griffith, who grew up in rural Kentucky and was the son of Confederate war hero

Colonel Jacob "Roaring Jake" Griffith. *The Birth of a Nation* told the tale of the miseries suffered by one small town in the aftermath of the war and the added indignities heaped on the population by the North. The result was the birth of the Klan. Despite the fact that the first shot of the film showed pathetic Africans being enslaved, and the second shot showed abolitionists at work, and film stunningly and vividly re-creating the assassination of President Lincoln in a way that brought history to life, what people remember is that it depicted the Klan as heroic. Which, to a man raised in Griffith's environment, it was.[4]

The film is effectively banned today. One has to search hard to find the 1905 novel on which it's based, Thomas Dixon's *The Clansman*. I have a copy and quote from the author's "To the Reader," in which he describes how Reconstruction was "the darkest hour of the life of the South, when her wounded people lay helpless amid rags and ashes," and adds, "The chaos of blind passion that followed Lincoln's assassination is inconceivable to-day [*sic*]." He flatly states that the policies of the North were regarded as a "bold attempt . . . to Africanize ten great States of the American Union."[5]

We know, of course, that this was not true. But in a time when communication between regions was slow at best and nonexistent at worst, when passions and humiliation coupled with resentment and shame were easily transformed to mass hysteria, it was easy for those ideas to take root. The novel, and the film, tell how that happened.

Leftists cannot and will not discuss the context of these works any more than they can discuss pretty much any topic with which the lemmings disagree. Griffith was so shocked by this reaction, even then, that his next film was the brilliant and widely lauded *Intolerance*, a saga of hate and hysteria through the ages. Unlike *The Birth of a Nation*, it was a commercial failure.

One terrible result of *The Birth of a Nation* was a surge of suppressed white pride and the resurrection of the Klan, not as a makeshift "police" force but as a well-organized tool for the cause of white supremacy. *The Birth of a Nation* was an early form of social media, carrying the same message across forty-eight states, that blacks are either shiftless (eating fried chicken in the legislature) or interested in chasing after white women (with the KKK riding to the rescue). Today the narrative by Dixon and Griffith is not interpreted as being in any way historical—which, in a filmed interview in 1930, is all that Griffith said he intended. He wanted to tell his father's story. President Woodrow Wilson supported that view. After a screening at the White House, he is reported to have said, "It is like writing history with lightning. And my only regret is that it is all so terribly true." The president did not say that just the antiblack parts were true. He used the word *all*.

Context matters. Of course, leftists don't want to hear that. If you want to cause instant mass hysteria among them, try arranging a screening of the film in any public forum, whether it's a theater or a college campus. It won't happen and, if it does, the venue will be picketed and attendees verbally or physically assaulted.

The left doesn't like to listen to anyone but other members of the left. When a liberal group like the Southern Poverty Law Center hides $69 million in offshore accounts expressly to target the sources and voices of disagreeable speech and to circulate discredited "data," what chance is there for a dialogue?

Like President Trump after the rioting and death in Charlottesville, I—like most historians who haven't been cowed to silence—will state that there was great wrong committed by *both* sides during Reconstruction, and that racism against blacks or whites or anyone is toxic and evil. Nonetheless, in addition to being evenhanded, I am prescient. Not at the level of Orwell or Andrew Jackson, but you can be sure that the reviews and memes of this book will call me an antiblack racist or a Nazi sympathizer just as they did President Trump for suggesting that soul-searching and calm dialogue is required by both the right *and* left. For citing the one accurate comment Goebbels made among the innumerable monstrous things he said and did, I will be labeled a "supporter." It's appropriate that the symbol of Twitter is a bird. It is, after all, the modern-day version of tarring and feathering. It's also fitting that the antebellum world of plantation owners and slaves has been replaced by the new generation of the plantation owners of leftist commerce (Apple, Google, Facebook) and their mindless, obedient acolytes. For all the blood spilled and strife endured, our nation has gone backward.

THE RUSH OF HYSTERIA

Reconstruction and its effects were a world away to the Americans who had gone west. Many had been drawn across the Rockies a generation before by the discovery of gold at John Sutter's sawmill in Northern California in 1848. Gold fever swept the land, thousands of "49ers" sold everything they owned and went west, and by the end of that year the population of the territory had jumped from eight hundred to twenty thousand. During the most profitable year of the Gold Rush, 1852, the yield was $81 million. By the start of the Civil War the Gold Rush was over... but not the hunger for prospecting.

It was always there, metals like silver or copper possessing the siren call of instant, if not easy, wealth.[6]

What turns fever to mass hysteria is when there is a pedal applied to the metal, such as a lingering economic downturn, like the "Long Depression" that began in 1873 and lasted for more than two decades. Like rootless veterans who have nowhere to go and nothing to do. Like displaced southerners whose plantations were ruined and roots destroyed. By the early 1890s banks began to fail, and then so did railroads, which were tied directly to America's financial fortunes. As the country lost its ability to transport goods, farms and manufacturers lost their revenue means. In 1893, the nation fell into recession and unemployment skyrocketed.

Enter potential redemption, when miners discovered a substantial gold strike in northwest Canada's Klondike region.[7]

The remoteness of the Klondike meant it took almost a year for the news to reach the States. But when the first ship bearing more than a ton of gold pulled into Seattle, the newspapers made up for lost time. "Gold! Gold! Gold! Gold!" trumpeted one headline.[8] Eager to profit from the excitement, newspapers throughout the country ran breathless front-page stories and featured cartoons of prospectors surrounded by fluttering dollar bills.

The lure of easy riches drew the unemployed and the desperate, who, as the 49ers before them, sold everything they had to finance their trip. But it also attracted office workers, shop clerks, policemen, and even the mayor of Seattle. If they had anything in common it was both a dream and a complete lack of knowledge about prospecting. Many probably didn't realize they faced a six-hundred-mile overland trip once they reached Canada. The nature of hysteria is such that few would have cared.

Prospectors may have been excited, but the Canadian government realized a swarm of miners unprepared for the country's terrain and weather would tax its rescue and supply resources. In 1897, the Northwest Mounted Police began requiring those seeking gold to bring a year's worth of food.[9] That, along with camping and mining equipment, meant each prospector had to carry more than a ton of gear, either by buying several pack animals or making multiple trips.

If the Canadians hoped these requirements would curtail fortune seekers, they were mistaken. Again, that's not how hysteria works. Within six months of the first reports, around one hundred thousand people sought the mining areas. The majority never reached their destination. Of the two overland trails that led to the gold-laden areas, one was too steep for pack animals. Miners taking the other tended to overload their animals and as a result three hundred horses and mules died.[10]

It was possible to reach the Klondike by boat, but the cost of tickets or vessels increased exponentially during the rush. The few who bought boats overloaded them until they sank. Those who bought passage were forced to leave much of their cargo behind. The ones who arrived at their destination soon realized the perils of less-traveled routes: they were often left in isolated camps along the river with no means to reach their destination.

By the time these first civilian prospectors reached the region, most of the valuable areas had already been claimed. Prospectors could still make day wages mining on behalf of others, but their earnings were far from the riches they'd imagined. Only thirty thousand of the initial one hundred thousand who set out reached the Klondike. The rest either turned back or died on the way.

Ultimately, only a few hundred prospectors became rich. Most were unable to claim stakes large enough to recoup the money they had invested in equipment and travel. But what really put an end to the Klondike gold fever was more hysteria. In 1898, the Klondike emptied out with the discovery of new gold veins elsewhere in the Yukon, and in Alaska.

As for the Long Depression? It ended with no help

from any gold rushes or hysteria, and there are lessons for today. Unemployment began to ebb as immigration slowed due to the shrunken job market. New jobs were taken by unemployed citizens. Nations worldwide turned to protectionist policies. The United States spent money on infrastructure to expand the West. New technologies made manufacturing, transportation, and construction more economical. More new jobs were created than old jobs lost. In short, everything that Donald Trump proposed during the election of 2016 worked in the 1890s.

In fact, you know who really got rich in the Klondike Gold Rush stampede? Donald Trump's grandfather Fred, and not from the precious metal. He opened restaurants and hotels in the region and walked away with half a million 1901 dollars. He wisely capitalized on the gold rush fever of others. By providing a service that was needed. That's not a knock. That's smart.

The takeaway from gold fever is what I was discussing earlier about racism. Hysteria creates tunnel vision and tunnel vision creates failed solutions. Head to the Klondike with nothing but a dream and you die. Fight racism with reverse racism and you motivate the original racists. Everyone jumps on an idea and careens toward the stated goal without objective thought. If a Powerball lottery is one million dollars, only regulars buy tickets. If it's one *billion* dollars, everyone wants in. Is one million dollars *not* worth the price of a two-dollar ticket? The lines will certainly be shorter.

There is no rational reason for most hysteria, other than that people want to be a part of something big and current and important. They want the adrenaline rush of opportunity and risk. They happily push every other stress or distraction from their minds to follow a simple task, even if that task is burning witches or burning crosses on the lawns of freed slaves. Hysteria is appealing to the masses because it does not require thought; some lunatic college professor or mainstream media pundit does all the thinking for them, even if those thoughts are vacuous or destructive.

A double tragedy takes place when there is actually a good idea that gets co-opted by hysterics. Independence from England was a good idea and the process was directed by reasonable men. Reconstruction was a good idea that was poisoned by hate. The witch trials were hysteria fired up for the sake of political gain.

Unfortunately, there was more of the truly evil kind on the horizon, hysteria in which the news media were willing purveyors of fake news.

Fake news kills. That's the lesson of out-of-control New York newspapers that revved up mass hysteria based on false tales of atrocities within Cuba and created the Spanish-American War. The war boosted newspaper readership—the equivalent of website "clicks" today—boosted the career of future president Teddy Roosevelt and resulted in more than three thousand Americans losing their lives. It also fed into the impulse to treat Hispanics and other immigrants, such as Germans, as second-class citizens. Once more, America is feeling the powerful forces of this hysteria more than one hundred years later.

9.

FROM REGIONAL WAR TO PROHIBITION
Hysteria Outside the Trenches

There's a line in the movie *Citizen Kane* in which newspaper publisher Kane tells a colleague, "If the headline is big enough, it makes the news big enough."[1]

That fits neatly with Goebbels's previously-stated philosophy that "a lie told a thousand times becomes the truth."[2] At the dawn of the twentieth century, both of those ideas converged to create hysteria that supported a war no one knew we needed.

The war involves people of Spanish descent. Before we get to that, however, it's useful to ponder just how marketable hate is in order to generate mass hysteria. By that I mean it is relatively easy to target a historically mysterious or outsider group like witches or Jews. How do evil-minded leaders and agenda-driven media get us to focus on people who are off the radar? Can anyone be targeted? The answer to the last question is yes. After the Civil War, General George Armstrong Custer built his short-lived career on the public's media-manipulated hatred of Indians. The answer to the first question, about concocting an enemy, is found in the kind of psychology I've been studying all my life, first as an anthropologist and then as a radio talk show host.

There are three primary ingredients necessary for whipping up mass hysteria. They are some combination of psychological stress, such as unemployment or debt or political strife within a family or group of friends; physical stress, as in illness caused by poor eating habits or drink or pot; and exhaustion from overwork, searching for work, commuting long hours, or lack of sleep due to the stress. These can occur naturally or they can be manufactured, especially today, when everyone is plugged in to some kind of device. You may not be thinking of a hurricane that probably won't affect you, but the media will force you to worry. You might not be concerned about North Korean nukes until the fear-mongering press tells you to be. You could be unaware of Ebola or some other disease until two people who visited Africa come down with it in Europe and we are suddenly warned it could become a worldwide epidemic. Bedbugs are always good for a news cycle or two.

You get the picture. Leaders distract us, and media sell ads based on our base instincts, whether fear or greed. So how does this translate to a particular group? How many people really have anything to fear from neo-Nazis who are few in number and essentially powerless? Why is the media obsessed with them, yet equally devoted to promoting love for Muslims who pose an immediate twofold threat: swiftly increasing numbers and well-hidden terrorists?

The answer is demographics. Neo-Nazis and their boosters represent a small voting bloc. Muslims and their bleeding-heart boosters represent a much larger bloc. In a free America, which this once was—with an unbiased press—these groups would have been reported upon only when they did something newsworthy. When the National Socialist Party of America marched in the predominantly Jewish town of Skokie, Illinois, in 1978, that was news. The march was intentionally provocative but, more important, it was constitutionally protected. It was reported upon and then it was gone.

There was no social media to keep it alive, pro or con. Indignation and fear were not headlined as if they were commodities to be sold. There was not a spike in membership for the NSPA.

When you have the bedrock causes of mass hysteria, the subtler effects take hold. In the short term, they are largely physical. Fear and excitation cause us to have panic attacks and to hyperventilate. Depleted of carbon dioxide, we experience symptoms from spasms to benign fasciculation (twitching) to temporary numbness. If these issues continue, hysterical psychology takes over and triggers hypochondria: It's a heart attack, it's colon cancer, it's a brain tumor. Others in our family become concerned. We feed off their fear and our symptoms amplify, whether they are imagined or real. We go online, playing amateur doctor, and zero in not on the voices of calm and reason but on the few fellow hysterics who say it really could be a heart attack, colon cancer, or a brain tumor. We actually *make* ourselves ill.

That same progression applies to the psychology of hate. We are annoyed by someone at work or on the bus. We find that other voices are aligned with our frustration—not at that individual necessarily but at that individual's race or religion. If the government or media decides there is a group we *should* hate (more on that in a moment), we fixate on that. If you are inherently stable, you won't bite. But how many of us possess that consistent level of benevolence? If the media feeds us someone to hate, anyone, we are likely to transfer our disgust and climb aboard. This is an insidious but very real, very human process. If you are a male attorney, normally rational, and a fellow female attorney takes maternity leave giving you her workload on top of your own, you *may* find yourself resentful of her ... and as the weeks and months pass, of feminism in general. You may be triggered into expressing your displeasure by all the hype around a movie like *Wonder Woman*. You may circle the wagons around all things male. And if the assault continues, if you read about (as I did) plans to make an all-girl film based on the all-boy novel *Lord of the Flies*, your resentment starts to set, like concrete. You find yourself on Election Day refusing to vote for any female candidates.

Psychological weakness of any kind, in any capacity, makes us yearn for a steadying hand, even if that hand is an agent of Goebbels or a once-reliable brand like CNN or the *New York Times*. Or Facebook, which offers you a rainbow gay flag for your profile but not a Confederate one. When all of these outlets and individuals have the same progressive agenda, you will either hate who they hate or love who they hate. The more these entities push an agenda, the more rabid your views become. As Goebbels said it would.

Which brings us to a perfect confluence of controlling factors to generate mass hysteria and hate near the turn of the century.

THE BIRTH OF A WAR

Shortly before the turn of the century, Americans needed new outlets for their energy. The frontier had been tamed, and the country's reach extended from the Atlantic to the Pacific. What was left? One of the last strongholds of the old colonial powers, and it was right at our doorstep. What to do about it? The answer was obvious.

The history of the Spanish colony of Cuba was four centuries of abuse, exploitation, and genocide. By 1896, Cubans had fought three wars over thirty years in their quest for independence. That year, occupying Spanish troops viciously cracked down on the rebels, relocating hundreds of thousands of Cubans from their rural homes into prison camps. What housing there was, offered scant protection from the elements. The Spanish provided little food for their prisoners and almost no medical services. Tens of thousands of Cubans died there or were shot for refusing to move to them. [3]

His eyes turned toward the Caribbean, Assistant Secretary of the Navy Teddy Roosevelt said, "I should welcome almost any war, for I think this country needs one."[4] President William McKinley preferred diplomatic and economic pressure, but William Randolph Hearst, publisher of the *New York Journal*, realized that a war with a substantial human interest angle would sell newspapers. Starting in 1895, the *New York Journal* and its rival the *New York World* competed for readership by publishing ever-increasingly lurid tales of torture, horrible living conditions, rapes, and murders within the Cuban camps. As Hearst had predicted, the camps were just the sort of outrage Americans could latch on to. The hysteria building continued, with help from members of the American government and Cuban rebels who sought an armed conflict. It had been more than thirty years since the end of the Civil War. A new generation felt the stirring of war fever.

Still, not everyone was convinced. Legend has it that in 1897, *New York Journal* illustrator Frederic Remington—the famed western artist who was stationed in Cuba to provide drawings of Spanish cruelty—sent a cable to Hearst reading, "Everything quiet. There is no trouble here. There will be no war. Wish to return." Hearst allegedly replied, "Please remain. You furnish the pictures and I'll furnish the war."[5]

Ultimately, a deadly incident in Havana Harbor removed the need for newspapers to peddle atrocities. The cruiser *Maine* had been stationed in the harbor—not, as President McKinley claimed, as a goodwill gesture, but to remind both the Spanish government and Cuban rebels that any activities that endangered American interests in Cuba would not be tolerated. On February 15, 1898, the *Maine* exploded and sank, killing 266 men.

Roosevelt and Hearst had their flash point. Here was destruction of American property. Here was a seeming attack on the American military. Never mind that the exact nature of the explosion was never determined. Two days after the incident, the *World* ran a piece debating whether the Maine explosion was caused by a bomb or a torpedo[6]— and further, whether Spain had even been involved. Recent investigations of the wreckage have led to speculation that it was an accident, an explosion caused by onboard ammunition and coal being stored too near each other.

No matter. The *Journal* took a firm stand, declaring "Destruction of the War Ship Maine Was the Work of an Enemy" and posting a "$50,000 REWARD! For the Detection of the Perpetrator of the Maine Outrage!" Since the perpetrator was never uncovered, the reward went uncollected. The next day, the *Journal* announced "The Whole Country Thrills with War Fever." That much, at least, was true. Around the country, newspapers embraced the tone set by the New York media. In tone and content and even in terms of monetary gain, this was no different than the billion-dollar Powerball.

The only person who was not ablaze with war fever, it seemed, was McKinley, who was not prepared to go to war based on the goading of newspapers and an explosion of inconclusive origin. For two months, he pursued a diplomatic end to hostilities. It wasn't until an April U.S. Navy blockade of Cuba resulted in Spain declaring war on America that newspapers got their war.

The newspapers weren't the only entities ready for war. As soon as the United States reciprocated Spain's declaration of war, Teddy Roosevelt resigned his post and formed the First U.S. Volunteer Cavalry Regiment. To complete the reality TV-style selling of the war, he gave his regiment a nickname bestowed in honor of the spectacular, live western attraction "Buffalo Bill's Wild West and Congress of Rough Riders of the World." Partly because of the fervor, partly because of Roosevelt's go-get-'em reputation, and partly because the whole matter seemed like a warm-weather vacation, volunteers swamped to join Roosevelt's Rough Riders. This, too, is mass hysteria: wanting to be a part of something that is big and trendy. In the absence of Facebook and Instagram, young men wanted to be able to send letters and photographs and trinkets to their wives, girlfriends, and mothers. Those were automatic "likes."

While the Spanish-American War was hardly a vacation, it did last only three and a half months. Mosquitos proved to be more fearsome than the Spanish: of the 3,289 American dead, nine times as many U.S. servicemen were felled by typhoid, malaria, and yellow fever than were killed in battle.[7] The brevity of the campaign had to be a relief to Hearst, not because he was a humanitarian but because he was a businessman. He knew then what we have since learned in Afghanistan—that over time even a necessary or at least publicly sanctioned war becomes tiresome...especially as the coffins and the maimed begin returning home.

The result of the mass hysteria caused by the American press was unprecedented and far-reaching. It didn't matter that it was based on a fabrication, just like the Associated Press and its lying use of the term "undocumented citizens." Spain left Cuba and gave Guam and Puerto Rico to the United States. For an additional $20 million we received sovereignty over the Philippines. Spain was no longer a global power while, for the price of ten weeks of war, the United States was. Cuba effectively remained an American colony and playground until Castro tossed us out in 1959. Roosevelt returned a hero (also helped by the press) and went from governor to vice president to president in just two years.

But there was a less obvious result, one that also resonates to this day. That was the treatment of all Hispanics as second-class citizens. We've seen a lot of racial hate in just the events we've talked about, and though the result isn't always obvious mass hysteria—rioting, burning, lynching—it is slow-burn hysteria nonetheless. It's a form of fight-or-flight. If you are of any ethnicity, with familiar practices, languages, traditions in your town, and someone with a different look and lifestyle shows up, you will go into self-preservation mode. Protect the herd. You needn't even express that to others of the town or neighborhood or jungle village. Fear and suspicion are palpable. Your people and your way of life are about to end. I am perplexed that the illegal immigration of drug dealers and killers that causes the death of citizens is okay with progressives, yet these same voices want to tear down statues of Columbus. That defies logic. Columbus made a difficult journey to go somewhere new. He sought a better life, too. He sent money home. He established a community within an existing community. He did not bother to learn the ways of the indigenous people but made them accept his ways, his nation's religion. Once a foothold had been gained, his numbers swelled. And by the way: he was sailing under the flag of the very people who are now demonized: Hispanics. They were conquerors then but victims now. Progressives are lucky to have logic that works like a pendulum, swinging wherever they want it to go.

Racism and bigotry have two defining parts, immorality and illegality. The problem for progressives is that the first is subjective and often clashes with the latter—for example, the bakery that refuses to make a cake for a gay couple. When any entrenched group feels threatened by a newly formed identity—be they married gays, freed blacks, or transplanted Hispanics who don't necessarily speak the language—hysteria on the local or national level is invariably the result. How that is manifest, whether by the formation of the KKK or massive deportations, depends entirely on the wisdom and broad-based compassion of our leaders.

These days, we've lost our ability to distinguish which causes are truly worth fighting for, which groups are truly worth championing. Propped by the profit-minded, agenda-driven media—now, as just before the Spanish-American War—the hysterical, vocal minority has come down hard on behalf of the new arrivals, be they legal or illegal. The problem for them is that they are not defending something they own. It isn't a rounded, functioning community with a consistent citizenry, shared history, and point of view. It is a subjective viewpoint with a shifting perimeter and ever-changing content, defined by whatever is the oppressed group of the moment: Hispanics, blacks, Muslims, women, gays. Never, of course, fetuses, whites, Jews, or job creators.

In addition to their selective vision, their moral indignation and constantly flapping tongues have blinded them to the larger reality, that in great numbers illegal immigration renders a community, a nation, incapable of lawful functioning, since not only is the immigration unlawful but the stopgap measures to permit it—the Deferred Action for Childhood Arrivals policy, or DACA, for one—are helplessly unconstitutional. How is a traditionalist supposed to feel in his or her home as the very fabric of its legal system no longer applies? How is a lawful American citizen supposed to react when informed that the dreams of nonlegal residents are more important than their own? When the taxes that American citizens dutifully pay are used to undermine, through progressive programs, the very nature of the traditional, vital, growth-oriented "American Dream"? There is only one dream DACA individuals should have, only one dream that should be encouraged by any right-thinking and compassionate individuals: becoming American citizens and participating in the legal process that has successfully embraced millions of refugees and immigrants since the earliest days of the colonies. Anything other than that is ruinous to the sovereignty and future of our nation. Of course, that requires assimilation to a large degree—something that the progressives also find offensive. In their view, anything that white Europeans conceived of, including American democracy, is de facto no good.

The progressive response to anti-DACA passion is *too bad...deal with it.* That isn't an answer, it's a loathing for an American system that, admittedly, has done the wrong thing from time to time. At one time we permitted slavery and put Japanese citizens in internment camps. We shot students at Kent State. Those were awful things, but they were aberrations in a history that has shown more respect for individual rights and human dignity than any civilization in human history. Those heinous black marks did not then and do not now define what America is in a larger sense. Tear our nation down from guilt, in atonement, and there is nothing. That is why I, and a lot of my fellow Americans. have a slow-burning rage. In 1969, President Richard Nixon popularized a half-century-old expression and called us "the silent majority." Originally, that phrase referred to the dead. Supreme Court justice John Marshall Harlan famously used those words in 1902 to refer to the losses on both sides of the Civil War. In his 1955 book *Profiles in Courage*, Senator John F. Kennedy changed the meaning somewhat to express the response of most Americans to "the screams of a vocal minority." That Pulitzer Prize–winning book was where Nixon encountered the phrase. Though we, the formerly silent majority, are increasingly becoming less than a majority, we still managed to elect Donald Trump against all odds.

One of my favorite pieces of writing in the English language—and I believe I can still say that without fear of being called a "white nationalist"— is Sir Walter Scott's poem *The Lay of the Last Minstrel*, which was written in 1805. It contains these immortal lines:

> *Breathes there the man, with soul so dead,*
> *Who never to himself hath said,*
> *This is my own, my native land!*
> *Whose heart hath ne'er within him burn'd,*
> *As home his footsteps he hath turn'd,*
> *From wandering on a foreign strand!*

I do not believe there are many progressives who can say that about themselves and their nation. They cannot see or feel history because their entire worldview is a hysterical tantrum. Like that girl in Roald Dahl's *Charlie and the Chocolate Factory*—Veruca Salt, the spoiled brat everyone remembers—they want what they want *now*. That is why I mistrust them as gatekeepers, as teachers, as journalists, as politicians. Not only do they fail to understand the concept of home, they repudiate it. They are about temper, not temperance. My own personal rage has been building since the first American flag was burned in protest during the Vietnam War. However justified the protests, the contempt for country made the flag burners unpalatable to me. The progressives and their hate is even worse because it skips from one issue to another in search of fuel to keep the rage burning.

Importing labor with open disregard for both the process of immigration and the people being relocated created decades of hardship for Hispanics. With the door open to Puerto Ricans and others from the Caribbean, especially the Dominican Republic, it opened wider for Mexicans as well. Throughout the early years of the last century, for example, the American government was content to allow Hispanics to immigrate as a source of cheap labor in factories, canneries, and in agriculture. In 1942, while young men were off fighting in World War II, Washington created the bracero program, which brought in thousands of Mexicans to work on U.S. farms. Eleven years later, the government initiated "Operation Wetback," which deported 3.8 million people—many of whom were American citizens.[8] The stereotype of these people as essentially interchangeable and disposable has not changed in more than a century.

Emotionally, this plays into the current uproar over the president's timely and overdue termination of the DACA program. Hispanics understandably resent the century of oppression and are vocally opposed to Trump's action; Americans who support the president are also understandably tired of the continued dilution of our borders, language, and culture. Critics of the right have said that we are anti-immigrant. That is demonstrably false. America has always been a multinational melting pot. What we are fighting, now, is a multicultural fascism—the left-spurred desire to destroy everything of European origin going back five centuries. But those are the old battle lines, the ones close to the surface that fan the hysterical reaction we've seen. The real issues today are more complex than Apple's Tim Cook or actors seem to understand when their knees jerk in defense of illegal immigrants. These issues require something more intelligent and comprehensive than Obama's illegal, free-pass document. The drug scourge has become a massive drain on this nation—costing billions of dollars annually in some states, like New Hampshire—and those narcotics are coming from south of the border. In fact, the Castro brothers, whom Obama welcomed into the fellowship of the civilized world, have been among the facilitators of their transport to these shores. Additionally, there are now a staggering thirty to fifty million illegal immigrants in the country, the majority of them Hispanic, most of them taking our jobs and/or straining our social welfare resources. And Islamic terrorists are almost certainly moving northward with the influx, along with the criminals we know about who are robbing and killing in our sanctuary cities.

As long as the left continues to fan mass hysteria over the supposed injustice of deporting illegal citizens, many of whom only "dream" of violent but lucrative criminal activity or shipping American dollars to their families in Guatemala or Mexico or Ecuador, the old biases will remain and grow stronger. In that respect, the resolution of another bias of even longer standing provides clues as to how hysteria can be managed and reduced. As long as the progressives refuse to reach across the aisle and acknowledge that half the nation cannot simply be trampled under, this nation will remain polarized. And polarization is the short road to mass hysteria and the evils of hate.

HYPHENS AND HYSTERIA

We've talked about how, in the nineteenth century, nativism caused a backlash against several non-WASP groups. This bias continued to be felt particularly hard among German Americans. The rage generated by the Hessians who fought alongside the British during the Revolution was forgotten; religion was not quite the hot-button issue it once was; but while the reasons were murky, the hatred remained and flourished with the coming of World War I.

Since 1914, when fighting first erupted in Europe, Americans had heard stories of German atrocities, whether burnings of libraries, strip searches of nuns, or wholesale rapes and massacres. And when German submarines sunk the British ocean liner RMS *Lusitania* in 1915, one in ten passengers was American.

Even after all this, Washington was not moved to fight Germany militarily. But American civilians felt no such restrictions, and their war frenzy manifested itself against anything that evoked the German people. In some cases this led to renamings reminiscent of 2003, when French fries popularly became "freedom fries" after France disapproved of the U.S. invasion of Iraq. In 1914, sauerkraut was out: the pickled vegetable was now called "liberty cabbage."[9] Frankfurters became hot dogs, and dachshunds were renamed "liberty pups." "German" hospitals in New York and Chicago were rechristened "Lenox Hill" and "Grant." Even German measles, which in theory should have been left alone to carry the stigma of illness, was renamed "Liberty measles."[10] Streets bearing names of German towns or leaders were given names to celebrate Americans such as Pershing or Wilson. (Ironically, the revered John J. Pershing, who became commander of our forces during World War I, was of German heritage, his family name having been Pfoerschin.)

Syracuse, New York, went a symbolic—and idiotic—step further, issuing a ban on the card game pinochle because of its roots in the German game *binokel*.[11]

But in the growing hysteria of the early twentieth century, these moves were seen as anything but silly. Indeed, a noted American seized upon the concept of nativism to publicly—and rightly— denounce a plague that is still with us, the hyphenate. In 1915, Theodore Roosevelt, now a private citizen, used an address to the Knights of Columbus to denounce *all* conflicting loyalties when he thundered:

The one absolutely certain way of bringing this nation to ruin, of preventing all possibility of its continuing to be a nation at all, would be to permit it to become a tangle of squabbling nationalities, an intricate knot of German-Americans, Irish-Americans, English-Americans, French-Americans, Scandinavian-Americans, or Italian-Americans, each preserving its separate nationality, each at heart feeling more sympathy with Europeans of that nationality than with the other citizens of the American Republic.[12]

German Americans did not help their situation. Their near-monolithic insensitivity and intransigence contributed to American panic. In 1916, not long before the United States declared war on Germany, a Chicago-based German pride organization made a point of loudly celebrating the kaiser's birthday.[13] Throughout the country, Germans—whose culture embraced brewing and consuming beer—were particularly tone deaf to the bourgeoning temperance movement, which we'll be getting to shortly, and campaigned avidly against it. With the start of World War I, temperance organizations made sure that anti-German propaganda often included images of menacing Germans with beer steins, or soldiers represented by marching beer casks.[14] And the German American media had long urged neutrality in the European war, but that was widely regarded as self-serving.

When the United States finally declared war in April 1917, everything German-related came under additional scrutiny. Schools eliminated German language instruction. Business groups that had tolerated multilingual employees—in particular, Germans—stopped doing so. And not all of the anti-German hysteria was paranoia. Germany secretly made overtures to Mexico, seeking a military alliance. While Mexico declined, Americans were infuriated by the potential of a two-front war instigated by Germany.

War removed the last restraint from rational behavior regarding German immigrants, and mass hysteria was everywhere. The Department of Justice began a tally of German aliens and imprisoned thousands under charges of espionage or supporting the German war effort. More than two thousand were arrested and sent to internment camps. Their cases were supervised and reviewed by a team led by young J. Edgar Hoover.[15]

German citizens not scrutinized by the U.S. government were made to show their patriotism by buying war bonds, often in amounts that exceeded what they could afford. Stores held bonfires of merchandise made in Germany. Shops owned by

German merchants had their windows smashed, or the word *kraut* painted across their fronts. And one German man living in Illinois had been put into protective custody but was dragged from the jail by a mob, forced to walk across broken bottles, and made to kiss an American flag before being lynched, hanged from a tree three times—as someone in the crowd put it, one time each for the red, white, and blue. The eleven men tried for his murder were acquitted in what a newspaper editor later termed "a farcical patriotic orgy."[16]

The film industry stoked the fervor as well. One of 1918's biggest movies was *The Kaiser, the Beast of Berlin*, which played to crowds that cheered the image of an American soldier punching the German leader. In Omaha, Nebraska, a truck advertising the film drove through the streets with an effigy of the kaiser hanging in its back. That same year, Charlie Chaplin's comedy *Shoulder Arms* depicted a French soldier who uses Limburger cheese against the Germans and gets past the dull-witted enemy disguised as a tree. It was the superstar's most successful movie to date.[17]

In a case of too little too late, German Americans trotted out the slogan "Germany is my mother; America my bride."[18] Americans weren't buying.

Echoing Theodore Roosevelt's earlier words, President Wilson said, "Any man who carries a hyphen around with him, carries a dagger that he is ready to plunge into the vitals of this Republic when he gets ready."[19]

The war was won, of course, and many of the symbolic name changes were rescinded. Others, however, took their place. Many German Americans changed their surnames and the names of their businesses. German-language newspapers were mostly gone. America and its outwardly contrite German American population healed their wounds, and all was very slowly and tentatively forgiven. It was a too-brief respite before Germany started a new and more terrible conflagration.

Just fifteen years after the end of the war, the rise of Adolf Hitler triggered a mass migration of Germans and Austrians to these shores, including filmmakers, actors, and composers who settled in Hollywood, and scientists like Albert Einstein. Mistrust of these émigrés was nothing like it had been in the previous generation. The reason was simple and there is a lesson for today. These new arrivals did not gravitate toward German enclaves in America. They immediately and proudly sought to assimilate into the culture and traditions of their new land, the land that saved many of them from destruction. They were grateful *and* respectful.

Contrast that with the Cedar Riverside section of Minneapolis, Minnesota, where it is impossible to know how many Muslims have settled from Africa, South Asia, Eastern Europe, and the Middle East. Because the Census Bureau is not permitted to ask question about religion, estimates range from 20,000 to 130,000.[20] Interviews with many outspoken youth not only advocate sharia law, but passionately refute freedom in general and criticism of Muhammad in particular. Andrew Luger, U.S. attorney for Minnesota, acknowledged that his state "has a terror recruitment problem."[21]

It *was* mass hysteria to turn on all German Americans in the early twentieth century, however little they did to address the hot-button issues. Despite their awareness of the challenges of being hyphenates, they stubbornly refused to capitulate. That wasn't anti-Americanism as much as it was German pride. They did not seek to make everyone celebrate Oktoberfest—and certainly not in place of another long-established American holiday.

The situation in Minneapolis and in other cities around the world—we discussed the dire condition of Great Britain earlier—is different. It is not irrational to be concerned about avowed enemies within one's borders. The lesson to be learned from the past, however, is that mechanisms already in place must be employed before we reach a point of no return and start burning witches or tarring and feathering former loyalists to the British Crown. There's a word that describes talk of tearing down the nation's laws and Constitution: *sedition*, a revolt or incitement to revolt against the lawful government. Much of this is not protected speech as defined by the First Amendment. Freely granted interviews, along with posts on social media, pass by a wide margin the threshold of a "clear and present danger."

Despite what the Social Justice Warriors and progressive champions of diversity would have the gullible believe, the loss of our national identity and character is the loss of America itself. And if sharia law ever comes, those liberals—the ones who embrace abortion, equality for women, religious freedom, gay and transgender rights, pot legalization—will be the first to be hanged or thrown to their deaths from rooftops. And then watch mass hysteria reach new heights as those frightened progressives stop toking long enough to seek the once-reviled police to protect them, or come sniffing around for NRA members who have the wherewithal to fight back. If you think it can't happen here, take a closer look at what is going on in France and Great Britain. The third world war will not be fought with North Korea or nuclear weapons. It will be to save Europe from the scourge that its own liberal insanity has allowed to take root and flourish.

Borders, language, culture. I will repeat those words as many times as it takes for them to register.

TEMPERANCE AND HYSTERIA

We were talking earlier about mass amnesia and the ravages of marijuana on generations of Americans. Apart from the anti-American propaganda to which we're constantly exposed from the left, brains and ambition continue to be dulled by the psychoactive alkaloid tetrahydracannabinol (THC).

The drug presents the difficult challenge for our nation of keeping the pendulum from swinging too far toward liberalism or fascism. But the truth is, we have a road map. We have already seen the social and political fallout of the attempt to define and control national habits and morality. It was the temperance movement of the previous two centuries.

The desire to curb alcohol abuse had been around since the colonial days, partly as a result of religious dogma and partly as a result of practicality: There was no time to grow anything but essential crops. Distilling and brewing were not considered appropriate uses for a garden's harvest. In the eighteenth century, taverns were the rough and bawdy heart of port cities. They were common, unsanitary, and downright dangerous. During the Revolution, British troops regularly picked fights with colonists and one another in pubs. If a patron so much as looked at them unhappily they could be arrested as a spy. More than occasionally there *were* spies, since drunk soldiers were talkative soldiers.

The first antidrinking movements advocated moderation rather than outright bans.[22] That attitude shifted by the mid-nineteenth century when women began to organize in support of causes such as prison reform, labor reform, women's rights, and temperance. The rhetoric shifted from advocating self-control to the idea that since people were not able to regulate their drinking, the government had to do it for them. The birth of the Prohibition movement was the forerunner of today's nanny state but it took hold with a hysteria that American women had not previously shown on these shores. By 1834, still early in the movement, the American

Temperance Society already had 170,000 members.[23] I suspect it had to do with women realizing that mobilizing gave them social and political power at a time when they otherwise had none. By organizing against alcohol consumption, they believed they could eliminate the source of many of their woes, such as wife abuse or husbands losing their jobs due to drunkenness. In 1873, women's groups aligned themselves with evangelical churches and formed the Woman's Christian Temperance Union,[24] a group that afforded the movement new levels of credibility, gave them great organizational power, and extended reach—from the pulpit. One religious group, the Methodists, declared, without obfuscation, that drinking was a sin.

For the most part, the deeds of early temperance activists were initially benign. Women would stand outside saloons singing hymns and shaming patrons, or enter the male-only bastions, kneel in the beer-soaked sawdust, and pray. These actions were more annoying than shaming, but they had the desired result of clearing out the room. But as the hysteria grew, not all actions were peaceful. And that fanaticism grew largely because of one woman.

Carrie Nation was a six-foot-tall, broad-shoul-
dered Social Justice Warrior whose dislikes included
corsets, tobacco, insufficiently long skirts—and
alcohol. In 1900, she began her crusade by marching into bars, singing, praying, and smashing
glasses, casks, and fixtures with a hatchet. Nation
did not do so unmolested. She was assaulted on
several occasions, and during the next decade she
was arrested more than thirty times. She raised
bail money through lectures, autographs, and selling miniature silver replicas of her hatchet. She also
sold copies of her biweekly newsletter the *Smash-
er's Mail*. She died in 1911, at age sixty-four, nine
years before Prohibition became law. Not surprisingly, she died after collapsing during one of her
fiery speeches.[25]

During the 1916 presidential election, both
Democrats and Republicans avoided addressing
Prohibition. Women did not. They spoke in numbers greater than ever, in voices louder than before,
and it was perceived—not incorrectly—that these
women had a sacred mission, which was to preserve
the American family.[26]

For women, the right to vote nationally was still
four years away, although women had the vote in
many states before the Nineteenth Amendment.

But politicians believed that universal women's suffrage was imminent, and more women than not were for Prohibition. The math put elected officials squarely behind the Eighteenth Amendment and by 1920 it was the law of the land.

The day before Prohibition went into effect, evangelical preacher Billy Sunday extolled its social benefits, saying, "We will turn our prisons into factories and our jails into storehouses and corncribs. Men will walk upright now, women will smile, and the children will laugh. Hell will be forever for rent."[27]

He was wrong. Americans were about to get a harsh lesson in unintended consequences, a lesson whose price we continue to pay.

REPEALING HYSTERIA

Welcome to mass hysteria. Many of the benefits temperance advocates claimed Prohibition would yield were based on false information, wishful thinking, or outright lies. One could make a list of almost every outcome promised and show that Prohibition achieved the opposite.

For example, Prohibitionists believed temperance would be accompanied by a rise in Christian faith. Church attendance got a bump at first, but that was because the Eighteenth Amendment permitted religious organizations to serve sacramental beverages. They came to be seen as self-serving institutions as religious leaders, especially priests and rabbis, foolishly touted their ability to procure wine. Churches quickly saw their attendance decline as the devout became disillusioned.[28]

Predictably, mass hysteria among religious zealots came to the rescue. When temperance groups raised concerns about alcohol in houses of worship, opponents branded them as anti-Catholic or anti-Semitic. Which wasn't far from the truth, as it turns out. Members of the Woman's Christian Temperance Union often belonged to the WKKK—a woman's auxiliary of the KKK.[29] Both Klans took Carrie Nation's fervor one step further, destroying speakeasies and tarring, feathering, and killing bootleggers. Instead of plunging, as predicted, homicides rose nationally over 1920–21, jumping from sixty-eight to eight-one per million.[30]

Prohibitionists had also sought to save families by shutting saloons and curtailing male drinking. But the saloons—which had been largely male bastions—were replaced by speakeasies, which welcomed women patrons.[31] Rather than reduce desire, Prohibition doubled the potential drinking population.

No one should have been surprised. By its very nature,

hysteria is produced by emotion, not thought. An idea may be a trigger. No one would argue that drunkenness is good. (Mothers Against Drunk Driving was formed in 1980 after a thirteen-year-old girl was killed in a DUI tragedy.[32] The idea was to sponsor tougher laws and increase public awareness of the scourge, both of which were needed. The execution was methodical and rational.) But Prohibition did not proceed in a smart, patient way. As a result, by 1929, it had fallen into such disrepute that a quiet but insistent counter group, the Women's Organization for National Prohibition Reform (WONPR), was formed.[33] WONPR executives argued that repealing Prohibition would reduce alcohol-related crime and corruption. It would also afford adults free choice and the obligation of taking responsibility for their own actions. In short, it was an early opponent of the nanny state. The rise of the WONPR played into the growing national sentiment toward smaller government, reduced interventionist attitude—libertarianism was not yet a party, but it was an active idea—and personal choice. This tone, compared with the hysteria that had heralded the temperance movement, also resonated with the American public, which, more and more, were hearing the voices of public figures over the radio, not just in print. Presentation mattered. Within two years, WONPR's membership was triple that of the WCTU.

The Great Depression all but guaranteed Prohibition's repeal. When the economy collapsed, Franklin Roosevelt incorporated bringing back legal alcohol sales, and the all-important tax revenue they generated, in his presidential platform. By 1933, what Herbert Hoover had dubbed "a great social and economic experiment" was finished. But a new and much greater hysteria lurked just over the horizon.

At the turn of the twentieth century—the American Century, as some have called it—the United States was growing as a global power. The country's enemies, both real and manufactured by fake news, had to reflect its new stature. Enter the anarchists and the communists, each of whom had their menace exaggerated by forces whose rise to power depended on presenting the populace with a virulent enemy. Ultimately, fate helped the power-mad when World War II provided new targets for hysteria—not just in a theater of battle, but at home.

10.

FROM REDS TO FASCISTS
Global Threats Produce
Greater Hysteria

I t's a largely forgotten terrorist attack, but two similarities to a later, bigger, more traumatic assault bear mentioning. First, the bombing in 1920 occurred a very short walk from where the future World Trade Center would be built. Second, the act of terror occurred in early September. There is something about a pleasant fall day, when citizens are out enjoying the last of the vanishing summer, that seems ripe for disruption.

At lunchtime on September 16, 1920, financial workers in lower Manhattan were out and about in great numbers. No one thought much of another overloaded, horse-drawn carriage on the cobbled streets. That's how deliveries were made then. It briefly stopped on the busiest corner of the financial district, across the street from the J. P. Morgan bank at 23 Wall Street. No one had any reason to suspect that the buggy was loaded with one hundred pounds of dynamite and, for shrapnel, five hundred pounds of iron sash weights that were used in windows.

The driver is believed to have left the cart and, at one minute past noon, the contents detonated. Thirty people died instantly, most of them in their teens and twenties working as messengers, secretaries, and clerks. Eight more succumbed to their injuries, 143 were gravely wounded, and hundreds more suffered minor harm. Automobiles were upended, windows were blown out for blocks around, and the interior of the bank was destroyed. Stubbornly, proudly—defiantly?—the famed statue of George Washington at Federal Hall, overseeing all, was undamaged. I have been to the site, and the scars of the blast—chipped walls and foundation—are still visible on the targeted building.[12]

By the next day, there were cries in the press and among influential Americans for local and federal authorities to root out and deport foreign radicals. Evidence and emotion converged on two possible groups: anarchists and communists. The investigation was thorough but immediately inconclusive. Six months later, the incoming administration of President Warren Harding favored and investigated the Soviets as the cause, most likely acting through their local agents in the Communist Party USA or through presumably sympathetic émigrés known as the Union of Russian Workers. But after three years, the perpetrator still was not identified. Now it is agreed that the act was likely committed by followers of the chronically hysterical sociopath Luigi Galleani, an Italian anarchist who—like the Nazi brownshirts who came after him—believed in the "propaganda of the deed," acts of terror and destruction designed to bring down any individuals or institutions perceived, by him, to be oppressive. The assassination of President William McKinley, which elevated Teddy Roosevelt to the presidency in 1901, was one such act.

Though the so-called Galleanists were the likely bombers, and ranked near the top of Washington's public enemies list, they were not feared as much as the communists. That's because with anarchists, the government was able to put faces on wanted posters. Cherry-picking and eliminating anarchists inspired much the same reaction as the drone killings of ISIS commanders today, a sense that the government was *doing* something. Contrast that today with government activity in North Korea.

The president startled the world by sitting down

with dictator Kim Jung-un and setting in motion the denuclearization of the Korean Peninsula. Did the world press give Trump credit for defusing one of the world's most dangerous situations? Before this summit the fake news media followed the situation in Korea like a championship tennis match.

China, which essentially controls the purse strings of Pyongyang, sits on its hands. Add to that a mainstream media determined to instill profitable fear—now, as then—and the result was several weeks of mass hysteria. The only time it goes away is when a hurricane or political scandal can briefly take its place. As those die away, Kim Jung-un once again becomes Public Enemy Number One. And even if Kim isn't terrorizing Japan and Guam, the press will cover Robert De Niro's hatred of Donald Trump surpassing his hatred of Kim because the president (along with many scientists) is unmoved by climate change.[3] And why, exactly, is De Niro so angry? Because in September 2017, Hurricane Irma, somehow the result of the president's neglect, severely impacted the actor's plans to build a luxury hotel in Barbuda. But we get ahead of ourselves on the "settled science" of global warming. And because the actor is very envious of Donald Trump's ascension to the power of the presidency. While the thespian remains a script reader. And so

Bobbie De Niro, a very small restaurant and hotel owner compared with Donald Trump, appears as the mouthpiece of Hollywood and the leftist press to attack the president using the language and the guttural mannerisms of one of his characters in a gangster movie.

RED SCARE

In 1918, a year after the Russian Revolution, communists were not seen as the primary threat. Granted, we didn't trust them, a feeling that fit neatly into our mistrust of Germans. Russian Marxism had its roots in the writings of German philosopher-economist Karl Marx. But fears of communist influence in America were fed by several incidents. The American labor movement had gained power, and two strikes—a stoppage by dockworkers in Seattle and a police strike in Boston—fueled the idea that labor organizers were following the Russian model and held communist sympathies. A sitting Senate committee investigating subversion folded communists into the mix. Though the report the committee made did not provide hard evidence regarding the extent of communist activity in the United States, it contained an alarmist picture of communist rule.

Media coverage of the report was awash in

hysterical prose. Rather than focus on the thinness
of the factual evidence, writers delighted in descriptions of Russian industrial corruption and salacious
tales about the "nationalization" of women, in
which Soviet women were allowed to choose sexual
partners.[4] Many "news" reports declared that communists were thriving in American cities and planning stateside revolutions.

The public's anxiety was heightened by a series
of race riots during the summer and fall of 1919.
While no clear link between communists and the
events was ever established, it seemed obvious to
white, middle- and upper-class Americans that
the lower status and poor employment prospects
of blacks made them likely targets for subversive
organizing.

On May 1, 1919—May Day, a Russian holiday—
leftist demonstrations in several cities turned violent. The following year, as the day neared, the U.S.
attorney general recklessly predicted a massive May
Day uprising that would feature assassinations,
bombings, riots, and an attempt to overthrow the
American government. Panicked states called out
their militias and cities required police officers to
work straight through the day. Armored police cars
with machine guns mounted on them patrolled the
streets.

The day passed quietly, and the hysteria deflated as the Red Scare became an object of ridicule.[5] Local and state governments bemoaned the expense of militarizing their streets, and newspaper editorials mocked what they termed "hallucinations."[6] Certainly the fear of violence on a mass scale was unfounded, but as hindsight has taught us, communism was making very real inroads into the American liberal movement.

The spread of sympathy for communism accelerated after the stock market crash of 1929. A nation in economic turmoil is vulnerable to foreign ideas, and communists gleefully exploited the crisis, presenting a utopian view of what life could be. In response to meetings, pamphlets, and public speeches, local, state, and federal governments cracked down on party members. By 1930, there was an alarming rise in prosecution of free speech to thwart the Communist Party actively organizing anti-unemployment and poverty relief rallies.[7] First the blacks, then the impoverished. The consensus in Washington was that the United States was ripe for destruction at the hands of an underground, ideological army.

The U.S. House convened the Committee to Investigate Communist Activities in the United States, which attributed the majority of American

communist activity to foreign-born agents directly
under Moscow's control. Once again, the press took
a legitimate concern and used it to whip up mass
hysteria about an imminent communist takeover.

The investigation hit upon a trope Americans
could grasp, regardless of the truth: This underground army was already subverting us. According
to the committee, Russia's slave-like economy was
enabling that country to further erode the crippled
American economy by shipping cheap lumber to
western states. While the veracity of this claim was in
doubt, its impact fired up the old suspicions. People
were not yet hysterical, but they were watchful.

And the reality was, Stalin's Russia was very successful in motivating liberals, especially in Hollywood, to align themselves with communism. After
all, actors, writers, and directors all felt they were
the oppressed slaving for studio moguls. There was
a quiet, and then vocal, war going on in the film
industry, with communist-controlled talent agents
openly smearing antagonistic heroes like Bette
Davis and Ronald Reagan. More on this later.

The committee had one other lasting impact. Its
recommendations included giving the Department
of Justice greater latitude to investigate communist
activity. These investigations would later form the
backbone of a congressional investigation and that,

too, would one day greatly impact the situation in Hollywood.

The West Coast turned out to be a hotbed of hysteria-triggering activity in the first half of the twentieth century.

Because the Naturalization Act of 1790 limited naturalized U.S. citizenship to Caucasians, it wasn't until the mid-nineteenth century that substantial numbers of Japanese started migrating to the United States, driven here by the return of Japanese imperial rule and its radical societal changes in 1868. Due to the convenience of ocean passage, most immigrants settled in Hawaii and along the West Coast. As that population grew exponentially, Washington passed the Immigration Act of 1924, which banned the immigration of nearly all Japanese.[8] The result was an effort to preserve their family's history in the titles they assigned to each generation: The original immigrants were known as the *Issei* while their offspring were known as the *Nisei*, Japanese Americans; the children of the *Nisei* were known as the *Sansei*—the names coming from *ichi*, *ni*, and *san*, the Japanese words of "one," "two," and "three."[9]

But whatever they were called, after December 7, 1941, the United States government regarded

Japanese immigrants as just one thing: potential enemies. Spies, saboteurs, liaisons for invasion—you name it, the Japanese were presumed to be ready, willing, and able.

Of course, our government itself is not capable of becoming hysterical. It isn't a monolithic mind, like North Korea or Nazi Germany. It's typically composed of a lot of little minds, each with their own agendas. Occasionally, these minds are fanatics: Lincoln about maintaining the Union, Governor George Wallace of Alabama about preventing racial integration, Barack Obama about minority causes. The difference between fanaticism and hysteria is instructional. The secession of the southern states was regarded as illegal, a view later validated in court. Jim Crow laws—named for a folkloric stereotype—were also legal in some states. In Obama's case he acted out, trampled the rule of law to have his way on health care, on immigration, on equal justice for whites accused of crimes. Fanaticism pushes boundaries. Hysteria ignores them. Obama's hysteria infected the vulnerable, horrified the inoculated, and divided a nation, perhaps irreparably. It didn't do this by empowering the marginalized but by enabling the selfish, lunatic left in every walk of life, from professional athletes kneeling during the national anthem to illegal immigrants finding no reason to obey any law to Muslims refusing to wash their hands of radical elements in their midst to actors of color screaming at fellow, struggling white actors who accept acting parts the Social Justice Warriors unilaterally don't think whites should be able to have. I'll discuss that further in the last chapter.

While our government cannot be hysterical, it is certainly capable of generating hysteria. It does so when our leaders have a mission to accomplish, whether for themselves or for the good of the nation. Winning World War II was one of those missions.

Suspicion of American-based Japanese did not start with the attack on Pearl Harbor. Japan had been enhancing its military and moving aggressively in Asia since 1931. As early as 1936, while conducting domestic surveillance, U.S. intelligence agencies had begun amassing lists of people to be placed in detention camps should hostilities break out between Japan and the United States.[10]

In late 1941, there were 112,000 Japanese living on the West Coast.[11][12] A majority were American citizens. Many others had lived in America for a generation or two. Once war was declared, the U.S. Department of State commissioned an investigation into these individuals' loyalty. Two separate reports indicated there was little cause to question Japanese allegiance, but both were suppressed because they didn't fit the narrative being crafted by Washington. The narrative was helped along by the Niihau Incident, in which a Japanese pilot crash-landed on a tiny Hawaiian island immediately after the Pearl Harbor attack. Three Hawaiians of Japanese descent, who did not know of the attack, aided the pilot in an ultimately fatal escape attempt.[13]

That story made headlines, and was used by President Franklin D. Roosevelt in February 1942 to issue an executive order allowing armed forces commanders to create "military areas" from which "any or all persons may be excluded."[14] All of California and parts of Arizona, Oregon, and the state of Washington were designated military areas.

The order said nothing about Japanese people. It didn't have to. By the end of spring 1942, any citizen within who was at least one-sixteenth Japanese—the *Yonsei*, or fourth generation—had been uprooted by the War Relocation Authority and placed in one of ten relocation camps, kept there by armed soldiers and barbed wire. Their number included orphaned infants of Japanese descent, whose threat as fifth columnists was never explained. It didn't matter. Hysteria, as we've seen, is a bootstrap operation. Propaganda makes the most susceptible people become fearful, with the unease causing fear in others. Pretty soon, the movement has metastasized as hysteria.

As the war raged and word of Japanese aggression and atrocities abroad circulated, and as American sons died in the Pacific Theater, popular sentiment held that all Japanese, including those interred on the West Coast, deserved their fate. The California legislature disseminated a paper claiming the loyalty of "ethnic Japanese" was with the Japanese emperor, and that Japanese schools in America taught racist ideologies. Media embraced these claims, endorsing internment so the military could avoid running "even the slightest risk of a major disaster from enemy groups within the nation,"[15] as the *Atlanta Constitution* put it. The *Los Angeles Times* refused to consider the possibility of American loyalty among the detainees, writing that "no matter where born, there is unfortunately no doubt whatever. They are for Japan; they will aid Japan in every way possible by espionage, sabotage and other activity."

Late in the war, in 1944, the Pentagon formed the 442nd Regimental Combat Team, a unit made of soldiers recruited from the Japanese internment camps. They fought heroically in Europe, were highly decorated, yet even they could not change public opinion.[16] Hysteria doesn't listen.

Of course, public opinion may also have been swayed by reasons other than patriotism. The Japanese on the West Coast were excellent farmers and irrigation specialists. Their internment opened jobs that white agriculturalists were happy to take. Unfortunately, there weren't enough whites to fill all the positions. To make up the shortfall, the United States welcomed massive waves of Mexican farmworkers, which we discussed earlier.

Ironically, in Hawaii, sugar and pineapple plantation owners needed Japanese workers. The United States needed the produce. As a result, very few of the 158,000 Japanese living there were relocated to camps.[17] Hawaii was far away and that news remained largely unreported on the mainland.

Legal action during the war went nowhere. Even the Supreme Court ruled the actions constitutional. Afterward, U.S. courts determined that while removing the Japanese from designated military areas may have been legal, imprisoning them was not. Most internees were given a pittance in cash and a train ticket to where they had been moved from—although their homes and businesses were long gone. Many returned to find that there was still so much hatred for imperial

Japan, so many American homes that had suffered loss of sons and fathers, that the American Japanese sons and daughters were no longer welcome. That wasn't hysteria, it was pain. And whether they understood or not, the Japanese Americans were forced to accept this reality. They settled elsewhere. I find this reaction both sad and touching. It displayed a level of dignity and empathy that spoke well of those immigrants. It is a lesson many Muslim Americans would be prudent to explore.

The U.S. government quickly moved to eliminate traces of its injustice. Rather than leave the internment camps as a reminder of what had happened, most were destroyed. However, in 1988, Congress did attempt to apologize for the internment by awarding each survivor of the camps twenty thousand dollars.[18] For many, the phrase "too little, too late" seemed to have been written for the compensation.

AN AXIS TO GRIND

The Japanese, of course, had company in the hell of the American psyche.

The Germans were there, too.

Part of the responsibility for this belongs to the news media, but part also came from comic books, radio, and Hollywood. When Superman or Captain America attacked Japanese soldiers or leaders, the Japanese were diminutive and buck-toothed, quite literally rodents. Germans were depicted as wild-eyed lunatics; often it was Hitler himself being punched or manhandled. Over the airwaves, there were news reports from foreign cities and from the front (typically censored to avoid creating too much hysteria) while Amos 'n' Andy and Fibber McGee and other popular characters battled spies. Walt Disney made some of the most famous anti-Nazi shorts beginning in 1943, with *Der Fuehrer's Face* starring Donald Duck as a beleaguered German factory worker. The poster showed Donald hitting Hitler in the face with a tomato.[19] That Oscar-winning cartoon also caricatured Mussolini as a jut-jawed thug and Japan's Prime Minister Tojo as a toothy dwarf. Feature films included the 1939 melodrama *Confessions of a Nazi Spy*, starring Edward G. Robinson. The screaming headline on the poster was something Obama might have found instructional regarding Islamic terrorists: "The Picture That Calls a Swastika A SWASTIKA!"[20]

The purpose of these films was flat-out propaganda, with the goal of creating not hysteria but something else. Roughly six million people within our borders—fifty times more than the Japanese population here—had at least one parent who had been born in Germany.[21] Rounding them up would have been impossible and also utterly destructive to our economy and war effort. There were internment camps for Germans, but only for those coming *to* America—a sensible precaution that we ignored when dealing with Syrian refugees under Obama. At the start of hostilities, America already had a historic mistrust of Germans. They didn't need a big push. What the government wanted was to create unbridled hatred of Nazis. Citizens had to be on the lookout for symbols of the Reich, listen for spoken support of Hitler, and honor the blackouts to protect us from aircraft and submarines dispatched by the Nazis.

As I've said, you cannot be consistently vigilant if you are hysterical. Mass hysteria permits you to go along with the unlawful incarceration of Japanese, which is why that had to be done quickly: hysteria subsides and passions ebb as the "enemy" vanishes. If the government had allowed its citizens to become rabid about Germans instead of Nazis, we would have turned on Dutch or Hungarians or Poles in much the same way that Sikhs were targeted as Muslims after 9/11 because hysterics confused their turbans with the Muslim keffiyeh.

The government knew that, unlike a potential

invasion of Hawaii, Alaska, or the American West Coast by the Japanese, any suspicious groups or lurking U-boats were looking for information. Fear Nazis, all American citizens had to do was keep their mouths shut, and Hitler's agents would come away empty-handed. That was the government's more measured response to Germany and lingering Germanophobia.

In our overly plugged-in day and age, it is difficult to imagine a government war policy having nuance. But this one did, and for all its flaws it kept the homeland safe. With hindsight, we can condemn the internment camps. With hindsight, we know that blameless people were herded into these places, their lives and livelihoods shattered. But we cannot forget that the "day that will live in infamy" was a national body blow. Rage—impotent rage—is a breeding ground for hysteria, and there likely would have been attacks on Japanese citizens who were still in their homes, in unguarded streets. That's what happened to blacks in the South at the hands of the Ku Klux Klan.

Hindsight is a great luxury, and any emotion other than sympathy in the face of lawless acts against our citizens is abhorrent to most Americans. It is the singular responsibility of historians to remind us of the way things were, not the way

things appear in the rearview mirror, or the way
things are through a distorted lens. Actor George
Takei, best known for playing Sulu on *Star Trek*,
was interned as a child and personifies the challenge. What he experienced was horrible. But his
view is entirely subjective. He commends Franklin Roosevelt for successfully battling the Great
Depression, then condemns him for "the horror
that he inflicted on a small group of Americans
who happened to look different...it was a racist
and hysterical act on the part of the government
and certainly the president of the United States
at that time. Seventy-five years later another person...I hate to give him that title."[22]

Takei is not correct. As we've seen, the internment was neither racist nor hysterical on the part
of the government. It *was* ultimately wrong, but it
was tactical and reasoned. Then Takei goes on to
condemn Donald Trump with a vague, noncontex-
tual brush informed by his own childhood experiences. That is not reason, that is emotion. That is
the stuff of which hysteria is made.

Angry subjectivity is particularly true in discussing the postwar era, when America was subjected to an unprecedented wave of mass hysteria,
one that not only had the traditional media but
also television to work its way with us.

Like the Internet and the liberal rallying cry of "net neutrality," the film industry was a natural target for hysteria. It was its own dedicated media—ideas went from the minds of leftist writers to screens nationwide—and it had glamour, which meant that accusations of treason against it would get front-page coverage in the news media. A U.S. House committee dragged one industry luminary after another in front of it, making and destroying careers indiscriminately. Once again, since children were seen as particularly vulnerable, comic books came under scrutiny as well. Congress pondered the extremely important questions: Was Wonder Woman a lesbian?

Were Batman and Robin homosexuals?

11.

FROM COMMIES TO COMICS
Congressional Witch Hunts Destroy Lives and Careers

In the same way that Great Britain decided to make me the token white, male American to ban from their country, Congress turned on a young man and made him a poster child for their own inability to control a plague sweeping the nation. To Congress—in particular, the United States Senate Subcommittee on Juvenile Delinquency—the problem with American youth wasn't bad parenting or Hollywood sensation-peddlers and the glorification of bad boy antiheroes like Marlon Brando. No, they said the problem was Bill Gaines, a man who published a small line of comic books. And like me, Gaines fought back.

What I learned as a botanist has served me well in life. For example, sometimes the seeds of hysteria grow in a flash, like bamboo or algae. That's how we get a *War of the Worlds* panic. The stock market crash of 1929 was like that as well—a triumph of self-preservation and impulse over reason. In August of that year, after a period of aggressive speculation, investors were becoming skittish because production had declined and unemployment had risen. Compounding these concerns were low wages, extensive debt, the questionable solvency of banks that were carrying that debt, and weakness in agriculture. Stock prices began to decline, resulting in a market "correction" that lasted from September into October. When the situation failed to stabilize, the pace accelerated and then—hysteria. On October 24, Black Thursday, a record number of shares were traded. Investors and banks calmed things by securing massive blocks of stock, causing things to look better on Friday. But then on Monday, Black Monday, after having had a weekend to work up balance sheets as well as panic, investors bailed and caused the market to plunge. On Black Tuesday, October 29, the panic became hysteria and the market collapsed completely. Investors lost billions and the Great Depression had begun.

Sometimes, though, hysteria takes time and careful watering. And like pollen grains or fungus spores, hysteria occasionally requires bees or a strong wind or rain to spread its seed to fertile ground. That's just how liberals have fomented another case of mass hysteria, this one in that second category I described earlier—denial of the existence of a threat despite overwhelming evidence that it does exist. That is the best way I can describe the American public's widespread belief that the investigations into communist influence in the 1940s and '50s were "witch hunts," based on exaggerated claims of communist influence in Hollywood, academia, the press, and the federal government.

Today *McCarthyism* is synonymous with witch hunting, paranoia, and government overreach, based on Senator Joseph McCarthy's activities in tandem with the House Un-American Activities Committee (HUAC) during the 1950s. There is only one problem with the liberal narrative supporting that meme: McCarthy was right.[1] Whatever you may think of his methods or alleged personal failings, his core proposition was true. Communism had made major inroads into all the institutions he alleged it had. As we'll see, most of the people identified didn't even deny the charges.

THE BLACKLIST

In 1938, Congress authorized the formation of the House Un-American Activities Committee.[2] The committee was empaneled to investigate subversive activities on both the left and right. HUAC began investigating Hollywood in 1940, when a former Communist Party member fingered forty-two film industry figures as "fellow travelers," a phrase that had originated in Russia in 1917 to describe those who were sympathetic to, if not yet active participants in, the Russian Revolution.[3] The names were huge and included Humphrey Bogart, James Cagney, Katharine Hepburn, and Lionel Stander.[4] Dashiell Hammett, author of *The Maltese Falcon* and *The Thin Man*, said this in defense of his colleagues: "At this crucial time when the cooperation of all democratic forces is so essential, this attack throws a very dubious light on the character of the whole...investigation."[5] The pressure temporarily subsided due to lack of evidence and popular support for fan favorites. The only one negatively affected was Stander, who lost his contract with Republic Pictures.[6]

World War II arrived and the uneasy alliance between the United States and the Soviet Union put a damper on anticommunist activism. The American Communist Party took advantage of this change in attitude to recruit aggressively. Membership hit fifty thousand.[7] Many ordinary Americans who went through the Great Depression were taken in by communism's utopian promises.

Parallels with the early 1940s and the tactics of socialist Bernie Sanders in 2016—with the entire Democratic Party, in fact—show how closely Sanders adopted the classic playbook while seeking the presidential nomination. Many see Sanders as an "idealistic," grandfatherly figure who is, at worst, unrealistic in his estimation of socialism's viability. I do not. I recognize Sanders for what he is, one of the most dangerous figures in American politics. It is precisely his unthreatening public image that makes him so dangerous, as it allows him to soft-sell the most inhumane and oppressive political system in human history.

Make no mistake, a Bernie Sanders America would eventually be the same authoritarian nightmare the Chinese under Mao and the Russians under Stalin endured. He is a communist pied piper who is leading our own children—no matter how old they may be—away before our very eyes. He's playing the same tune to twenty-first-century Millennials that communism played to the left in the twentieth century.

In October 1947, with the war won and the

Soviet Union now our biggest concern, and with television becoming more and more influential, HUAC began hearings into communist infiltration of Hollywood.[8] Almost at once, heavy hitters in the motion picture industry formed the Committee for the First Amendment and flew to Washington to testify and protest. Among their numbers were Bette Davis, Judy Garland, Gene Kelly, Humphrey Bogart, Groucho Marx, Henry Fonda, and Lucille Ball.[9]

They argued it wasn't just a question of free speech, but of ingratitude. The stars had raised countless millions for their country selling war bonds, sponsoring rubber drives, or enlisting to fight—Fonda, Kelly, and the great Jimmy Stewart among them—and had worked with the USO to entertain troops around the globe.[10][11][12] Now *they* were being investigated?

Because of the big names involved—the kinds of names that sold newspapers and got radio listeners to stay tuned—anticommunist sentiment surged. Hollywood came under withering fire from many right-leaning columnists, such as the powerful Hedda Hopper, and from the Hearst newspapers. Citing the 1940 hearings, the press declared celebrity members of the Committee for the First Amendment communists or communist sympathizers. Defense of the group was limited since, for one, the charges were largely true, and also because many commentators were afraid of losing their jobs. One exception was former first lady and left-wing icon Eleanor Roosevelt, who emerged from the where-are-they-now file on October 29, 1947, to write:

> The film industry is a great industry with infinite possibilities for good and bad. Its primary purpose is to entertain people. On the side, it can do many other things. It can popularize certain ideals, it can make education palatable. But in the long run, the judge who decides whether what it does is good or bad is the man or woman who attends the movies. In a democratic country I do not think the public will tolerate a removal of its right to decide what it thinks of the ideas and performances of those who make the movie industry work.[13]

In late 1947, HUAC began subpoenaing people named in a series of *Hollywood Reporter* articles as communists. The committee wanted to determine whether sympathizers had been introducing procommunist ideas into U.S. films. Ronald

Reagan, then president of the Screen Actors Guild, testified that communists within his union had tried to influence its policies. Walt Disney affirmed that communist influence in the film industry was a serious problem. And actor Adolphe Menjou expressed his desire to send all Hollywood communists back to Russia. In a prescient statement designed to undercut the left's defense of the conspirators, he remarked, "I am a witch hunter if the witches are communists."[14]

These assertions came only a few years after Hollywood had released a string of procommunist movies. A 1942 thriller, *Miss V from Moscow*, highlighted the daring of Russian espionage exploits. *The Boy from Stalingrad* and *The Battle of Russia*, both released in 1943, championed Russia's resistance to the Nazis. That same year, *Mission to Moscow* idealized Russia under Stalin, as seen through a U.S. ambassador to the Soviet Union.

These are but four examples from an entire genre of procommunist films, all of which were geared toward manipulating the American public's view of the Russian government and people. Given the role movies played in shaping attitudes, they helped create an environment in which people coming into contact with subversives would feel sympathetic toward their cause.

Many of the actors who stood accused doubled down, disastrously, noting that membership in the Communist Party was not illegal, that the real threat to American values was the demonization of people in the entertainment field, and that, under the First Amendment's free association clause, HUAC's inquiries were unconstitutional.

Note that this First Amendment argument is missing one very important element: It doesn't deny the charges. For the most part, those accused of being communists didn't say it wasn't true; they made the argument that being a communist is a First Amendment right, being free speech and free association. Part of the mass hysteria over this issue is people blindly accepting that proposition. The other is believing the majority of these people were wrongly accused. They weren't; they didn't even deny the charges!

The First Amendment gives wide latitude to the expression of ideas and the right to meet and discuss them. But it doesn't sanction criminal conspiracies. No reasonable person would cite the First Amendment to defend conspirators meeting to plot a murder or set up a modern slavery ring. Yet that is exactly what any organization seeking to impose communism on a free country is doing.

If you think that's an extreme position, you're

in for a surprise. In August 1954, the Communist Control Act made the existence of the Communist Party illegal and membership in it or support of it a criminal act. The bill passed the Senate unanimously, 85–0, and the House, 305–2. Those vote counts are a striking illustration of just how clearly patriotic Americans of the time recognized the threat communism represents. The bill was signed into law by President Dwight Eisenhower on August 24, 1954, and remains in effect to this day. Only future presidents neglecting to enforce the law allows the Communist Party of the United States to continue to exist.[15]

Then, as now, there were conservative members of the Holly-wood community who provided bulwarks against the socialist Hollywood mindset. Jimmy Stewart, for example, nearly ended his friendship with former roommate Fonda over the latter's left-wing ideology. In 1944, John Wayne, who was a big enough star not to care what people thought, was one of the founding members of the Motion Picture Alliance for the Preservation of American Ideals. Loyalty oaths were printed and signatures were required by the studios. Among those who joined Wayne were his frequent film collaborators Ward Bond, Walter Brennan, and director John Ford, along with big names like Gary Cooper, Cecil B. DeMille, Walt Disney, Clark Gable, Ginger Rogers, Barbara Stanwyck, and Robert Taylor.[16] Taylor was a huge star at the time and, when he finally testified, identifying by name the so-called fellow travelers, film-loving but left-leaning France was so incensed that they called for his films to be banned. Good old France. I'll tell you more about Taylor later.

Institutionally, the film industry responded by blackballing acknowledged, or even suspected, communists. Just before the war, studio heads were called to Washington and had acceded to the wishes of President Franklin D. Roosevelt, who asked them not to make movies about anti-Semitism. Though the media was aware of the true nature of the concentration camps, Roosevelt knew it would be tough selling another European war to Americans—tougher if they thought it was about liberating Jews. Unlike his Republican predecessor Lincoln, the great Democrat issued no form of Emancipation Proclamation.

Among actors, the professional casualties over the course of the HUAC hearings were midlevel names like Zero Mostel, Howard Da Silva, and Larry Parks,[17] who starred in the 1946 hit *The*

Jolson Story. Henry Fonda and Edward G. Robinson were among the "gray-listed" actors, men who
were big enough names that they would be permitted to work if they acknowledged the error of their
ways. Robinson did; Fonda did not. He didn't act
in Hollywood for six years.[18]

But the big haul for HUAC was the screenwriters.
Unlike the actors, these people were intellectuals who
could make the First Amendment argument, valid
or not. They showed up at the hearings and defiantly refused to cooperate. HUAC would eventually
charge a double handful of writers—the Hollywood
Ten—with contempt of Congress for refusing to
name names or for attempting to make pre-testimony
statements. Members of the Hollywood Ten served
sentences of between six months and one year.

But that was only the start of their punishment.
Before they were imprisoned, the Association of
Motion Picture Producers declared all ten would
be ineligible for employment in the film industry
until the contempt charges were cleared and they
swore they were not communists. Nearly all left
prison to find themselves unemployable. Only one,
writer-director Edward Dmytryk, was able to work
steadily, and only after he declared he had, indeed,
been a communist and named twenty-six others.[19]

The furor burned on for years, during which

time the film industry released dozens of anti-communist films just as it had earlier made anti-Nazi movies. Among those produced were *The Red Menace* (1949), which depicted an innocent soldier being seduced to join the Communist Party; *I Was a Communist for the FBI* (1951), about a covert agent who had infiltrated a communist cell; and *My Son John* (1952), which posed the question: What is greater, loyalty to one's country or to one's family? (Answer: the USA.) In the same year, John Wayne and James Arness played heroic HUAC investigators in *Big Jim McLain*, in which Duke kicked down doors and took prisoners.

By 1951, the tactics of those subpoenaed had changed. Rather than argue on behalf of the First Amendment, most invoked their Fifth Amendment right not to incriminate themselves as a result of refusing to implicate others. Again, let me point out they were not denying the charges. In fact, they were admitting answering the question of whether they were communists would tend to incriminate them, although the 1954 Communist Control Act was not yet law. Of course, those refusing to cooperate were placed on a blacklist.

Fittingly, the medium that had nearly killed Hollywood by causing movie theaters to shut down in droves ultimately came to Hollywood's rescue. By the early 1950s, television was starved for fresh, quality content. Movie stars, movie directors, and movie writers felt the young medium that sold detergent and mouthwash to the masses was beneath them. The studios, forced to make more and more shows for TV, were also forced to hire new talent. That's where names such as Charlton Heston, Jack Lemmon, James Dean, and writer Rod Serling got their start. As late as 1957, producers were still fearful of hiring the previous pariahs.

Producer Sam Spiegel was told not to give blacklisted screenwriters Michael Wilson and Carl Foreman credit for *Bridge on the River Kwai* or else the film would have trouble getting bookings.[20] Instead, in a small show of resistance, he gave the credit to the author of the book, Pierre Boulle, who did not speak any English. The Best Screenplay Academy Award it earned was not rightly attributed to the actual screenwriters until 1985. It took another three years before actor Kirk Douglas and director Otto Preminger took aim squarely at HUAC and the blacklist. Both Douglas's epic *Spartacus* and Preminger's sprawling *Exodus* hired blacklisted writer Dalton Trumbo *and* put his name on the screen, in defiance of the blacklist.[21]

The left would have you believe that communists in Hollywood and in other American institutions were an oppressed minority who had—as they would have you believe—been turned into political victims, rather members of an anti-American conspiracy to impose a political system that had already resulted in tens of millions of civilian deaths, with tens of millions more to come in the decades that followed. And they have turned the studio heads who blacklisted them—private business owners who had every right to refuse to allow their property to be used to spread this abhorrent message—into totalitarian villains.

The widespread belief in this completely false narrative is one of the most insidious mass hysterias to ever have gripped the American public. Since dissolution of the HUAC in 1975, we've seen the rise of a new, radical left. In 2009, acting White House communications director Anita Dunn publicly praised Mao Zedong as "one of my two favorite political philosophers."[22] In a 2017 article, Establishment mouthpiece Bloomberg gleefully ran an article titled "Get Rid of Capitalism? Millennials Are Ready to Talk About It," citing a Harvard University poll in which 51 percent of eighteen- to twenty-nine-year-olds in the United States said they opposed capitalism.[23] As of this writing, the communist pied piper Bernie Sanders plans to run for president again in 2020.

SEEING RED

As avidly followed as they were, the HUAC hearings on William Gaines in 1954 were just Washington's warm-up for bigger game.

In the 1950s, television became the most powerful medium for generating hysteria to date—possibly more powerful than today's Internet. The Web is fragmented among countless social media venues and competing shriekers. Unlike today, channel choices were limited during the early days of television, and there was little in the way of countervailing information. Fortunately, we had some stalwart professionals like Edward R. Murrow vetting and delivering the news.

A new medium needs narrative, and Joseph McCarthy had been a storyteller all his life. While in the Marines, he attributed a broken leg to a variety of battle-related causes, depending on what story he felt like telling. The truth was, he had suffered the injury during an on-ship party. His critics claim he exaggerated his war record to qualify for a Distinguished Flying Cross and several Air Medals. Probably untrue.[24] He was a tail-gunner on a bomber. During his successful Senate run in 1946, he accused his opponent of cowardice for not serving during World War II—despite his opponent having been forty-six when America entered the war, past the age of enlistment.

These character flaws, along with his likely alcoholism[25] even before his downfall, have fueled the left's portrayal of McCarthy as a paranoid, vindictive, witch-hunting bully. Maybe their estimation of the man himself is correct. Maybe it is exaggerated. Either way, it doesn't change the fact that his fundamental claim that communists had infiltrated the government and other highly influential institutions was true.

In 1950, McCarthy claimed to have a list of communists who had infiltrated the U.S. Department of State. McCarthy's story had circumstantial credibility. Communists were old enemies, as we've seen, and their corrosive influence was feared by most Americans. But that was before the war, before they had been our allies in defeating the hated Nazis.

By 1950, however, the Soviet Union had successfully grabbed chunks of Eastern Europe, notably half of Germany and half of Berlin. Reports of their repressive rule were everywhere. In addition, civil war in China had left that country under communist control as of 1949—the same year the Soviet Union belatedly tested its own atomic bomb using secrets stolen from the United States. The world seemed to be turning an unpleasant shade of red.

As a result, there were legitimate reasons to be concerned about Soviet influence in the United States. McCarthy's fellow Republicans in the Senate were receptive to his claims. The Democrats, who were in control at the time, were less impressed. A report from a Democrat-led committee said McCarthy's allegations were a hoax. In response, Republicans charged the Democrats with perpetrating a whitewash and went so far as to suggest it was potentially treasonable.

That reply—excessive, full-throated, and handed to a concerned public—was the first giant step toward what the left now claims was red hysteria. It was an assertion so bold there was no backpedaling. Especially for McCarthy.

The Republicans' support emboldened the senator from Wisconsin, who expanded his allegations of subversive activity. In addition to those he suspected purely of communist connections or sympathies, he began exposing alleged "homosexuals" in the U.S. Foreign Service, who were considered high risks for blackmail and, thus, treason.

There is no doubt there was potential to do harm to innocents under circumstances like these.

Once an allegation was made, even by innuendo, the victim was tarred. It stuck. One powerful senator, Millard Tydings of Maryland, had labeled McCarthy's State Department accusations a hoax. McCarthy retaliated by accusing Tydings of being in league with communists. That year, the four-term incumbent lost his reelection bid.[26]

After the fall of Tydings, few senators were willing to oppose McCarthy. In 1952, even Dwight Eisenhower—the hero of World War II, the mastermind of D-Day, and that year's ultimately successful Republican presidential candidate—offered only tepid criticism of McCarthy's investigations. In fact, it could hardly be called criticism; he said that while he disagreed with McCarthy's methods, he approved of his goals.[27] While this is today viewed merely as political pragmatism, Eisenhower may have seen through the convenient opposition to McCarthy's investigations by liberals who were just a little too eager to defend the rights of communists.

A year later, Arthur Miller would release his play *The Crucible*, which was a fictionalized account of the Salem Witch Trials. Miller had come under scrutiny for his communist sympathies and was questioned by the House Un-American Activities Committee in 1956.[28]

Miller was wrong in many ways, but none bigger than this: the McCarthy hearings, unlike the witch trials in which there were no witches, were predicated on a real threat. There *were* subversives in the United States, in the government, and in sensitive positions. The threat was there, even if Senator Joseph McCarthy was not the perfect man to lead the charge. Not, as it turned out, in the television age, when the alleged overreach of a serious crusade could be replaced by the media-fueled mass hysteria against McCarthy, a feeding frenzy that ultimately toppled him.

But that fate would be a few years later. In the early 1950s, the Wisconsin senator increasingly felt as though he had no restraints. When Eisenhower refused to replace a diplomat who wanted the United States to establish relations with now-communist China, McCarthy updated an earlier characterization of the communist-neutral presidencies of Franklin Roosevelt and Harry S. Truman from "twenty years of treason" to "twenty-one years of treason"—the addition being Eisenhower's first year as president.[29]

While Roosevelt and Truman had a war to win and needed communist Russia for that, we now know the alliance with Russia for those purposes wasn't the only reason to make that allegation against them. But McCarthy considered even the war alliance bad judgment and possibly worse. Many people believed him. They remembered how Russia entered the war against Japan at the last moment, grabbing land in the region as well as placing occupation forces in Korea, which eventually led to the creation of the north and south states—and continues to impact us today. So there was a lot of truth in what McCarthy said, whether his criticism of the alliance was ultimately valid or not.

As I said in the opening chapter, history has for the most part vindicated McCarthy. During the 1980s, details began emerging about an anti–Soviet Union counterintelligence program called the Venona Project.[30] Intercepts of Soviet intelligence messages revealed that there *had* been communist infiltration of a wide range of American institutions: the diplomatic corps; the Manhattan Project, which was responsible for creating the United States' first atomic weapons; the U.S. Treasury Department; and even Franklin D. Roosevelt's White House. Even before World War II ended, America's so-called allies in the Soviet Union had pipelines into our most valuable secrets—and our hearts and minds. The papers also named

Hollywood writer Walter Bernstein and producer Boris Moros as fellow travelers.

While there were indeed subversives to be rooted out, McCarthy's style did not help his cause. He took no prisoners, and in 1953 he was given the chair of the Senate Committee on Government Operations. While this wasn't the Senate committee that had been investigating communist influences, its subpoena power and purpose were broad enough that McCarthy was able to launch his own investigations into suspected communists.

McCarthy initially focused on the Voice of America, the U.S.-run foreign propaganda arm that broadcast behind the "Iron Curtain." While the charges of communist infiltrators in that essential resource haven't to date been proven, the allegations were enough to ruin careers and cause at least one suicide.[31] McCarthy's investigators then went through State Department libraries, looking for names of authors who were communist sympathizers. The State Department cooperated, ordering international libraries to remove works by authors who McCarthy and his staff deemed inappropriate. When the list of authors was made public, domestic schools, libraries, and personal book collections were purged as well. There, I believe McCarthy and his movement went too far.

McCarthy's reign was not without unintended consequences. One of his lieutenants wrote an article accusing Protestant clergy of actively supporting communists. McCarthy's Catholic followers, including Joe Kennedy, father of future president John F. Kennedy, loved the allegation. Protestants, understandably, didn't. Influential clergy, politicians, and, most important, the electorate successfully demanded the lieutenant's resignation. While McCarthy himself was not deflated, it was a dent, the first indication he was vulnerable.[32]

McCarthy certainly overstepped his bounds when he challenged the loyalty of an army dentist. President Truman himself had issued an executive order in 1947 demanding that government employees sign a loyalty oath. While the dentist had refused to sign the document, there was no evidence he was a communist. Undeterred, McCarthy went after the dentist as well as whoever had arranged for his promotion to major.

As it happened, the dentist had been given his rank under a law that rewarded medical professionals in the military—a law for which McCarthy himself had voted.[33] A war with the military had begun, but the brazen McCarthy forgot that one thing an army knows very, very well is how to counterattack. In drafting their defense, army lawyers realized that McCarthy's vulnerability wasn't his allegedly overzealous prosecution of communists; there was too much truth in his allegations to muster enough support in Washington. Instead they portrayed him as a hypocrite. When one of McCarthy's aides was drafted in 1953, the senator's office had sought special privileges and commissions for him, including a stateside posting.[34]

McCarthy wasn't intimidated by this tactic and actually increased his vitriol. He accused the army of using that aide to blackmail his committee into dropping its investigation.

Had McCarthy backed down, it might have saved his career. When the so-called Army-McCarthy hearings began in April 1954, they were broadcast live on television. Overnight McCarthy became a national figure, as did his infamous bull-dog attorney, Roy Cohn. Robert F. Kennedy might have, too. McCarthy named the young attorney assistant counsel of the U.S. Senate Permanent Sub-committee on Investigations. But Kennedy found the senator's methods unacceptable and resigned after seven months.[35]

With hindsight, this image was not one that McCarthy would have crafted for himself. What Americans saw in this and other exchanges was a rash and bombastic senator attacking a member of the military, perhaps the nation's most well-respected institution—one that had defeated Hitler and Tojo, had given them the much-beloved Ike, and had been a part of the lives of a whole generation of young men who had sworn an oath of loyalty when they donned the uniform.

The McCarthy hearings were must-see TV until they ended in June. What survives from those hearings—what is burned into the memory of everyone who saw them—is the exchange between McCarthy and Boston attorney Joseph Welch, who had been called to testify about fellow attorney Fred Fisher. Fisher had been a member of the far-left National Lawyers Guild (NLG), which was suspected of being a communist front group at the time. The NLG has long been active in far left-wing causes, including filing several lawsuits on behalf of the Occupy movement in 2011. Disgusted with McCarthy's questions about Fisher, Welch said:

> Until this moment, Senator, I think I have never really gauged your cruelty or your recklessness. Fred Fisher is a young man who went to the Harvard Law School and came into my firm and is starting what looks to be a brilliant career with us.... Little did I

dream you could be so reckless and so cruel
as to do an injury to that lad. It is true he is
still with Hale and Dorr. It is true that he
will continue to be with Hale and Dorr. It is,
I regret to say, equally true that I fear he shall
always bear a scar needlessly inflicted by you.
If it were in my power to forgive you for your
reckless cruelty I would do so. I like to think
I am a gentleman, but your forgiveness will
have to come from someone other than me.

When McCarthy persisted, Welch's riposte was
one for the ages:

Let us not assassinate this lad further, Senator. You've done enough. Have you no sense
of decency, sir? At long last, have you left no
sense of decency?[36]

It is an iconic moment in the history of television. Welch, who would later star as Judge Weaver
in the Jimmy Stewart classic *Anatomy of a Murder*, was raised to heroic status as the man who
ended "McCarthyism." But there is one, stubborn little fact the Establishment glosses over and
that the public, in the grip of this mass hysteria,

isn't curious about—McCarthy's allegations were true. Fisher had indeed been a member of the far-left group, whose mission today remains to be "an effective force in the service of the people by valuing human rights over property interests,"[37] according to the National Lawyers Guild's own website.

Television was not kind to McCarthy. On-camera, he came off as an angry, waspish bully, while army officials came off as righteous and solid.

Newspapers that were once afraid of denouncing McCarthy now turned on him. Editorials and the coverage of the hearings were extremely unflattering, and popular opinion of McCarthy plummeted. On December 2, 1954, the Senate voted to censure the senator, effectively rendering him powerless. Regardless of the validity of McCarthy's suspicions and accusations, he was no longer a viable messenger for the cause.

Three years later, at the age of forty-eight, McCarthy died of hepatitis, a broken, alcoholic man.[38]

Perhaps the most effective characterization of McCarthy's efforts as abuse of power was delivered by the aforementioned Edward R. Murrow on a 1954 television broadcast of his program *See It Now*:

The actions of the junior Senator from Wisconsin have caused alarm and dismay amongst our allies abroad, and given considerable comfort to our enemies. And whose fault is that? Not really his. He didn't create this situation of fear; he merely exploited it— and rather successfully. Cassius was right: "The fault, dear Brutus, is not in our stars, but in ourselves."

Thus the official story was written. McCarthy was a vindictive bully who exaggerated communist influence and ruthlessly destroyed many innocent people. Sixty-four years later, a generation of Americans who accept this mass hysteria about McCarthy as reality now believe socialism is superior to capitalism.

JUVENILE DELINQUENTS

After World War II, television and postwar prosperity moved forward in lockstep. The suburbs expanded thanks to low-interest loans from the GI Bill; veterans received an education; jobs were created; and television—which had been demonstrated effectively in 1927—took off in earnest. By 1951, TV was coast-to-coast. Almost at once, Americans were better informed, and more immediately and accurately so, than at any time in our history.

But the 1950s were not as innocent as many people remember them to be. There were, for example, two kinds of hysteria over rock and roll in general and Elvis Presley in particular. First, the kids lost their minds when Elvis swiveled his hips or even when Buddy Holly just stood still singing about Peggy Sue. Second, parents, clergy, and psychologists teamed up to decry the music as sexual and barbaric—the very same arguments that had been leveled against the "swing" music they had listened to in their youth.

Movies contributed to the hysteria. I remember soldiers who returned with technical skills becoming backyard mechanics, some of them tinkering with motorized go-carts, motorcycles, and hot rods, often with their sons. That led to drag racing that was legal in some places, lawless in others—and thus, movies about hot rods and juvenile delinquents. Some of these movies were geared toward adults, like Marlon Brando in *The Wild One.* Some were done with intelligence and insight, like *Rebel Without a Cause,* starring James Dean. But most of these movies were aimed at the younger audiences and were sensational by design, with titles like *Hot-Rod Girl, The Ghost of Dragstrip Hollow,* and *Red*

Ball Express. Those same clergy, parents, and psychologists became concerned that these movies were not cathartic but aspirational. Many adults then became many *hysterical* adults, and were very vocal about these concerns—especially when writing and calling their representatives in Congress.

The result was predictable. Showing concern about juvenile delinquency was a no-lose proposition for politicians. The United States Committee on the Judiciary is a standing group of twenty senators who, in 1953, formed a subcommittee called the United States Senate Subcommittee on Juvenile Delinquency. It was decided the hearings would be televised. State politicians would have a national audience; their faces would become known; their reputations could be whatever they wanted them to be. And the public would respond as the politicians directed, by both their manner and words. Hysteria could be turned up and down like a TV dial.

It was a dangerous new power and the subcommittee used it to destroy. Incredibly, the target was not Hollywood this time, though it was the most visible promoter of the sexy juvenile lifestyle. The industry donated heavily to political campaigns, and theater owners were having financial difficulty. Television had killed movie attendance and lurid movies—these so-called exploitation films—were bringing kids back to theaters. So the subcommittee turned, instead, on a vulnerable medium whose postwar sales were also shrinking.

Without Nazis and the Japanese to fight, superhero comic books were failing. I was their target audience, and at ten and eleven years old even I wasn't interested in reading them anymore. Publishers turned to other genres like war, western, romance, science fiction, and humor, which fragmented the audience even further. Furthermore, those genres left them competing with TV as well: if you had a TV, you had access to Hopalong Cassidy, the Lone Ranger, and old western movies...for free. All those World War II movies were sold to television as well. Even hysteria about the atom bomb didn't help sell comics, since you can show a mushroom cloud over New York or a cratered London just so many times before it wears thin.

And then someone tried a Hail Mary pass that briefly showed the way for comic books—and got him in a load of trouble.

The story of William M. Gaines is one of the greatest comebacks in American history. It is also an example of how a businessman in fear of losing his livelihood should fight back when his government threatens him—not necessarily with protests or violence, not with an army of street thugs, but with a handful of bold conspirators... and wit.

Gaines was the son of Max Gaines, one of the most important men in the history of popular culture. Odds are you've never heard of him, but all of us have been impacted, in some way, by what Max did. In fact, we wouldn't be discussing this topic without him. His is the kind of story I love because it reeks of ethnicity (he was born Maxwell Ginsburg),[39] [40] city streets, and guts.

Max Gaines was a loud, aggressive New York printing company salesman who was bothered by the fact that the color presses, which were only used to run off the Sunday newspaper comics, sat idle for six days a week. He came up with an idea to reprint those Sunday newspaper comic strips in a color book alternately called "funny books" or "comic books." All you had to do, he reasoned, was take those big pages, fold them in half, then in half again, and staple them between two covers. The result of his vision was *Famous Funnies: A Carnival of Comics*, which debuted in 1933.[41] Other comic books followed, including one featuring a comic strip that had been rejected all over town but which Gaines thought would work in the new medium he had created: Superman. Having partnered with others for his previous endeavors, Gaines set up his own publishing company, Educational Comics. When he died in a boating accident in 1947, his twenty-five-year-old son, William, fresh out of the Army Air Corps, took over the firm.

Under Max, Educational Comics—or simply "EC"—published tales from the Bible, about science, and about U.S. and world history. William expanded into more commercial topics like horror, war, and science fiction. You may be familiar with one of his titles, *Tales from the Crypt*; long after its demise, it spawned a popular TV series and films during the late 1980s–'90s.[42]

The new EC titles contained shocking, violent, and often lurid tales that were enormously popular among the youth of America...and equally unpopular among educators and psychologists, who were concerned about their impact on young minds and morals. With no reliable evidence or methodology, one particular attack caused shock waves: the bestseller *Seduction of the Innocent*, published in 1954 by psychologist Fredric Wertham,[43] in which he charged that comics and comic books were systematically corrupting and destroying America's youth. He suspected that Wonder Woman was a lesbian and regarded Batman and Robin as living in a homosexual paradise—which is why Aunt Harriet was added to the 1966 TV show.[44]

The result of Wertham's book was mass hysteria in schools and among parents, which dovetailed into the ongoing Senate Subcommittee on Juvenile Delinquency, chaired by Tennessee Democrat senator Estes Kefauver. It's incredible to think that the party of the progressives, which now approves of transgender schooling in kindergarten, was once alarmed because one hysterical, glory-seeking psychologist claimed (without proof) that young America was being dangerously exposed to alternative lifestyles.[45]

Gaines was hauled before the committee in order to explain himself. The transcript of his testimony is available online and I urge you to seek it out. Bullied relentlessly, the young publisher fell back on giving honest, steadfast answers, which ultimately doomed him. For example, consider this classic exchange:

> *Senator Kefauver:* Here is your May 22 issue. This seems to be a man with a bloody ax holding a woman's head up which has been severed from her body. Do you think that is in good taste?

Mr. Gaines: Yes, sir; I do, for the cover of a horror comic.[46]

While Gaines was telling the truth, there was
also something disingenuous about his testimony.
His comic books *were* often sadistic. It was not
uncommon for him to run stories in which a slum-
lord was left at the mercy of ravenous dogs in a
maze lined with razor blades or a corrupt young
man's heart was cut out and given to his father for
Valentine's Day. Yes, wrongdoers were usually punished and punished grotesquely. And yes, the publications may have been protected speech under the
Constitution. But to feign complete innocence in
the face of the allegations was coy at best, insin-
cere at worse. Gaines knew his audience, and he
was delivering what it wanted.

The story wraps up much as the hysterics would
have hoped: Senator Kefauver went on to become
the vice presidential running mate of Democrat
Adlai Stevenson in 1956—a losing ticket—while
Gaines ended up losing almost everything. The
result of the backlash against comics was preordained: the establishing of a self-policing censorship board known as the Comics Code Authority.
Gaines tried to operate under its restrictions, but

titles like *Tales from the Crypt* and *Shock SuspenStories* simply didn't lend themselves to sanitizing, and even the kinds of morality tales he had always told, the *only* publisher to do so—objecting to racism, anti-Semitism, corruption—were now considered too intense for children and were thus off-limits. Gaines ended up folding all of his titles, save for one. It was a comic book he transitioned into magazine format to avoid the restrictions of the Comics Code Authority. A magazine that skewered the kinds of people and institutions that had pilloried him. It also took on Madison Avenue, Hollywood, politics, and every aspect of human nature.

It was called *Mad*.[47]

Mad made Gaines wealthy and, through it, he and the "usual gang of idiots" (as he called *Mad*'s contributors on the masthead) influenced more young minds than Estes Kefauver and Fredric Wertham could have ever imagined. *Mad* continues to this day, while few remember Kefauver and Wertham. The Comics Code Authority? Dead and buried like one of the corpses from Gaines's comic books. Inevitably, youthful fascination with hot rods ended with the decade as teen interest and movies shifted, as they always do, to activities such as surfing, guitar bands like the Beatles, our space race with the Russians, and, eventually, the drug culture. The "problem" would have self-corrected, in time.

Perhaps the first and last lines from Kipling's poem "If" apply:

If you can keep your head when all about you
Are losing theirs and blaming it on you . . .
Yours is the Earth and everything that's in it,
And—which is more—you'll be a Man, my son!

Today's Muslims pretend they are oppressed in America, and they have vocal allies. That was not the case when anti-Catholic hysteria crested and broke with John F. Kennedy's election in 1960. As a result, Christianity overall struck back with hysterical self-defense when an offhand remark by a prominent musician triggered a massive pro-Christianity hysterical backlash. That was just the beginning of the 1960s. Hysterical overreaction dominated the decade, from the Black Lives Matter movement of its day, the Black Panther Party for Self-Defense, to the anti-Vietnam activists, ban-the-bomb radicals, and—once again—the uprising of impressionable, pliable youth. As today, anti-Establishment hysteria was the new normal. Then, as now, most would-be Social Justice Warriors were focused more on tearing down than on what would replace what they had destroyed.

12.

FROM THE CATHOLICS TO FLOWER POWER
When Everyone Had a Pulpit

JFK AND THE BALANCE OF PANIC

The new decade brought with it the shadow of an old hysteria, only now that panic had a face: John Fitzgerald Kennedy, senator from Massachusetts, who was running for president. And this time, though that hysteria kept resurfacing, it was successfully beaten back.

I was a teenager in 1960, and I was fascinated by politics—especially where ethnicities were involved. Back then, when you grew up in a poor neighborhood in Queens, you got to know people who came from everywhere on the planet. That's still true, to a degree: you can go to Astoria and find a Greek restaurant next to an Indian restaurant next to a

Chinese restaurant with Japanese, Turkish, Ethiopian, and others a short walk away.

It didn't seem strange to me that a Catholic was running for president; Catholic churches were everywhere in my neighborhood. But there was talk about Kennedy's candidacy at school and in the streets. I found out only one other presidential candidate had been Catholic and that was New York's governor Alfred E. Smith in 1928. Among the allegations made against Smith were that he would amend the Constitution to make Catholicism America's official religion, and that he would build a tunnel from the White House to the Vatican. He didn't win. He didn't even come close. In fact, he didn't even carry New York.

The reason the talk never became hysteric in JFK's case was that he didn't let it go unchallenged. He confronted the issue early in the campaign in a speech to the American Society of Newspaper Editors when he asked, in the televised address, "Are we going to admit to the world—worse still, are we going to admit to ourselves—that one-third of the American people is forever barred from the White House?"[1]

The speech insulated him from Alfred Smith's fate, even as 150 Protestant ministers gathered in

Washington and challenged Kennedy to repudiate the teachings of the Catholic Church to prove his independence.[2] He didn't. Instead he gave another speech, this time to the Greater Houston Ministerial Association. After expressing sincere frustration that he was being forced to address this issue again, he said, "I believe in an America that is officially neither Catholic, Protestant, nor Jewish; where no public official either requests or accept instructions on public policy from the Pope, the National Council of Churches, or any other ecclesiastical source."[3]

The address became JFK's stump speech whenever he felt it was needed, though his rival—Republican vice president Richard Nixon—felt JFK deployed it cynically, using it in Catholic neighborhoods to remind voters there that he was one of them. It is understandable *why* Nixon was frustrated. In the closing days of the campaign, Catholic bishops in Puerto Rico forbade Catholics from voting for any politician who was in favor of birth control or abortion. The edict received widespread coverage and when Kennedy did not challenge it, Nixon began to gain on him dramatically in an already tight race. JFK held on to win, but by the thinnest margin.[4]

I bring this up not because of the supreme irony of the Democrats nearly being brought down because of their silence on the twin issues of abortion and birth control, but because it's one of the few times hysteria was tamped down. I could talk again about the platitudes—a lie told often enough becomes the truth and all of that. But after nearly a quarter century on the radio and writing books where I unfailingly speak my mind, I can tell you that like JFK, like William Gaines, like Joseph Welch, all it takes to deflate hysteria is the truth.

People are emotional, at times they're reactionary, and too often they are stupid. But ordinary people—what I call the Eddies and Ediths—don't have the innate capacity of a Barack Obama or Hillary Clinton to live with hypocrisy or lies. If you don't believe me, sit around the dinner table with family, friends, or even strangers. You will have a pretty good idea, within a minute or two, who is trustworthy and who is not. It's language, it's body language, it's narcissism, it's talking instead of listening, it's many qualities. How long or how many times will you go to that dinner table before saying something about what you know isn't true or honest?

When a politician or a media outlet lies to create mass hysteria, it's like someone new has joined the table. For a minute or two—or a week or two—we may buy what they are saying. But then our fundamental humanism rises to the surface, like armor, and disavows that fear and falsehood. It's like the autonomic nervous system. We cannot ignore what we know to be true. We can only choose not to act. Which is how the Cotton Mathers get to execute innocent women. Which is how the Obamas and Pelosis get to let in refugees who common sense tells us likely conceal terrorists in their midst. It is still fundamental humanism to harbor sincere concerns and take reasonable precautions about people whose brothers and sisters celebrated in the streets after the attacks of 9/11.

John F. Kennedy assured the nation that the pope would not sit by his elbow in the White House. He told the truth. Barack Obama assured this country that he was a good Christian. He did not tell the truth. But he did have Pope Francis, "Lenin's pope," as I have called him in other books, sitting by his elbow. Francis's socialist pronouncements have become the new orthodoxy of the Church of Liberalism. It is so explicit that more than two hundred scholars and priests signed a letter accusing Francis of spreading heresy, according to *Politico*.[5]

Kennedy's policies were permitted to continue by the election of Lyndon B. Johnson. Obama's policies were repudiated by the wholesale rejection of Hillary Clinton in the 2016 election—a rejection that turns out to have been even larger than we knew, now that voter fraud in a state she "won," New Hampshire, has been proven.

I mentioned earlier that there are nine Muslim mayors of cities in Great Britain. One could argue that there is no cause for hysteria because none of them has said anything incendiary or contrary to Western values. Let's assume that's correct. This is also true: There are presently fifteen–twenty million Muslims living in the European Union. That number is expected to double by 2025—just a few years from now.[6] Should the United Kingdom just assume everything is going to be fine? Should the English be complacent about Tower Hamlets in East London, a borough that is referred to locally as the Islamic Republic of Tower Hamlets?

I am by nature a thoughtful man. I do not want to participate in spreading unrest or being caught up in mass hysteria. But I am also not naïve. Unless and until some of these British mayors come forward and acknowledge the simmering fear and concern, the way JFK did; until just one of them takes actions that repudiate the transformation of the nation into a sharia or Islamic state; until then,

I will continue to be vigilant. The joke buried in all of this is that while unvetted Muslims are permitted in the United Kingdom, I am not. In 2009, without specifying *why*, Home Secretary Jacqui Smith—whose U.S. counterpart, perhaps coincidentally, was Secretary of State Hillary Clinton—made me one of sixteen people banned from her country's shores as a "threat to national security." Others in that group include Yunis Al-Astal, who heads the terrorist group Hamas, and former KKK grand wizard Stephen Donald Black.[7]

On one level, I don't care. I live in a sanctuary city that is being devoured from within; I don't need to visit a sanctuary nation undergoing the same transformation, the same fate. But as a humanist, I do care. Hysteria against reasonable voices of dissent can be just as damning as hysteria promoting a false or dangerous narrative.

JFK wasn't a great president. He mismanaged the disastrous Bay of Pigs invasion, which failed to overthrow Castro. He allowed the Cuban Missile Crisis to spiral out of control, causing a short-lived mass hysteria that the United States was going to suffer a nuclear attack. He even went on television to suggest the risk was real and that he intended to establish a naval blockade to isolate Cuba. If JFK had known anything about his Soviet adversary, Nikita Khrushchev, he would have understood that the man was a game player. Khrushchev had risen to power in 1953, in the power vacuum of the post-Stalin era, partly through inimitable bluster that played exceptionally well in the media, including his famous threat "We will bury you!" leveled at the West in 1956 as well as removing his shoe and pounding it on a desk at the United Nations in 1960 to protest comments about Soviet repression in Eastern Europe.

Kennedy was a man who understood the importance of image but not of political theater. Think of him as the Kim Jung-un of his day—well-heeled, armed, and tucked snugly into a phalanx of yes-men and repression. JFK and his advisers believed Khrushchev *might* be crazy and acted accordingly. While the media in the United States went berserk for two weeks in October 1962, showing Kennedy and his advisers meeting late into the night, looking grim and haggard, the Soviet premier smiled and went to the Bolshoi Theater.[8][9][10]

Eventually, a backroom deal ended the crisis. The Cuban missiles were removed in exchange for the United States dismantling missiles in Turkey that were aimed at the Soviet Union. The deal should have happened on day one, but the hysteria revved up by the crisis team in Washington and disseminated by the media had to play out. Unfortunately, there had been no one at Kennedy's side to say, "Jack— remember how you rationally and intelligently confronted the Catholic issue without overreacting? Do that here."

THE NEW HYSTERIA

Mass hysteria did not accompany the assassination of John F. Kennedy in November 1963. I remember spotty concerns about whether the republic would fall, but those seemed more emotional than realistic. Television helped us through: it was the first time such extensive remote coverage had been attempted, and it came off in a way that did the medium proud. The nation mourned as one. It would be six years before we did anything in unity again, briefly coming together to celebrate the landing of Apollo 11 on the moon— an event that also caused a growth spurt in television as live pictures were broadcast from the moon. Before and after that historic day, however, the nation was defined by bitter divisions on the left and right, among races, among pacifists and warriors, among the young and the old, among dopers and straights. In short, it was as if everyone had become hysterical.

It was not like any kind of hysteria we had seen before. In 1964, young girls went crazy for the Beatles, but we had seen that for Frank Sinatra in the 1940s and Elvis in the 1950s. Today Instagram is the new mass hysteria for girls. They seem to believe they cannot exist without constant "likes" of their computer-augmented self-portraits. There was a war in Vietnam but, at first, when President Johnson escalated the conflict in 1964–65, it was still much less of a war than Korea, which was just a little over ten years old and remained fresh in people's minds. There was concern about civil rights, especially after JFK and his attorney general and brother Robert kicked open some college doors in the South. Johnson applied real federal muscle to the problem, and while there was spotty panic in the South, the nation generally approved of what he was doing. I remember thinking at the time, I wonder if the South will try to secede again? but the question was more rhetorical than practical. Blacks represented a double-digit percentage of the population in most southern states. And their voting rights were federally protected now, thanks to the Voting Rights Act of 1965.

But that era also introduced new hysterias and

new hysterics, as well. The Beatles were a tremendous, unprecedented, and for nearly ten years a nearly unstoppable force for change in music, coiffure, clothing, spiritualism…pretty much everything. Why do I say "nearly" unstoppable? Because in 1966, John Lennon created a hysteria that nearly derailed an upcoming United States tour and featured a cameo from the always-ready-for-a-fight KKK.

Lennon had given an interview in 1966 in which he said, without malice or judgment, that the Beatles were "more popular than Jesus right now," and added "I don't know which will go first—rock and roll or Christianity."[11]

The quote first appeared in an English newspaper and caused no reaction whatsoever. Nor should it have. It was not theological or judgmental. It was simply about numbers. But when it was reprinted in an American magazine, southern radio stations misrepresented it in an attempt to try to stop the changes being wrought by the Beatles juggernaut. They stopped playing Beatles songs and organized bonfires that were fueled with Beatles records and memorabilia. Images of hysterical, enthusiastic crowds were frighteningly reminiscent of the book burnings in Nazi Germany just a quarter century earlier. The band came close to canceling the tour; when it didn't, the Ku Klux Klan picketed the venues where the Beatles were playing.

Nevertheless, the hysteria over Lennon's comment frightened the Beatles and helped motivate the group to abandon touring in favor of focusing on its studio work. As Lennon would later remark, "[I]f I hadn't said [the comment about Jesus] and upset the very Christian Ku Klux Klan, well, Lord, I might still be up there with all the other performing fleas! God bless America. Thank you, Jesus."[12]

The Beatles' reaction to the threats proved to be to culture's benefit: the first album the group produced after its renewed dedication to studio work was *Sgt. Pepper's Lonely Hearts Club Band* in 1967, a revered recording that helped give birth to the "concept album."

Hysteria elbowed its way in again toward the end of the decade when those demographic and sociological schisms I mentioned above converged and clashed over two issues: the out-of-control war in Vietnam—our nation's first televised war, with unfiltered footage shown nightly on the news, in color—and the militancy of the black population. And what triggered the eruption of mass hysteria on both sides were the back-to-back assassinations in 1968 of civil rights activist Dr. Martin Luther King in April, and then antiwar icon and 1968 presidential candidate Robert F. Kennedy in June.

For a nation still coming to terms with the murder of a president, the outrage over these killings was unable to be contained. The death of Dr. King in April resulted in the so-called Holy Week Uprising, with riots taking place in the nation's capital, Baltimore, Kansas City, Detroit, and Chicago, among other places. President Johnson wanted force applied where it was needed and believed—perhaps rightly—that the violence wasn't just about Dr. King but about the war draft, about the war itself, about poverty, about countless other social ills. As Johnson told his press secretary, George Christian, "When you put your foot on a man's neck and hold him down for three hundred years, and then you let him up, what's he going to do? He's going to knock your block off." For that reason, Johnson also seized this opportunity to push the wide-ranging social programs that were stalled in Congress. I remember one reason New York City was relatively calm was because Mayor John Lindsay went up to Harlem to urge calm and reassure the black community that City Hall was doing everything it could to fight poverty. Like

JFK before him, Lindsay was in earnest, and they believed him.

The hysteria quickly burned off and turned to mourning. The holdout was the Black Panther Party, founded in 1966 as the Black Panther Party for Self-Defense and devoted to that cause.[13] By the end of 1968, however, with group-high membership at two thousand, the mission and tactics had changed. Violence, robbery, extortion, and murder were its tools, and the FBI branded it a "black nationalist hate group." The group increasingly lost influence through the next decade, to be replaced in these times by the equally hostile, violent Black Lives Matter organization—funded to a great extent by that all-around disturber of civil societies worldwide, George Soros.

The Black Panthers dissipated because anger and hysteria cannot be sustained, especially when people refuse to sign on. The vast majority of blacks were too busy trying to educate their children and build their communities to dedicate the time, energy, and resources to being militant. Many knew great strides had been made in a few short years and were willing to work with the Establishment. At the time, the name of the game was still one America.

HIPPIES, YIPPIES, AND HYSTERICS

Vietnam was a different matter. Everyone knew someone who was serving there. Most of us knew of someone who had died there. And the death count continued to rise as progress against the communists continued to slow. It wasn't so much spoken of at the time, but I got the feeling America was sick of fighting communists. It was like crying wolf. Where was the threat? Our system was clearly not in jeopardy. Communism was no longer a monolithic, Stalinist entity. It was openly repressive in Eastern Europe, impoverished throughout the Soviet Union, and militarized in sections of China...but poor and starving elsewhere in the vast nation. Cuba was a puppet state without the means to do us harm. And Vietnam had less meaning to most Americans than any of those.

For the most part, the hysteria was initially one-sided. The news wasn't good and musicians fanned the flames. With the exception of Staff Sergeant Barry Sadler's "Ballad of the Green Berets," which was the nation's number one song in 1966,[14] and Victor Lundberg's prowar "An Open Letter to My Teenage Son," which was number ten the following year,[15] every other song about the conflict was a protest. I remember that vividly because I was listening to a lot of music then. I had just met my wife, Janet, in 1967, and I even worked for a short time with LSD advocate Timothy Leary in Millbrook, New York. I wasn't personally interested in the drug, but he represented the avant-garde of thinking at the time, which was complementary to my own outside-the-box view of the world. He gave me a tent at the front of the mansion and I was literally the gatekeeper. Why? Because I did not use the drug and could be counted on to be sober.

The songs of the time were pervasive and powerful. Jim Morrison and the Doors mourned "The Unknown Soldier," Edwin Starr sang disapprovingly of "War," John Lee Hooker announced, "I Don't Wanna Go to Vietnam"—the tunes came one after the other. Pete Seeger's "Waist Deep in the Big Muddy" was cut from the *Smothers Brothers Comedy Hour*[16]—as were the brothers themselves when their hit show became too controversial for CBS. Even softer rock groups like Gary Puckett and the Union Gap sang longingly of "Home," the Association gave us "Requiem for the Masses," and the Monkees—the *Monkees!*—put out the thinly disguised "Zor and Zam" about warring nations.

The antiwar drumbeat was quite literally constant, especially when President Nixon escalated the conflict into Cambodia, where Viet Cong soldiers would hide to avoid South Vietnamese forces. And while campus protests and media disapproval did not constitute hysteria but fear of the draft, they spurred an anti-Establishment backlash that *was* hysteria. The counterculture, as the hippies were called, all wore peace symbols or spray-painted them on walls and streets. Children of prosperity attacked their own status. Students and the hippie dropouts denounced the once-proud achievements of NASA as a waste of money, stupidly oblivious to the spin-offs like microchips, handheld video cameras, and even Teflon. They turned on the police, whom they referred to as "pigs" or "the fuzz," and promoted slogans like "Never trust anyone over thirty" and "Make love, not war," to which the Establishment replied, "America, love it or leave it." There were impromptu riots, like the one at the Stonewall Inn in New York City in the summer of 1969, which started the gay rights movement in earnest.[17] Draft cards were burned alongside flags and brassieres, the latter in the name of "women's liberation." Hippies in particular didn't believe in work, they believed in playing Frisbee. As we've discussed, they also saturated their systems with pot, psychoactive drugs, and other substances that not only colored their hysterical reaction to everything but bred a fast-growing antagonism from Americans over thirty. To them, the kids were mostly bums.

In every city, and on every campus, it seemed as though everyone had lost their minds and was acting out. It was different from today, where people are manipulated by social media on a daily basis. This was a generational hysteria in which even the fading HUAC got involved when it subpoenaed Jerry Rubin and Abbie Hoffman in 1967, two founders of the Yippie movement—a coy play on "hippie" that described a group of disruptive, theatrics-loving clowns who infiltrated the New York Stock Exchange and threw money (real and fake) at the traders, held "sit-ins" and "be-ins" in public places, and threw Nazi salutes and blew gum bubbles during the HUAC hearings. These self-described "Groucho Marxists" were every inch the hysterical lunatics they appeared. I thought at the time, and nothing has changed my opinion, that they were half-baked anarchists without the skill set to promote an alternative to whatever they protested.

The anti-Establishment lunacy continued until two events put an end to it. The first was the 1974 resignation, in disgrace, of Richard M. Nixon as a result of the Watergate break-in. The second was the end of direct U.S. military involvement in Vietnam, although fighting continued until 1975. The targets were gone. The insanity passed.

The end of this hysteria wasn't like pulling the plug on a computer, where a vital machine goes silent. It was like a clean breeze blew in and swept rotted flower petals away. To borrow a phrase from Bob Dylan, they were "blowin' in the wind." A smattering of the hard-core lunatics and radicals emerged from hibernation a few years ago, pulled their gray hair into ponytails, loaded their iPods with as much Joni Mitchell as Tim Cook's little devices could hold, and showed up to join Occupy Wall Street, rally for Bernie Sanders, and participate in other hysterical protests. Because, you will notice, the old hippies and young radicals never show up to support anything *for* all citizens, like eating healthy. It is in their DNA to destroy. But while they were never very dynamic, these modern-day hippies are just sad relics, the by-product of a dazed, reactionary youth that grew into something mentally, emotionally, and physically stunted. And people wonder why the nation is on the verge of having a nervous breakdown.

Because that deformity is another by-product of hysteria. If you subscribe to it at a young age, as a matter of course, you stop listening—except to your own voice and the simplistic mantras of your fellow airheads in an echo chamber. You fail to take in ideas that are intellectually nutritious. And part of that pathology is you want everything else to be the way you are: no restrictions, no literate words, no tradition. In short, no borders, no language, no culture. With these people as role models, with the rebellious sixties held up as an exemplar of pro-test, we are breeding a generation of equally vapid youth, of lemmings, of people who know only one setting: hysteria. We see it in the reaction to the election of Donald Trump—which, almost two years after the fact, continues to reduce a portion of the electorate to a vocabulary of inarticulate cries. They just nod obediently, like zombies, whenever Bernie or Lizzy Warren speaks.

Domestic hysteria often has a real trigger. During the 1970s, a manufactured gasoline shortage led to long lines, fights, and riots. Wage and price controls caused the impotent rage of the populace to toss out elected officials. When attention shifted during the Reagan administration to rampant pornography—including the exploitation of children—it became a flashpoint for hysteria on both sides as religious leaders, feminists, free-speech fanatics, free-sex fanatics, and many others were fiercely polarized by a single subject. The fallout of this long hysteria was that nobody wanted to be "politically incorrect," even if, once again, innocent youth had to suffer.

13.

FROM GAS LINES
TO REAGAN
Not All Hysteria
Is Manufactured

The Arabs of the oil-producing nations won a war against the United States without firing a shot.

It was October 1973, and America had come to Israel's aid after Egypt and Syria launched a surprise attack. The fighting was over in three weeks, the attackers defeated, but the Arabs were not done with us. In November, under the umbrella of OPEC—the Organization of the Petroleum Exporting Countries[1]—they reduced oil output by 25 percent.[2] Their goal was to bully America into a foreign policy less friendly to Israel.

The result was hysteria at the pumps. Gas prices jumped by more than 40 percent—when you could get it.[3] The summer of 1974 is captured in two iconic images: endless lines at filling stations that had gas, and filling stations that had sold their inventory and were closed. Some closed for the day;[4] others closed permanently. Every day, Americans drove by gas stations that had once been brightly lit twenty-four hours a day. Seeing them gone did not help the national mood.

And it got worse. Open gas stations came under fire for selling gas by appointment to longtime customers,[5] or for supplying black market vendors who sold their product at whatever prices the market would bear.[6] By summer, fights at gas stations were common.[7]

This wouldn't be the last time in the 1970s things got ugly at the pumps. In June, 1979, there were protests over gasoline shortages. In Levittown, Pennsylvania, police wore riot gear and used dogs to stop frustrated motorists from burning cars and vandalizing buildings. That same weekend, fewer than fifty gas stations were open in the entire state of Connecticut, and of six thousand stations in New Jersey, barely five hundred had their lights on. The cost of delivering goods by truck skyrocketed, as did consumer prices. Everything from food to clothing to goods was impacted.[8]

As all wars do, this one endangered our children.

Starting in January 1974, the United States went on year-round Daylight Savings Time in an effort to preserve precious reserves of oil.[9] Before the sun had risen, kids were crossing streets, waiting—sometimes alone—at bus stops, and stumbling around in the dark.

Hysteria was present in every corner of the nation, in every industry—and in Washington, D.C.

War frequently makes governments do dumb, hysterical things, and this war was no exception. In 1974, the Nixon administration imposed a national 55 mph speed limit to boost fuel efficiency.[10] Truckers, the lifeblood of our economy, felt this harder than anyone. Many were paid per delivery, and the reduced speed limit meant more time per load. Rather than work for reduced pay, they struck, which further damaged the economy. But President Nixon stood firm, as did Presidents Ford and Carter after him, and the national speed limit wasn't rolled back until 1995. Ford was flat footed for his short tenure in office following Nixon's resignation, but Jimmy Carter leaped into action to expand government as only a Democrat can. In 1977, the government bureaucracy swelled by another cabinet-level department, the Department of Energy.

The war almost brought rationing back to our

country. Gasoline ration cards, like those used during World War II, were printed. There was a truly rebellious tone to the hysteria as this new burden was readied for distribution.[11] Thankfully, we'll never know what impact those ration cards would have had on national morale. After a combination of conservation efforts that threatened to impact the economy of the Arab states permanently, and Middle East diplomacy that briefly settled tension in the region, petroleum-producing countries reopened the taps.

It turned out crisis was only on hiatus, though. The Iranian Revolution of 1979 and the Iran-Iraq War in 1980 created additional supply disruptions. Oil prices again shot up.[12] And again, government intervention made the situation worse. Under President Carter, controls were removed from oil and gas prices. That placed a momentary burden on consumers, but it was supposed to spur domestic exploration and production. Carter and the Democrats couldn't resist tacking a "windfall profit tax" on oil companies, however. That took away any impetus for them to explore for new sources. Had the government not interfered, rising gas prices would have made exploration affordable and we could have moved from dependency on the Arab states.

Supply was down, costs were up, and Americans again faced long lines at the gas pumps. The government tried to moderate the situation by, among other schemes, alternating days when cars could fill up based on even or odd license plate numbers.[13] All summer, anyone with a screwdriver and at least two vehicles was busily switching plates. Illegal? Yes. Jimmy Carter made almost everyone a criminal. But like backyard distillers during Prohibition, idiotic laws enacted during periods of hysteria make people do illegal things, whether as acts of rebellion or simply coping.

Here's the ultimate joke played on, and then by, the left. It was under Carter that alternative energy exploration began to take root, whether solar panels like the ones he put on top of the White House, or coal and natural gas. But the hysterics found something new to be hysterical about. This time it was the nuclear industry, which currently provides a cheap source of 20 percent of this country's needs.[14] It was unsafe, there were going to be meltdowns, we would all be sterile. You can't win.

The 1979 oil crisis resolved itself as industrial nations turned to alternative fuels. By 1981 there were oil gluts and oil prices were dropping.[15] It is perhaps a fitting denouement to the Arab-manufactured crisis that a line from Galatians in the New Testament applies: "For whatsoever a man soweth, that shall he also reap."

COMMUNITY STANDARDS

Born-again Christian Jimmy Carter was the presidential candidate who famously told *Playboy* magazine, in 1976, "I've looked on many women with lust. I've committed adultery in my heart many times."[16] He wasn't alone and he did no one any favors by setting the bar for morality so low.

Ronald Reagan came along at the right time for a number of reasons. One of them was to call attention to a scourge that has always caused me more than a little concern, if not *quite* hysteria. Pornography.

When I was a teenager, there was only one place anyone could buy girlie magazines like *Nugget*, and *Cavalier*, and *Swank*: under the counter at certain newsstands. For the harder stuff, you had to go to Forty-Second Street in Manhattan off Seventh Avenue. Heading west, closer to Tenth Avenue, were the last holdouts of the burlesque houses along with the theaters that showed porn and "all-male" movies. It was a sleazy area that got even more degenerate until Rudy Giuliani cleaned it up when he became mayor. People say he "Disney-fied" it by allowing the New Amsterdam Theater to be renovated and for the Disney musicals *King David* and then *The Lion King* to take up residence. They're right. He did. And it was the best thing that could have happened. What had been three avenues of crime and perversion became a safe tourist attraction.

I'm not a prude, but what people do behind closed doors should stay there. It's no one else's business. In the early 1980s, before the Times Square cleanup, though, our nation was subjected not just to a proliferation of full-frontal nudity in once semi-artistic magazines like *Playboy* and *Penthouse*—and worse in Larry Flynt's *Hustler*—but to a surge in the number of porn films as the new medium of home video leaped on the genre as a valuable source of revenue.

That was the state of things when Ronald Reagan was elected president, and law professor and former army second lieutenant Edwin Meese was named attorney general of the United States. As Governor Reagan's chief of staff in California, Meese was a law-and-order man who was the impetus behind the hard National Guard crackdown on student protesters at Berkeley in 1969.[17]

One of Meese's signature efforts was the exhaustive report of the Attorney General's Commission on Pornography, which was released in the summer of 1986.[18] The report was, on the one hand, a politically charged document. It was a repudiation of the earlier President's Commission on Obscenity and Pornography report, released on October 24, 1970, which was against censorship of pornography and advocated stronger sex education programs in schools.[19] That report had been commissioned under the Johnson administration, was denounced by Nixon, but stood as a liberal lighthouse for three administrations. Meese finally undid that. The topics the document covered, in great detail, were a history of pornography, an interpretation of First Amendment protections, the dangerous sociological impact of pornography, and the ways in which pornography enriches organized crime.

Few could disagree with the social and criminal aspects of Meese's findings. I had friends in the 1970s who worked in the Midtown South Precinct of Manhattan. Many pornography shops on Forty-Second Street were fronts for criminal activity. Many of the films were used to launder mob money. A large number of people who frequented these establishments were not looking for a one-time-only stag film for a bachelor party. They were obsessed individuals who should have been seeking help, not more books and magazines. If it were alcohol, the liberals would have been urging the users to join AA.

Liberal hysteria exploded over two topics: that it was impossible to define pornography vis-à-vis art, and that free speech was under attack by the Reagan administration. Both of those arguments were absurd and were ably dismissed by the Supreme Court in the mid-1950s. The members of Chief Justice Earl Warren's Court came up with what I consider to be a wise and applicable yardstick: It's pornography if "to the average person, applying contemporary community standards, the dominant theme of the material taken as a whole appeals to the prurient interest."[20] In other words, the nudes of Michelangelo are art. The movie *Deep Throat* is pornography. Pornography is demonstrably destructive to our society, to our economy, to our families, and cannot be considered protected speech. End of discussion. In its own way, even the free-speech advocates at the *New York Times* inadvertently supported the Supreme Court definition when they refused to publish the Meese report because they deemed it too pornographic. It was one of the richest hypocrisies in the history of journalism as the press censored a document whose view of censorship was contrary to their own. To their credit, many religious bookstores that agreed with the report sold published copies under the counter.

Sadly, maybe that isn't the definition the Supreme Court should have been worrying about. Today, the question is: What's a community? Is it Muslims in Minneapolis? Scientologists in Clearwater, Florida? Progressives melting down history in New York City? The justices never envisioned a nation where the very concept of community was no longer viable.

Thirty years ago, there were still community standards. But no legal finding has ever stopped the ACLU and other liberal juggernauts, and they defended both the pornography shops and the businesses that provided the wares. In fact, showing just how repugnant they are, the ACLU issued this directive in 1994 under the banner of pornography and the First Amendment: "The sexually abusive acts committed against children should be criminalized, but once those acts are in the form of visual depictions, they are protected forms of expression."[21] I do not believe I need to comment further.

Communists were of the opposing view, critical of anything that promoted sexual inequality among workers, thus chauvinism, thus pornography. Feminists were actually torn. While most of pornography treated women like sex objects, the women who appeared in these magazines and films were exercising their right as liberated women to do as they pleased. The Feminist Anti-Censorship Task Force held that view.[22] The group Radical Women took the former view.[23] There is nothing so validating as watching liberals tear at one another with greater and greater frenzy. You can see their dilemma. Are women who do a lesbian sex scene being used or promoting gay rights?

There was also a very fundamental question of legality, which the liberals ignored—just as they have always ignored the law of the land. Models and actors creating pornography were paid. They were being compensated for having sex. That's prostitution. That's illegal. For that reason alone, the industry should have been shut down.

But it wasn't. The debate died down with the coming of the Internet and the notion that everyone can be a porn star on pay sites catering to every taste, every fetish. That is what the liberals have wrought, the easy promulgation of mental pollution to every device in everyone's pocket or purse and the regular, ceaseless consumption of work hours, family time, and economy. And that's not all. There is one area of the report that I find particularly fascinating and especially relevant today.

Surgeon General C. Everett Koop conducted
workshops and one of his conclusions was that "[p]
rolonged use of pornography increases beliefs that
less common sexual practices are more common."[24]
We need only look around at the nation today to
see how that truth has flourished. Every gay pride
parade grows thicker with flags for different subsets
of lesbians, gay, bisexual, transgender, questioning, and supporting persons. And those are just the
public expressions. I am unaware, but would not be
surprised, to find that there are flags or symbols for
sick fetishists, bondage enthusiasts, sadomasoch-
ists, and acts your mother could not imagine.

I strongly disagree with people who say that
these obsessions are nature, not nurture. Even if
I allowed that homosexuality is nature, I do not
believe it is what God intended. There is increasing and persuasive evidence that the chemical
changes to women's bodies, caused by the advent
of the birth control pill in the 1960s, has created
a generation of sexual abnormality. A science has
grown up around that idea, epigenetics, and one
of the foundational ideas is that since every fetus
is exposed to hormonal fluctuations, the artificial
hormones in the pill may have triggered an increase
in homosexuality.

What Surgeon General Koop posited has come

to pass. Artificially bred sexuality, masquerading as "nature," and psychologically impaired nurture have conspired to legitimize qualities that should properly be dealt with on a psychiatrist's couch. We do that with rapists, flashers, pedophiles, and nymphomaniacs. I'm not talking about degree, because violent sexual beings should be taken off the streets, not gays or transgenders. But to Gilberto Vitale, New York's infamous "Cannibal Cop," who, in 2013, allegedly wanted to abduct for gang rape, and then cook and eat, women.[25] *That* was normal. I did a quick check on his fetish. It's got a name, gynophagia, and it has a Twitter presence with hundreds of followers.

The question is, why should *any* nonnormative sexual expression be treated as nature? Does anyone emerge from the womb already thinking they should pursue gynophagia? Why is "nature" the default, and who gets to decide what is or isn't natural? I can answer that. The primary purpose of sex is procreation. Yes, there are ancillary aspects such as love and intimacy and pleasure. But any other *primary* justification does not come from nature. As I have stated numerous times over the years on my radio program, I am a sexual libertarian. If it is consensual and does not harm or include children, it is not the business of government.

Of course, a quiet conversation about the previous paragraph cannot be had. The hysterical, screaming liberal advocates of anything goes (except heterosexuality, even if you agree to be called the profoundly unnecessary new coinage "cis-gendered," which means you identify as the gender of your birth)—these pathologically irrational progressives won't allow the discussion to be had. I believe strongly in many positions but I am not a strict ideologue. If people have rational ideas, I want to hear them. It's what I do every weekday on the radio. But it is almost universal that liberals who phone my radio show are hysterics who place the call to shout memes, spit bile, and depart—convincing no one and hearing nothing.

MANUFACTURED EVIL

Children can be manipulated. We saw this in the Salem Witch Trials, when it was done with malicious intent, even if the full repercussions of their actions weren't clear to them. Sometimes, though, children manipulate adults often without trying. There was a little-known phenomenon from Louisiana, in 1939, that illustrates this point. The Twitching Epidemic of 1939 began when a teenage girl started to suffer uncontrollable twitching in her right leg during a school dance, either from anxiety, using muscles she didn't ordinarily use, or a medical cause like alkalosis (the amount of acid in her blood). The twitching continued for weeks and soon a half dozen of her female classmates were experiencing it as well. Hysterical parents took their children out of the school, and shortly thereafter the malady stopped just as suddenly as it started. It turned out the cause was psychological; "Twitching Mary" did not really know how to dance and her malady was a subconscious expression of that. It was also a way of getting attention from her boyfriend, whom she apparently didn't want dancing with other girls. Her fellow students? They became what they beheld. Psychosomatic illness caused by hysteria.[26]

A similar hysteria happened in 1989 at a youth center in Florida. Sandwiches were provided each lunchtime, and when one girl vomited because of what she'd eaten, other kids started complaining of nausea, headaches, cramps, and similar ailments. In just over half an hour, 63 of the 150 children were ill and more than a third of them had thrown up. The children were taken to hospitals, but no illness was uncovered. Laboratory tests on the sandwiches also came back negative. As with the twitching, it was the power of suggestion—group hysteria.

But sometimes, adults manipulate children—and this has the potential to ruin lives and destroy communities.[27] I know I don't have to say this, but I will: our children are sacred. It breaks my heart to see latchkey kids around my own city, getting into trouble while they are still adolescents because they are being raised by a single mother who is working and have no strong male role models who are willing to step up and fill the role of absent fathers. If there is any deep-set rot in American society, the decay of the family is it. Children who do not have their parents around often look for attention. That is what happened in the summer of 1983, when a new wave of hysteria crisscrossed the nation, fueled by moral horror. That new panic was the preschool Satanism scandals.

It began with the McMartin Preschool in Manhattan Beach, California, which was run by Virginia McMartin and her daughter Peggy. A male boy's painful bowel movements led to an investigation of sodomy—a teacher and the boy's estranged father were the alleged perpetrators—and though the boy's testimony was wildly inconsistent, he added that McMartin staff had sex with animals and that the teacher could fly. The charges shifted to embrace the existence of a satanic cult operating in the area, possibly as a result of abuse therapy clinic interviews that, to put it mildly, asked leading questions. Arrests followed that year. After years of highly publicized criminal trials with no convictions obtained, the charges were dropped in 1990. Everything from withheld prosecution evidence to false memory syndrome was blamed for the witch hunt and its failure. What is astonishing is that the hysteria whipped itself up again as parents engaged an archaeologist to investigate whether there were secret tunnels under the school. There weren't. A fact that the trial did find, however, is that the mother who had first made the allegations, the mother who was having trouble with her former husband, had psychological issues.

What was sickeningly prophetic about this trial—which was the most expensive ever, at $15 million, if not quite "the trial of the century"—is that the media generally bought the point of view of the Los Angeles County prosecutors that something *was* going on there. You know, where there's brimstone there's fire. Leave it to the already-corrupted *New York Times* to put a self-serving face on what was widespread media rush to judgment: "Publicity surrounding that case helped focus attention on what many experts saw as a long-neglected problem."[28]

The McMartin travesty caused a spate of allegations nationwide about Devil worship going on at day care centers with ritual abuse (sexual and otherwise), blood-drinking, animal sacrifice, and more. It was so widespread that the phenomenon even got its own acronym, SRA—satanic ritual abuse. One of the last of the thirteen major cases in North America occurred in 1992, in Saskatchewan, Canada. In overturning the conviction of the woman who ran a babysitting service, the Royal Canadian Mounted Police finally called the nine-year odyssey what it was: "emotional hysteria."[29]

What is particularly tragic is that it is possible that somewhere amid all the wild lies about all various centers, there may have been some tragic truth—not about satanism but about child pornography or abuse. We will never know. The opportunity to get to the truth was crowded out by hysteria over the most sensational charges, which discredited similar claims.

HYSTERIA BEGETS HYSTERICALS

There's an absurdist, surreal juxtaposition of the McMartin case with another event that involved children in 1983. Despite all this, adults were *again* willing to act irrationally and hurt one another based on the words of the young...only this time it had nothing to do with the Devil.

In 1983, the manufacturer of Cabbage Patch Kids dolls had woefully underestimated demand.

Stores that had received a few hundred of the dolls faced thousands of determined adults... if someone unwilling to say no to a six-year-old can be called an adult. Nonetheless, parents wanted their children to have the pinch-faced rags for all the reasons any child would want a doll—but also for status.[30]

This hysteria was manufactured in perhaps the truest sense of the word. In 1982, toy company Coleco licensed the dolls from the original manufacturer. At that time each doll was made by hand, a distinctive creation. The next year, instead of hand-crafting Cabbage Patch Kids, Coleco mass-produced them. They also cut the price from $125 to $25 and mounted an aggressive television campaign.[31] The company held a mass adoption ceremony in Boston; part of the gimmick was that these dolls came with names and birth certificates. They weren't bought, they became part of your family.[32]

Coleco executives expected a modest hit. What they got was a craze. The company had made two million dolls. Thanks in part to each doll's perceived uniqueness, and in part to their resale value, adults weren't just buying one per child. The entire run sold out by early October but the demand continued.

Humorists picked up on the craze. A disc jockey announced that two thousand dolls would be air dropped on a stadium. Anyone who wanted one should bring a catcher's mitt and, if lucky enough to catch one, should hold up a credit card so people in the plane could photograph it for payment.

A dozen people, gullible and hysterical, showed up.[33]

Coleco stepped up its production. But as each new shipment hit stores, it sold out. Some retailers advertised for shoppers who had bought several dolls and who might be willing to part with them for above what they had paid, but below what the store would resell them for.

With Christmas approaching and the demand not slacking, parents began to panic. There was no Internet to spread the word in real time as to which stores had received new shipments, so parents would line up and wait for toy stores to open. Those lucky enough to grab a doll had to run gauntlets in order to get to a checkout counter, and many had the dolls ripped from their grasp by other shoppers. When shoppers fell, they were often trampled.

A riot in a Wilkes-Barre, Pennsylvania, store may not have been the worst of hundreds of similar incidents, but it was captured on video—a rarity for the time. I get sick when I watch it, not because of the unchecked consumerism, but because of the feral hysteria embodied in each and every shopper like rogue coyotes. In the footage, a clerk stands on a counter waving a baseball bat at crowds of shoppers and screaming at them. In the background, panicked store workers throw dolls into the crowd. At least one shopper suffered a broken leg.[34]

The riots meant more media coverage. The additional million dolls Coleco produced before Christmas still didn't meet demand.

One would expect children to be upset and disappointed, which is why parents have a responsibility to step in and manage expectations. But that assumes someone managed *theirs*. At the time, mothers freely voiced their tremendous indignation at the lack of dolls. In news reports they wondered aloud what they were going to tell their children on Christmas morning? That you were good but Santa ran short? The elves were unionized and took too many breaks?

The hysteria was pathetic, and it died down as Coleco caught up with its back orders; the gotta-have-it mania passed because people could have it. There was no natural selection, no survival of the fittest. Yet the company actually managed to go broke in 1988,[35] in large part because management believed that the hysteria was about the inherent superiority of their product and not about the underlying greed, status-craving, and inability to treat children like children rather than as entitled little tyrants. Their video game system, ColecoVision, and add-on computer, Adam, were massively overproduced for a demand that never materialized.

The hysteria was neither unique nor informative. Some of us had seen it before, such as with the national craze in 1954, coonskin caps from Disney's *Davy Crockett* TV series. They suffered a shortage because, selling at a rate of five thousand a day, there were no more raccoons from which to remove the tails that hung down the back of the cap.[36] The key word, in both this instance and that of the Cabbage Patch Kids instances, is *shortage*. In 1958, the nation had a Hula Hoop craze, those plastic rings you twirled on your hips. The manufacturer was making more than fifty thousand hoops a day. But there were enough to go around—thus no hysteria.

None of that must-have mania was new, but here's what *is* informative about the Cabbage Patch Kids. The girls and boys receiving those dolls are in their early forties today. The grandchildren of the indulgent parents are in college. Seen in that context, self-centered righteousness on university campuses makes sense. Each of those students at Berkeley and elsewhere who protests speeches by conservatives is acting out the same hysteria they saw modeled for them by their parents; they, and their "muscle" AntiFA, conspire to decide who gets trampled. Never mind that another kid wants a doll, or to hear a speaker with a different viewpoint. They can't have that. And the parent—in this case, the university—indulges them. Cause and effect is as predictable as the seasons.

And not everything changed after the Cabbage Patch Kids craze died. Every Christmas season still brings "door buster" sales with temptingly low prices for a limited supply of hot items. What used to be a President's Day car sale is now an "event." Each new Apple device debuts with long lines outside each Apple Store. Hyperbolic marketing is now designed to stir hysteria. If it hadn't been for a decade of severe recession ended by Donald trump, one can only wonder in what uncharted territory consumerism would have taken us.

POLITICAL MADNESS AND THE DEATH OF COMMON SENSE

There are few terms in the English language that have done more harm and stirred more passion than *politically correct*. It suggests a kid-glove approach to reality that offends by failing to offend; that is, it self-censors many of the very topics we should be talking about. And it has changed from being a thoughtful way to crafting speech to

frankly a dumb form of self-censorship to something much more dangerous—a repudiation of the
very differences that the Social Justice Warriors
and diversity police claim to want.

The term *politically correct* appears in a 1793
Supreme Court decision discussing the difference
between "the United States" and "the people of the
United States." According to the Court, the latter is "politically correct," since it is the people who
brought the United States into existence. That is why
the people and not the states should be protected. A
subtle adjunct to this idea occurred after the Civil
War. Until then, many reporters and ordinary civilians said of our nation, "The United States are."
Afterward, we were one. "The United States is."[37]

Over the past two-hundred-plus years, the phrase
has been perverted. Today's idea of American political madness shifted from its noble origin and has its
roots in Marxism. Ninety years ago, Italian communist Antonio Gramsci envisioned a state in which people couldn't resist a progressive agenda because it was
impossible to articulate countering views. According
to Gramsci's scheme, such views would have been
labeled shameful, and the actual vocabulary for chal-
lenging them would have been eliminated.[38] This was
Orwellian theory before Orwell, and leftists learned
well. By labeling something politically incorrect, they

believed they would stifle debate. For example, in Marxist thought there can be no class structure. The idea is that if you remove the language that indicates any ties to groups from the past, be they economic, religious, cultural, or educational, you remove the barriers between people.

In those terms, it sounds acceptable. If you stop to think about the deeper implications for just a few seconds, however, the sinister, manipulative quality of that kind of erasure is at once apparent. A banker is just a man, a worker is just a man, and society is scrubbed of its color and texture. Our individual distinctions are the basis for our national identity: borders, language, culture.

It wasn't until the 1980s that modern political madness gained its toehold in the United States, thanks to academia. Professors who had been students in the Marxist-embracing 1960s now had tenure, and they wanted to use their status for power. The question was how to do it without a Russian-style revolution—which, indeed, many of them advocated. What grew, like mushrooms in this intellectual darkness, was modern political madness.

The Western system would be permitted to stay intact—at least, that's what radicals among both the faculty and students told administrators. They just wanted representation for their own thinking. Since "do your own thing" was the byword of the counter-culture, universities went along with this. Nobody but the rabid radicals thought that their impact would weather the decade. Because the radicals were not yet hysterical but intellectually grounded, they would prove the administrators very wrong.

The attack began under the cover of gender fairness. This was a tactical move. In liberal arts institutions, more than half the students are female, and women are well represented among the faculty. Anyone opposing these efforts would have to face colleagues and fellow students within a college's closed environment, what someone—I forget who—called "mini North Koreas."[39]

Professors started penalizing students for using the standard *he* as a gender-neutral indicator in academic papers. Administrators who might have told professors to cut it out would have been vilified. Students who protested the cleansing of the language were mocked—and if they were in humanities classes, in which grades are awarded based on subjective criteria, they were penalized.[40]

At the time, letting the classroom standard become *he/she* or even the grammatically incorrect *they* seemed like a small concession. Ignore the fact—which the left regularly does—that according to the English language's Germanic roots, *he* is a perfectly acceptable gender-neutral pronoun. But a little he/she was not enough for the left. Once its foot soldiers had tasted the joys of bullying, the Politically Correct Army wanted more. So the quest became to find causes they could champion, causes that would give them power but not make them the new top-dog target. The left knows that by shaming any existing structure, they have a theoretical high road with no real responsibility. That is the major, inherent flaw in leftist hysteria. It revs up passions without actually *doing* anything constructive, within the system, to help those they allegedly care about. In the recent uproar over DACA, all you heard was *illegal* aliens screaming about rights *they do not possess*. That is what the left does. And that is why the hysteria evaporates because, again, there is no real, actionable structure.

Political correctness soon began influencing curricula. In 1988, a year after Jesse Jackson led five hundred students in chanting, "Hey hey, ho ho, Western culture's got to go,"[41] Stanford University eliminated a required freshman course in Western civilization and replaced it with the purposely vague, Marxist-based "Cultures, Ideas, and Values." This new curriculum featured courses such as "Forging Revolutionary Selves," and "Our Bodies, Our Sheep, Our Cosmos, Ourselves,"[42] which focused on Navajo Indians. Thirty years later, Stanford would accept a Muslim student whose application "essay" on what mattered to him consisted only of the phrase "#BlackLivesMatter" typed one hundred times.[43] In other words, a hysterical protest reduced to type, without thought.

Throughout the late 1980s and early 1990s, conservative authors attempted to sound an alarm against the culture of victimization and the dilution of the Western canon that was infiltrating academia. Liberals accused them of promoting a culture war, all the while blind to the irony that, in making their own accusations, they were waging just that sort of war against the traditional American thought. Literature was a particular target. During those years, leftists didn't just advocate the jettisoning of classic literature and essential history, they lost a sense of modern history as well. They never got the pathetic joke they had hatched. During the 1950s and 1960s, college students fought for integration. In the 1980s, in the name of preserving multiculturalism, dorms were set aside for exclusive ethnic or academic experiences—at students' request.

By 1990, in a cowardly preemptive strike that has become standard operating procedure today, college faculties had begun discussing political correctness in regard to what should and shouldn't be taught and what could or couldn't be talked about. This is how cool intellectualism on the left translates to hysteria among everyone else. The public still wasn't fully aware of what was going on until 1991, when President George H. W. Bush noted that political correctness "replaces old prejudice with new ones. It declares certain topics off-limits."[44] Bush's speech did as much as anything else to cement the phrase as a pejorative among conservatives.

Later in the decade, education took a backseat at schools—yes, you read that correctly—when students were petitioning to have Ebonics, a supposed "black dialect" of American English, accepted as a valid alternative language.[45] In other words, the inversion of *axe* for *ask,* rather than be corrected, was going to be embraced. Twenty years later, we see the idiocy of that in our daily concourse.

At the same time, increasingly segregated "studies" majors exploded. These majors had their beginnings in the 1960s and 1970s, when students first demanded black and women's studies majors. Okay, that was a legitimate request. Like mental Cheerios, it was part of a nutritional intellectual diet. However, by the end of the 1990s, a college student could spend—some of us would say "waste"—four years immersed in ethnic, sexual, geographic, or other studies, while giving short shrift to the works that had defined social, cultural, and intellectual norms for centuries. It is one thing to teach, say, black authors. It is another to do so to the *exclusion* of Shakespeare, Dickens, or Jane Austen as though they simply do not matter—or that the very act of excluding them somehow demonstrates moral courage and intellectual enlightenment. The academic process, which by definition should involve having one's ideas challenged and expanded, had been supplanted by self-righteousness certainty about what was good or necessary. Students stopped thinking of faculty as educators and started thinking of them as servants. At forty thousand dollars a year, they reasoned, shouldn't the customer always be right? And God help the white male professor who dared to stand up for classical education.

Worse, these ideas trickled down to high schools, to junior high schools, to elementary schools so that we now have what are effectively gay studies to seven-year-olds. This is not an exaggeration. In 2016, California became the first state to make LGBT rights an official part of their required curriculum for children beginning in the second grade.[46]

In the decades since they first set out to destroy our educational system, the left has delighted in coming up with new means of oppressing free speech. Consider "safe spaces," where political correctness warriors could hide without molestation *or* contrary ideas . . . after they smashed windows or burned cars because something offended them. I would make the analogy that it's like the Gypsy girl Esmeralda seeking sanctuary in church in Victor Hugo's *The Hunchback of Notre Dame*—but I'm sure it will be only a matter of time before hunchbacks, churches, and victimized women are banished from literature. Yet think of how absolutely counterintuitive safe spaces are. When you designate an area of a campus—*an institution of learning and supposedly free thinking*—a safe space, you are de facto announcing not only that the world beyond the ivied walls is unsafe, but that the rest of the campus itself is also unsafe. The solution? Join AntiFA or some other anarchistic group and make America a safe space for all Marxists.

Here's the real kicker, though. When students are denied their safe spaces, they cry. They're doing a lot of crying these days. Pretty much anything can set them off, including unconscious, unintended, and ultimately unreal "microaggressions," such as calling a meeting and having only white people show up—which is an actual example of a microaggression cited by a University of Illinois at Urbana–Champaign study.[47] Yes, that is considered a *microaggression* although it's unclear who in the room is actually being aggressed against. By this definition, a yoga class can violate tenets of political correctness, since white people doing yoga is cultural appropriation,[48] just as serving Vietnamese *banh mi* sandwiches without the authentic bread is.[49] Guess what: college student have protested both.

The absurdity does not even stop there. In September 2017, a black woman shopping at a Texas Hobby Lobby became offended, and went online to say so, about a raw-cotton display at the store. Here is what she posted on social media:

> This decor is WRONG on SO many levels. There is nothing decorative about raw cotton. . . . A commodity which was gained at the expense of African-American slaves. A little sensitivity goes a long way. PLEASE REMOVE THIS "decor."[50]

This is real. The ellipses are original—nothing was omitted from what she posted. A woman actually expected the world to bend to her hysterical will. She seems to think that people should self-censor for fear of offending every possible person who could be offended for any conceivable reason, even when those reasons, like this one, are absurd.

The madness of attacks on American institutions such as the Bill of Rights, which high school kids have adopted from their older siblings, is in ascension. We've discussed how safe spaces are a barely disguised attack on the First Amendment. Now comes the kiddie crusade focusing on the Second Amendment.

The attacks are being led by a teenage agitator who is seeking to do what left-wing youth movements have done before him—strip the means of defense from citizens and patriots, leaving them unable to defend themselves against propaganda, politically correct thought, and when ultimately necessary, "reeducation." For those unable or unwilling to be reeducated, there can be only one end result: prison.

This demagogue's targets are National Rifle Association members and other legal gun owners.[51] As high school students often do, they are convinced they have better knowledge, that by exercising "gun control"—which make no mistake, is their code word for gun elimination—they will save countless children.

There is a reason why the word *sophomore* literally means "wise fool." The sophomoric bully is using tear-jerking sympathy to whip sympathy—appropriate sympathy, for the victims of the mentally ill school-shooting butchers—into the ultimate mass hysteria, the surrender of a right established nearly 230 years ago. Disarming a population to maintain control is nothing new: Hitler, Stalin, Mao, the

Castro brothers, Muammar Quaddafi, Idi Amin, and Pot's Khmer Rouge all understood it. King George III, from whom we won independence by keeping our guns in defiance of royal order, certainly understood it. Maybe if this spawn of Marx spent less time walking out of classes and more time learning in them, he would understand it, too.

Or maybe he already does. Do I think this bullying fanatic knows what he is doing? Yes, and he is probably laughing at all of us. He and his sister have gone as far as to create armbands with peace symbols on them, armbands to be worn while marching in formation during school walkouts and other forms of sanctioned civil disobedience that educators and parents have been browbeaten and shamed into condoning.

This little corporal—and those of you who know history know what despot I mean—mixed the signs of hatred from the left in his speeches and actions. He can't just be satisfied with armbands that evoke the Hitler Youth: When he gives speeches, he holds his fist up in the militant Black Power salute. And all the while he seeks to destroy rights in the name of "public good" and "keeping our children safe." Won't someone think of the children, he asks?

I think of the children. The legions who have come before him: the original Hitler Youth, the youngest of the Red Army soldiers during World War II, the

United Kingdom Home Guard, the child soldiers of the Khmer Rouge, the adolescent beheaders of ISIS, various children in armed youth gangs and death squads throughout Africa and South America . . . and the United States. I think of them all. While many of them were abused by adults into participating, every once in a while a truly "special" child emerges, one who fully embraces a path to either fame, power, or a chance to vent his childish rage.

And time and again we enable them. We allow emotions and fear of disapproval or denunciation from children to overrule rational thought. And we all suffer for it.

Hypocritically, of course, the left does not care if anyone on the right feels unsafe. For instance, many people are made uncomfortable by explicit sexual discussions. Leftists love this discomfort and they demand the world confront sexuality on their terms, which means acknowledging more than the standard two genders and three types of sex—heterosexual, homosexual, and bisexual. These days, leftist public sexual nomenclature includes *GBLTTQQPIA*—gay, bisexual, lesbian, transsexual, transgender, queer, questioning, pansexual, intersex, asexual—and doubtless a few more terms that will emerge between the time I write this and when the book comes out. And that's before we get into whether someone is bigender, cisgender, genderqueer, or heteronormative. God protect the poor student or teacher or kindergartner who uses the wrong word to describe someone, or assumes that a female wearing a dress identifies as female. For all they know, this individual is a female who identifies as male who is exploring whether he should identify as female. That sounds as idiotic as it is, but political correctness at that level of absurdity actually exists.

Don't bother learning what these words mean. For one thing, they will probably change before long. For another, they aren't used to clarify or illuminate. They are codes that separate those in the know— like some secret Masonic coded hand gesture— from those who really don't care and would be just as happy for everything to stay behind closed doors. The terms are used so the speaker can feel that he, she, whatever possesses superior knowledge.

Sadly, the people raised in this environment of moral superiority, exclusion, and entitlement during the first decade of the twenty-first century have moved into the "real" world. As they have, a number of professions have changed to reflect their thinking. Newsrooms, bastions of the left, have abandoned the pretense of gathering and presenting facts and have become forums for crusades and bombast. Human resource professionals (no longer the Personnel Department, of course), who once focused on hiring the best talent and making sure payrolls were met, have begun spending time rooting out anything that might be a "trigger" to employees who had never faced a viewpoint they couldn't shout down. In fields such as climatology, geology, and medicine, a practitioner's failure to embrace leftist doctrine can result in being ostracized or even job loss, whether through removal or resignation due to hostile work environment—hostile to conservatives, which means human resource departments rarely get involved. Military religious leaders can have their careers derailed if they refuse to perform gay marriages, no matter how bravely or heroically they had previously served.

We have had to accept *chairperson* for *chairman*, *firefighter* for *fireman*, *postal carrier* for *postman*, and—okay. Those are relatively painless, but only as language. The madness doesn't stop there, however. Hollywood studios are now adding "inclusion riders" to their contracts. Unlike the brave Freedom Riders of the 1960s, *these* riders promote a new form of racist, antiwhite hate in which producers promise to go out of their way to hire women, people of color, members of the LGBTQ "community," and the disabled. Failing to do so, the studios agree to contribute to scholarship funds for those groups. By the way: There is nothing about senior citizens in that rider. It's still okay for the young, the so-called inclusionists to send experienced, highly qualified older folks out to graze.

Political madness has put us all in physical danger by changing the requirements necessary for firefighters. Can't carry someone a minimum distance, or complete an exercise involving pulling down a ceiling quickly enough? Not a problem— fire departments are changing the job's physical requirements to avoid lawsuits. And what about Yale, Columbia, Dartmouth, and other universities having decided, now, to replace ancient, hallowed language like *upperclassman* and *freshman* with "first-year students" and "upper-level students." Were they concerned that women would be utterly at sea being called a "freshman"? Prep schools like Canterbury, in Connecticut, have moved from *headmaster* to "head of school." What was wrong with having a headmaster or a headmistress? At least then you'd know how to properly address your letter or email. Because we surely need more land mines in our politically correct communications. Early in this process of sanitizing our language, the term *Indian* was replaced with *Native American*. The anthropological record is pretty clear. There were no "native" Americans. Everybody, except the

Pleistocene animals, came here from somewhere else, from the south and from the land bridge that used to connect Asia with Alaska. What it is, of course, is a form of built-in apology for genocide and for Columbus's misunderstanding of who he had encountered—neither of which makes any linguistic sense. That word *Indian* took on a secondary meaning more than half a millennium ago.

There's more. Political correctness knows no bounds and no shame. In 2009, as many of you know, a Muslim army psychiatrist at Fort Hood in Texas went on a shooting spree, killing thirteen and wounding thirty-two others. Colleagues had noted erratic behavior from him for years.[52] He was a loner, and he had been written up for doing substandard work. Furthermore, the army knew of communication between him and a religious leader who had been named a security threat by the National Security Agency. But he wasn't watched more closely specifically because he is a Muslim and nobody wanted to be chastised by the PC police. They had been told, time and again, that political correctness required them to be religion-blind . . . and that included a religion whose adherents are actively killing infidels. And it got more abhorrent. Refusing to call it what it was, Islamic-inspired extremism, the Obama administration called it "workplace violence." That

was an insult to the military, to the American people, and most of all to the victims. Not that our
politically correct president cared.

In the name of political correctness, any level
of bad behavior can be excused, if it is cloaked in
the protective armor of heightened racial or cultural sensitivity. Diversity training materials teach
that requiring people to show up on time may not
fit into their culture, so this behavior should be
accommodated instead of corrected.

In 2018, corporate America is seeing in full, grotesque flowering what we have been discussing, what
took root in academia during the preceding decades.
The student snowflakes who have been brainwashed
into politically correct thinking are now flexing
their muscles now that they are older people—I'm
not going to say adults—in the business world.

If there is a chance that some consumer or some
viewer may not like something, it gets jettisoned . . .
fast. No hearing. No due process. Just a professional
execution. That is the very definition of hysteria.

You know those disclaimers on home video, about
opinions not necessarily expressing the views of management? Artists—whose job is to comment and interpret,
after all—artists no longer have that right or courtesy.
Just like under Hitler, though now serving the socialists.
They toe the leftist line or they are history.

This is the year hysterical reaction trumped sound business sense in several notable instances. It is the year Starbucks lost sales from more than eight thousand stores during an afternoon coffee rush when it closed all its locations for sensitivity training after an incident in a single store, when a single barista overreacted to the presence of two black men who were loitering without buying anything.[53] It is the year the Disney–ABC Television Group canceled its hit *Roseanne* reboot after a tweet from its star. Not an official tweet from the network or the show, not even a tweet about the show—just an unfortunate comment from an actress.[54] It is the year the National Football League, one of the great American entertainment brands, tied itself in knots trying to come up with a solution to its employees publicly damaging that brand, rather than just firing the employees outright.

In these cases—and many more like them—a truth about our universities, which graduated the dummies who made these decisions, became apparent. For all the time they spent in classes learning about cultural overreaction, and the virtues of victimhood, they apparently skipped basic economics. Because these hysterical reactions, which they did voluntarily, had serious economic repercussions for the businesses. Starbucks lost an afternoon of sales .

. . and still had to pay to keep the lights on and pay the wages of the employees who were being indoctrinated. As a by-product the coffee chain had to close hundreds of stores, permanently. At the *Roseanne* show, in which even Roseanne's costars rose against her, hundreds of backstage techs, support staff, and other workers lost work (the show was revived sans Roseanne). The NFL's compromise solution of having player-employees who wanted to protest not take the field—without penalty— during the national anthem satisfied no one, cheapened the product, and has and will cost the league revenue and brand equity.

This is very real damage. It's damage in Hollywood, it's damage throughout the country in places where the left loves to huddle for hours over its expensive Apple laptops, and it's damage to a great Sunday pastime. But the left isn't going to see that. The left got its pound of flesh in return for a transgression, and when a few more people join the unemployment lines, well . . . that's a small price to pay. Especially for people who don't have to pay it.

We will be in for more such actions, but I hope 2018 marks the high-water mark for them. I hope that someday, somewhere, someone who has a classic education, who has been trained in economics and classics and sanity, will stand firm against mass self-flagellation reactions that only hurt the people the left supposedly wants to help. I hope that someone with a degree that doesn't end in the word "studies" will be able to make a sane case for measured responses—including the word "no."

If there *is* hope, it is with the few universities that refuse to kowtow to the hysteria and those that are starting to challenge this nonsense. One university president recently informed students that his institution was a college, not a day care center. And the dean of students at the University of Chicago informed the incoming 2016 freshman class:

> Our commitment to academic freedom means that we do not support so-called trigger warnings, we do not cancel invited speakers because their topics might prove controversial, and we do not condone the creation of intellectual "safe spaces" where individuals can retreat from ideas and perspectives at odds with their own.[55]

Because reason will always trump hysteria, this mania will die of its own oxygen deprivation. In the meantime, however, a generation of minds is being ruined.

The first victim of hysteria is fact. The modern era has seen several great hysterias fueled by nothing more than dubious science. Unproven science renewed its long and ugly reign when dietary experts held that food we have been eating for millennia has turned against us and continues, today, as alarmists try to convince us that the planet is baking itself to death.

14.

FROM CONSUMABLES TO CLIMATE CHANGE
The Nation Creates New Venues for Hysteria

POISONOUS IDEAS

I have always read and cherished the Bible, which is what inspired my previous book, *God, Faith, and Reason*. Whether or not you believe the stories as literal history, the morals are profound and the wisdom indisputable. I turn to the ultimate authority again for a few thoughts on our next topic.

Let's go back to the beginning:

And to Adam He said, "Because you have listened to the voice of your wife and have eaten of the tree of which I commanded you, 'You shall not eat of it,' cursed is the ground because of you; in pain you shall eat of it all the days of your life; thorns and thistles it shall bring forth for you; and you shall eat the plants of the field. By the sweat of your face you shall eat bread, till you return to the ground, for out of it you were taken; for you are dust, and to dust you shall return." (Genesis 3:17-19)

Jumping ahead:

"This is the bread that comes down from heaven, so that one may eat of it and not die." (John 6:50–71)

And this:

"Or which one of you, if his son asks him for bread, will give him a stone?" (Matthew 7:9–11)

The answer to that last question is relevant. The food industry is trying to give you something indigestible. Despite millennia of tradition, despite having been a dietary staple of the human race for some thirty thousand years, society has suddenly done an about-face on bread. In particular, on wheat. And in specific, gluten.

As a trained nutritionist and botanist, I have always been aware of what gluten is. The word is from the Latin *glūten*, which unappetizingly means "glue," and it's a protein complex that accounts for most of the protein found in wheat used to make bread. In addition to nutrition, it helps dough to achieve added volume. It's true that some people are sensitive or allergic to gluten. We are not a monolithic species, and environment, genetic mutations, and other triggers have caused us to diverge over the eons. For example, celiac disease is a disorder that impacts the small intestine and other sections of the gastrointestinal track. It can be caused by rye and barley as well as wheat. It also affects only about 1 in 133 Americans.[1] So how did one syndrome, which at its most extreme can cause diarrhea and malabsorption, turn gluten into public food enemy number one? How did it go from being an unknown protein to a word everyone tosses around (even if they don't really know what it is or does)?

That happened in 2010, when doctors came up with a catch-all phrase to describe a condition that wasn't celiac disease or a simple wheat allergy. They called it "nonceliac gluten sensitivity." While the public became hysterical about the possible health impact of this terrible condition, the food industry went into overdrive creating a new market: gluten-free foods. This, not long after the same food industry came up with a market to service people who believed or feared they were "lactose intolerant," unable to digest the sugar lactose found in food products. According to some estimates, roughly two-thirds of the world is lactose intolerant. Verifiable or not, that's far more than the estimated 6 percent of the population who are gluten sensitive[2]—and given that a lot of the "studies" that are aimed at making us change the products we buy are written with a very liberal perspective, I suspect there's a lot more "not" than "verifiable."

Some scholars have suggested—and I share many of their views—that one of the worst things that ever happened to humankind was the invention of agriculture. Once we started producing crops and breeding animals that thrived in specific regions, people living in those areas ate just one kind of diet in abundance. Talking about the Bible, the Jews freed by Moses were headed to a land flowing with milk and honey, which was supposed to be a good thing. Milk maybe not, at least not for adults, according to some dieticians, and while there are antioxidants in honey that strengthen our cells, it is also an ideal medium for botulism bacteria. I can just imagine the overly health–sensitive in the wandering tribes trying to point that out, along with discussing trichinosis in pork. They'd have left these people eating manna at the foot of Mount Sinai.

But agriculture inadvertently damaged us. Instead of enjoying a balanced variety by remaining hunter-gatherers who spear fish, pick berries and fruit, and spit-roast boar, as our taller and stronger prehistoric forebears did, we loaded up on foods that caused a variety of ailments, like heart disease and diabetes, that continue to this day. A phrase, popularized by nutritionist Victor Lindlahr in a 1923 *Bridgeport Telegraph* article said it best: "Ninety per cent of the diseases known to man are caused by cheap food-stuffs. You are what you eat."[3]

But the reverse is also true. We are what we do *not* eat, and for most people who have become hysterical and given up gluten, there is a dangerous precedent. Hysterical consumers assume, in what is commonly and tritely referred to as "an abundance of caution," to simply avoid any undiagnosed risks by avoiding gluten. Or lactose. Or beef. Or chicken. Or beer. Or anything else that *might* not be optimal for our health (though the juries are still out on many of those). The first thing to be aware of if you *are* gluten sensitive is that turning to gluten-free products will likely cause you to gain weight. That's because you will now absorb caloric bulk that your body was rejecting before.[4]

Furthermore, there is a misconception that if something is gluten-free, it is de facto healthy. That is also not true. The replacement ingredients for wheat typically contain more sugar and less protein and fiber. Neither of those options is healthy. There are also social pressures that can lead to stress, which can cause countless health issues. It used to be you could go to a restaurant or friend's house and just eat what was served. Now people want vegan or gluten-free or lactose-free or organic-only. They want substitutes like "mock duck"—which, ironically, contains gluten. Social stress is not a good thing for anyone. And I'm sure you've seen it, people are not moderate about this. They *will not touch* anything with gluten. They will sit at the table and eat nothing but the salad—no croutons—if you've failed to accommodate them.

There is something else to consider, and that's the fact that U.S. growers add folic acid to many grains. Folic acid has been proven to reduce birth defects and anemia, among other ills. Grains also contain necessary B vitamins, and of course there is the energy that comes from carbohydrates.

But hysteria doesn't respond to reason and you aren't about to get reason from the food industry.

The gluten-free market is now a $4 billion business in the United States.

I would be the last person to suggest anyone behave foolishly or irresponsibly with food. Be informed, be sensible, but do not become hysterical. It isn't necessary to go through your kitchen and throw out everything that is on someone else's dietary watch list. Especially when you're researching online, and it's often impossible to tell real news (as much as that exists any more) from sponsored content.

While we're on the subject of food hysteria, for years consumers have been told to fear foods made with GMOs, genetically modified organisms, also cynically called "Frankenfoods" after the famed monster. Here's the hysteria the activists were peddling. First, a scientifically enhanced plant or animal would damage the environment because it would no longer be subject to natural selection. It would become the Superman of calves or potatoes or whatever it happened to be. Second, it would force farmers to buy costly seeds—a burden on developing nations. Third and most damning, they would corrupt human genes and cause autism, diabetes, obesity, cancer, and more—all of these claims made with hysterical fear and not a scrap of evidence.

So, what have we actually learned since 1994, when the first U.S. Food and Drug Administration approved product, the Flavr Savr tomato, hit the shelves? These startling facts: they have done no damage to consumers as far as medical science can tell and they have actually reduced the amount of toxic pesticides used by farmers, actually improving the health of consumers . . . and the environment.

End of story. Except that hysterics on the left will now move to some other topic—like the climate.

CLIMATE HYSTERICS

I'm going to list, in order of importance, the events that cause climate change.

First: orbital cycles. Earth revolves around the sun in a nonconsistent way, and has for at least the last two millennia. This has resulted in a general cooling of 0.02 degrees Celsius per century, and is expected to continue into the predictable future.[5]

Second: solar activity. Sunspots—cool areas on the sun—decrease the temperature on our world and were apparently responsible, in part, for the Little Ice Age that afflicted Europe in the seventeenth and early eighteenth centuries.[6]

Third: volcanic activity. Increased eruptions send ash high into the atmosphere, circling the globe, cutting off sunlight, and cooling the planet.

In 1883, the eruption of Krakatoa caused summer temperatures in the Northern Hemisphere to drop roughly 1.2 degrees Celsius.[7]

Fourth: ocean circulation. Fresh water entering the oceans can cause a shift in the air currents, such as the Gulf Stream, which can heat the polar regions and cause climate shifts.[8]

Fifth on the list, and way down at that: human activity. If we, as a species, tried to affect any one of the first four, we could not. That is how little our impact matters. How much do you think your campfire or your car or even all the world's private jets affect the climate? Less than Krakatoa. And the effects of that, the biggest explosion in human history only, endured for a year.

So why all the uproar about global warming, which was phrase-changed to "climate change" and is now "extreme weather"—because the first two, like the third, is riddled by bad-science holes?

The answer, of course, like the hysteria over gluten, is money.

People don't want to accept that. They call my show, post on my Facebook page, insist that I know nothing and that this is "settled science"—spoken with only the confidence that a drugged hippie or Millennial who still lives at home can muster. Sure, there is settled science on many subjects, like smoking cigarettes is bad for you and unprotected sex with a stranger can give you any number of diseases. But there is also science that is absurd on the surface. I just read an article about why people are afraid of clowns, as if the hype about the subject somehow makes it true. They even gave it a name: *coulrophobia*. The Ringling Brothers and Barnum & Bailey Circus would not have stayed in business for 146 years if people were inherently afraid of clowns! A few people may be, but it has nothing to do—as the article said—with the nuances of pattern recognition or the distortion of the human face. It has to do with the fact that clowns are frequently the antagonists in horror movies.

The "settled science" of climate change is like that. It's being forced on us by the Al Gores of the world and their Oscar-winning "documentaries" like *An Inconvenient Truth*. People have gotten rich from spreading hysteria on the topic. An example of how shallow their arguments are can be seen in the fact that no one went to see *The Inconvenient Sequel* last year. I guess there was not enough of a hysterical tailwind. Remember, I said these hysterias burn out of their own accord. Perhaps Gore and Obama and their associates even managed to convince themselves there's truth to what they're selling. Certainly their screaming minions—people who are not climatologists—think so. But it's all just wind, and not even gale force at that.

Nevertheless, the money keeps flowing. A recent study reported by the *Daily Caller* found liberal foundations spent nearly $567 million on global warming–related funding between 2011 and 2015. Al Gore's Alliance for Climate Protection got $20 million before merging with the Climate Reality Project, also founded by Gore.[9]

And what does an Al Gore do when that revenue stream burns out? He whips up another cause with such transparent, shameless contrivance that only chronic hysterics could embrace it. He and others have decided that a massive conglomeration of floating garbage in the Pacific Ocean should be its own country, called Trash Isles, of which Gore is already the First Citizen. If you can't become president of the United States, I suppose this is the next-best thing. Gore has somehow convinced one hundred thousand other people who have too much time on their hands to sign on as citizens of this mass of detritus they say is the size of France. They've even petitioned the United Nations to recognize it as the world's 196th country. Achieving that, they hope to get the UN to clean it up under its Environmental Charter. They are also planning to mint Trash Isles currency, called "debris," which would feature images of afflicted sea animals.

No one is saying that garbage in our oceans is a good thing. But it is sad that, as these people claim to be trying to salvage civilization, they are destroying it by turning pollution into *Lord of the Flies* for environmentalists—a barbaric power scramble in which dissenters are eliminated.

What these radicals fail to understand is that no one alive has seen more than a century of weather, and the record written in our planet's surface tells a very different story. Russia's Vostok Station, in Antarctica, is the coldest place on the globe. Ice cores taken from this site tell us about the climate of the region going back some 420,000 years. The findings? The rise and fall of global temperatures is a natural cycle on our world. Today's temperatures are the same as they were at peaks throughout history. Despite the carbon dioxide we're pumping into the atmosphere, people have added very little to the process and are not the cause of global warming. I have to add, though, that I was disappointed to see NASA join the fray when they tweeted, "This year's Arctic sea ice minimum extent is the 8th lowest on record, according to new data."[10]

So? What exactly does that say? First, "on record" is limited to roughly a century. And eighth lowest... relative to what? When was the lowest, what is the context, what does it mean besides the fact that NASA is funded by the government and studies like these help keep the dollars flowing?

But even NASA is not impervious to the truth. In late 2017, it released evidence of a mantle plume—a naturally occurring heat source—deep below Antarctica. The new findings revealed that water levels within Antarctica's rivers and lakes ebb and flow rapidly. Where this happens, there's friction. Where there's friction, there's heat. And where there's heat, ice melts.

NASA's conclusion was that changes in geothermal conditions cause warmer water to move closer to the ice sheet covering Antarctica, which in turn generates natural loss of ice.

If you haven't heard about this study—"Influence of a West Antarctic Mantle Plume on Ice Sheet Basal Conditions"—don't be surprised. There's more money in creating hysteria over climate change allegations than in understanding and explaining natural phenomenon.[11]

The data cannot be much plainer, but activists who have experienced twenty, thirty, forty winters in their lives are convinced that it's getting warmer, that hurricanes are more ferocious and frequent, that our actions will doom us the way acid rain did in the 1970s. Except that that particular hysteria du jour, acid rain, went away with reasonable desulfurization processes. I daresay that most young climate hysterics never heard of that end-of-the-world phenomenon.

But the use of weather as a terror tactic and profit center does not stop there. No one would say that islands and cities in the way of hurricanes should not take precautions to protect themselves. Hurricanes *are* unpredictable by nature, and the so-called cone of uncertainty in their tracks is valid meteorology. And certainly Hurricane Harvey hit Texas with merciless destructive force. There, the alerts were appropriate. But as I've said elsewhere in this book, the more viewers tune in to the weather on TV and the more they click on weather apps, the more money the providers make. So weather-focused media outlets are going to push the limits of responsible forecasting to ramp up doom scenarios. And not just a day or two before, but a *week* or two before. The weathercasts make these "events" part of our pop culture psyche with their superlatives of "the biggest" or "the strongest" storm ever.

During the Florida landfall of Hurricane Irma in the fall of 2017, I know people who were watching it unfold on a Sunday night as if it were reality TV. After Irma, Hurricane Jose came barreling through the Northern Leeward Islands, causing stunning devastation.[12]

Almost at once, it was setting its sights on the East Coast of the United States. We were warned this was the first time that the Atlantic had two hurricanes with winds of more than 150 mph at the same time. Obviously, climate change had to be the cause and the North Atlantic states were on edge over the trajectory, fearing a catastrophic rerun of Hurricane Sandy from 2012.

That was September 8. By September 18, Jose had vacillated between a tropical storm and a Category 1 hurricane but, in any case, it was only going to graze the Sandy-traumatized region. That didn't stop the news media from headlining that Jose would "hit" Long Island. You had to click on the story to find there was only going to be rain and waves. The populace could relax...until the next Atlantic storm could be turned into the "worst ever." But the meteorologists had another one in the batter's box, Hurricane Maria, which was going to impact the Leeward Islands again. But to tweak some fear, we were also told that would cause dangerous surf and rip currents from Delaware through Massachusetts. I have been to a lot of beaches around the world and I have never seen one that is not regularly subjected to dangerous surf and rip currents. How is that even newsworthy, except to stir fear? How is it newsworthy, in the United States, for a Maria headline to say: "To go outside... is to play with death" with no more information than that. It is lurid, in the way that yellow journalism has always embraced.

We have seen enough megastorms in our lifetime to treat them with great, great respect. There was Katrina in 2005. Before that, I remember Hurricane Carla slamming Houston on TV. Coverage of that storm in 1961 gave young Texas reporter Dan Rather his first national exposure. But quiet caution and occasional updates does not fix people's eyes to their TVs or devices. Constant attention and hysteria are needed for that. What's astonishing is that we keep falling for it in every walk of life. Not just *the* big storm but *the* big game, *the* news item you won't believe unless you click on it, *the* trial of the century, as if O. J. Simpson mattered as much as the Scopes Monkey Trial in 1925, in which the subject of evolution being taught in schools was the issue.

I'll say it again because it merits repeating. The subject is not climate or extreme weather, it's money. The greening of earth is not about grass but dollar bills. That is the real inconvenient truth.

We are now in the era of "treason chic," in which activists hysterically subvert the United States as a way of expressing their individuality. Hand in hand with this hate-filled hysteria are the daily baseless accusations against President Trump, which range from the conflated to the absurd. The left has moved mass hysteria from an organically occurring phenomenon into a social justice tactic. In the process, it is cutting its own collective throat—and potentially taking us with it.

15.

FROM TREASON
TO TOMORROW
Mass Hysteria on Overdrive

I n 1791, a middle-aged white man published his memoirs. I read it in high school. I doubt many people do so, today. They should. *The Autobiography of Benjamin Franklin* lays out in concise, witty language how a nation is born and how individuals can participate in or even precipitate that process.

To the latter point, while aware that colonials who proposed war with England were committing treason, Franklin explained how a native military came to be born in Pennsylvania. One word: *need.* He wrote:

With respect to defense, Spain having been several years at war against Great Britain, and being at length join'd by France, which brought us into great danger; and the laboured and long-continued endeavour of our governor, Thomas, to prevail with our Quaker Assembly to pass a militia law, and make other provisions for the security of the province, having proved abortive, I determined to try what might be done by a voluntary association of the people. To promote this, I first wrote and published a pamphlet, entitled Plain Truth, in which I stated our defenceless situation in strong lights, with the necessity of union and discipline for our defense, and promis'd to propose in a few days an association, to be generally signed for that purpose. The pamphlet had a sudden and surprising effect. I was call'd upon for the instrument of association, and having settled the draft of it with a few friends, I appointed a meeting of the citizens in the large building before mentioned.[1]

Once armed and, more important, organized to defend the motherland in proxy wars, a colonial army was able—and willing, and eventually motivated—to defend itself.

Treason was slippery, then. We were Americans,

we were British subjects, we were torn. Good men like Benedict Arnold, who had a heroic record of leadership during the early days of the Revolution, were driven by circumstance or pride to return to the service of King George—to Arnold's eventual discredit, since he picked the losing side.

Franklin defended our revolution by declaring, "Rebellion to tyrants is obedience to God."[2] He is not incorrect, of course, though there is some wiggle room in the definition of *tyrant*. That leeway does *not* apply to the hysterical traitors who sought to undermine the United States over the last few years.

Hysteria—and treason—do not require a long fuse. At times they only need paranoia and a desire to lash out at someone or some institution.

Chelsea Manning, thirty-one, served as a U.S. Army intelligence analyst in Iraq while she was still Bradley Manning. In 2010, WikiLeaks began posting some of the 750,000 classified and/or sensitive military and government documents Manning had smuggled out and forwarded. Why? According to an army psychiatrist, Manning felt isolated due to his gender identity issues in the extremely masculine environment.[3] Which begged the question: What did Manning expect to find in the army? Arrest, court-martial, and prison followed.

What came after that is beyond belief: prison treatment to correct his "gender dysphoria," paid for by the military, and then her thirty-five-year sentence commuted by that traitor of a different kind, Barack Obama. Just how much does that man hate this nation? And just how hysterical is the nation? Obama got a pass for that, but Trump was derided for pardoning former Sheriff Joe Arpaio of Arizona for criminal contempt due to his supposed racial profiling of people he suspected of crossing into the United States illegally through his jurisdiction along the nation's southern border. The reaction to Trump is, at every level, hysteria. Yet the fawning over Manning wasn't finished. In September 2017, there was very briefly an offer for Manning to be a "visiting fellow" at Harvard's John F. Kennedy School of Government. That incomprehensible honor was very quickly withdrawn.[4]

And then there's Michael Isaacson, twenty-nine, an adjunct professor at John Jay College of Criminal Justice, who tweeted this on August 23, 2017: "Some of y'all might think it sucks being an anti-fascist teaching at John Jay College but I think it's a privilege to teach future dead cops."[5] Technically, that does not fall under the category of treason. But it does smack of sedition and reeks of stupidity. John Jay College let Isaacson go—eventually.

What these three individuals share are flashes of indignation that resulted in an impulsive act—hysteria—that allowed each of them to burn, briefly, like a supernova. Not one of them professed an ounce of thought, of talking their deed out with another, and only Manning was ever apologetic, which people being court-martialed often are. His explanation, in court, is stupefying:

> I am sorry that my actions hurt people. I'm sorry that they hurt the United States. I am sorry for the unintended consequences of my actions. When I made these decisions I believed I was going to help people, not hurt people.... At the time of my decisions I was dealing with a lot of issues.

I am not a psychiatrist and have not personally met Chelsea Manning or Michael Isaacson. I cannot say what is inside their heads, only what they did. I would not *like* to meet any of them over dinner, since I value digestion, though I'd be happy to interview them on my show. But that will never happen. Even if they agreed, they would say everything they have to say in about ten seconds. There's nothing more to say about hysteria.

As long as we have left-leaning organizations

leaping like panthers to defend these extremists—
as the ACLU and GLAAD did with Manning—
there will be no incentive to act responsibly and
serve the common, national, rational good.

And while they may not fit the legal standards
of treason, acts like these are in a tragic, antisocial,
or even sociopathic class by themselves.

HYPOCRISY AND HYSTERIA

Mass hysteria in America has had a long, destructive journey. There is something almost biblical about its immortal nature and its ability to take
many guises—now a serpent in Eden, encouraging
the rejection of authority. Now a frenzy at the foot of
Mount Sinai, as monotheism is repudiated for a traditional Golden Calf. Now a crowd calling for the
life of the thief Barabbas over that of Jesus, driven
to hysteria by the whispers of pro-Roman voices.
And it's not yet through. Like an infectious disease, hysteria continues to morph. It can be big and
global or it can be scalpel-precise. Today, uniquely,
it can be both. Whereas it took some effort for a
Cotton Mather or Carrie Nation to get into a position where people noticed, while the communists
in czarist Russia had to print handbills on con-
cealed presses and clandestinely pass them out—all

it takes now to start a social fire is a blog, a tweet, or a hashtag.

In late summer 2017, a pair of liberal Holly-wood lions stirred mass hysteria from their den on the West Coast. Rob Reiner—who began his career as "Meathead" on *All in the Family*—and Morgan Freeman helped launch a group predicated on a delusion I told you about at the start of this book, when I wrote about "positive hallucinations or hysteria"—people believe things are real, absent evidence, just because someone says so. According to a statement on the website of the Committee to Investigate Russia, "The Russian Active Measures campaign aimed at the United States has been exposed. Using hacking, Twitter armies, and fake news, the Kremlin engaged in an aggressive effort to subvert the American democratic process." In a video he made for the launch, Freeman says, "We need our president to speak directly to us and tell us the truth. We need him to sit behind the desk in the Oval Office and say 'My fellow Americans, during this past election, we came under attack by the Russian government.' "[6]

The website and Morgan Freeman both declare, as fact, something that is not only untrue but is *demonstrably* untrue. Why? Because their own hysteria dies hard. They still cannot accept that Hillary Clinton lost the election. In effect, what they are asking is that Donald Trump tell the electorate that if not for Russia, Hillary would be sitting behind his desk. What is at once amusing and painfully sad is that neither of these men seems to be aware of how much the name of their group, "Committee to Investigate Russia," sounds like something from the McCarthy era, when anti-Soviet rhetoric was coming from the far right. Rhetoric that, to a one, they all decry.

Almost at once, nearly sixty-five thousand people followed the Facebook page of the Committee to Investigate Russia. That is how mass hysteria works today. A celebrity promulgates positive hysteria and the doped-out and/or starstruck and/or aging hippie population listens. The good news is, social media "events" tend to have the life span of a mayfly. As the days pass and the committee asks for donations or sends email updates that blend into the dozens of other email updates these people receive, their attention will wander. As the committee fails to present real evidence to support its thesis, those followers will turn their hysteria to the next fad du jour. And on and on.

Actually, most of those followers probably forgot about the committee in a day or two after attending a Paul McCartney concert. The college kids, ex-hippies, and urban leftist elites group-hugged by singing former Beatles bandmate John Lennon's "Give Peace a Chance." Arriving or going home stoned, they lacked the mental faculties to process reality. Did they imagine Kim Jung-un was listening? Will that stop him from publicly executing McCartney's fellow musicians by strapping them to the muzzles of antiaircraft guns, as the Transnational Justice Working Group in Seoul has reported? Will a song prevent Kim from turning countless North Korean girls into sex slaves? What about the ayatollahs in Iran? Would Hitler have listened to the message of "Give Peace a Chance"? *Should* Abraham Lincoln have listened, allowing the Confederacy to coexist with the United States and permitting slavery to continue by giving peace a chance? Barack Obama did that in Iraq, to his eternal shame, and gave the world ISIS. It's on *his* head that the terrorists he dismissed as "JV," junior varsity, killed 170,000 Christians and Shiites, and took thousands of women as sex slaves. Where is the Rob Reiner/Morgan Freeman committee or peacenik sing-along for them? You won't see one, of course. Reality does not fit these people's pie-in-the-sky narrative. That is the fundamental flaw of liberalism: the inability to carry a thought beyond a mantra.

The stoners on the left can barely carry a cogent thought beyond the time it takes to swipe left or right on Tinder, yet they can carry grudges for decades. Remember how I told you during the HUAC hearings actor Robert Taylor testified against communists in his industry? He had been so popular everywhere else in the world, his films made so much money for MGM, that the studio named one of their soundstages after him. By 1990, MGM had vacated the Culver City lot and it was then Lorimar Studios. The already leftist Hollywood decided that Taylor did not merit that honor because he "named names" during the hearings. His name was removed. The political madness as conceptualized by Antonio Gramsci was already taking root. Remove the identity and you socialize the community.

Thousands of sociopaths and haters, their mania still immature, can find countless reasons to explode into full, hysterical flower. And there are equally underdeveloped thinkers, especially in the entertainment industry, whose narcissism spurs them to "lead." (If they didn't crave attention, they wouldn't be actors and musicians who intentionally place themselves in the public eye.) There may even be a valid social point in what someone is saying. But carried aloft on the shoulders of a mob, its impotent rage suddenly unleashed, power and attention inflate a conversation into a confrontation, a query into a demand, a thought into a mandate. This can happen overnight, without the time it takes to refine or rethink an idea. It took intellectual giant Thomas Jefferson seventeen days to take to write the approximately 1,300 words of the Declaration of Independence. Tweets and blogs are authored by emotion-charged narcissists, out-of-power politicians, and bitter, entitled whiners in a snit at Starbucks.

ACTING HYSTERICAL

I'm going to leave you with what may be some of the most important cautionary tales of the book, since they are happening now. They involve our entertainers and cherished, pervasive art forms, and they show the dire results of mass hysteria sharpened to a laser point, what I call "focused hysteria." Focused hysteria allows you to destroy more things faster—not just institutions but careers. Like the Nazis in occupied nations, it allows you to line citizens up against a wall to be shot, creating a fearful object lesson for the rest of the population.

One of the big Broadway hits of 2016–17 was *Natasha, Pierre & The Great Comet of 1812*, a musical version of *War and Peace*. I heard about it when it was nominated for a slew of Tony Awards, including one for its star, Josh Groban. I didn't know who he was, and when I was told I forgot. To me, a Broadway star is Mary Martin or Zero Mostel. If you don't know those names, you'll have to do what I did—ask someone. Turns out Groban is a huge musical star and a massive box-office draw. He also happens to be white.

When Groban's contracted time was up and he left the show, he was replaced by Okieriete Onaodowan, who had played several roles in the Broadway musical *Hamilton*. Yet even that association, with the most hyped show of the last decade, wasn't enough to sell tickets. The producers of *Natasha, Pierre & The Great Comet of 1812* decided to what any sane businessperson would have done: they offered to buy out the rest of Onaodowan's contract and replace him with a major box office name, Mandy Patinkin—who, like Groban, happens to be white. The problem is, Onaodowan is black—as is most everyone in *Hamilton*; whites are encouraged not to audition for any of the major parts and would not be hired even if they were brilliant. (Why aren't the SJWs protesting *that*?)

As soon as the Patinkin plan was announced, members of the Broadway community, Social Justice Warriors, and diversity zealots made the absurd charge that producers were being insensitive by replacing a black actor with a white actor—despite the fact that the part was created by a white actor, which the whiners neglected to consider. Patinkin, a champion of liberal causes and underdogs, withdrew immediately, tweeting, "I hear what members of the community have said and I agree with them." Okay, he's entitled to believe that. But what the producers said in their statement was craven capitulation to what was focused hysteria:

> We had the wrong impression of . . . the casting announcement and how it would be received by members of the theater community, which we appreciate is deeply invested in the success of actors of color—as are we—and to whom we are grateful for bringing this to our attention. We regret our *mistake* deeply, and wish to express our apologies to everyone who felt hurt and betrayed by these actions.[7]

The italics are mine. The insanity was theirs. The producers not only let themselves be deafened by a handful of loud voices, they self-flagellated for having made a sensible business decision. End result? The play closed. Onaodowan was unemployed anyway, along with everyone else involved with the show. Well done, Social Justice Warriors.

Have the angry SJWs learned anything? Of course not. They remain not only hysterical but *hypocritically* hysterical. They gleefully created audience confusion with "color blind" casting in shows like the New York revival of *1776* in 2016, in which, among others, Martha Jefferson was played by a black actress, leading some audience members to mistake her for Sally Hemings; and in *Kung Fu*, a 2014 show about Bruce Lee in which the white actor James Coburn was played by a black actor, the SJWs refused to allow historically accurate portrayals of real people.

The justification for this nonsense is the bogus claim of "white privilege," a mantra that was upended, as we've noted, with affirmative action in 1961. Now the claims of white privilege are simply hate. They are designed to justify punitive actions against a perceived enemy. Instead of writing new shows, instead of being creative and resourceful, frustrated actors blame the white man for their failure. The notion that casting directors should simply hire the best people isn't even acceptable. White people must be excluded, punished.

In the summer of 2017, the esteemed North Shore Music Theatre in Massachusetts cast non-Hispanics in the three lead roles of *Evita*—as was done when the show was first produced on Broadway, whence Mandy Patinkin rose to fame as Che. One of those actors, Constantine Maroulis, may not have been a household name for me, but he was a finalist on *American Idol* and that obviously carries some box-office heft.

One young New York actress, Lauren Villegas, founder of Project Am I Right?, posted this gem: "Blackface does not happen in theater today, yellowface largely does not happen, but Latinx characters do not get the same kind of care when being cast," she wrote.[8] Incidentally, *Latinx*—pronounced "Lateen-ex"—is a genderless alternative to *Latino* and *Latina*. That term is being foisted on a public that is largely unaware that the theater term *bravo* is for a man, *brava* for a woman. I suppose *bravx* is next.

North Shore Music Theatre *Evita* director Bill Hanney responded in an interview: "If a Latino person came in and they were the best, they'd be in my show. We found the right people. Our focus was not to find a Latino. It was to find the right Eva, Che, and Peron, etc."

But that line of reasoning did not matter to Villegas, who responded, "Authenticity comes from lived experience. Actors do more than pretend;

we draw on who we are. I hope people realize that choosing to appropriate a culture they don't know will only perpetuate shallow stereotypes."

By that logic, no one but a Jew can ever again play the major roles in *Fiddler on the Roof.* Only the French can appear in *Phantom of the Opera,* which, after all, is set in the Paris Opera. Only Jersey boys should be able to act in *Jersey Boys* since there is a unique voice and culture few non-Jerseyites would really get. And unless we can find a Kryptonian, don't count on seeing Superman in a movie or TV show again. I'm being facetious about the Man of Steel. But in a world insanely scrubbed of traditional gender identity, Villegas and those who echo her sentiments seem strangely obsessed with something called racial identity. I would add that Daniel Day-Lewis won the Best Actor Oscar for *Lincoln* in 2012, and Day-Lewis is British. Should his Oscar be taken away for this blatant example of "cultural appropriation"?

"Lived experience"? According to Villegas's "logic," the role of Jenny Diver in *The Threepenny Opera* should be played exclusively by prostitutes, the role of Che can only be acted by mass murderers—and forget Macbeth, which requires an actor who has committed regicide. What an arrogant assumption to declare that someone cannot "know" another culture or profession, while at the same time giving people of color a free pass to take any classically and historically "white" role from Julius Caesar to Willy Loman. As an anthropologist, not an actor, I can assure you that that opinion is as naïvely knee-jerk as traditional nativism. I have a friend, who is white, who has been studying martial arts for sixty years in New York City's Chinatown and also among Japanese martial art masters. He is Daoist, and more "Asian" in thought and deed than many Asians I've met who were born in the United States. Is his dedication to studying, preserving, and sharing the culture of martial arts an act of ignorance, aggression, or insensitivity? Or could it possibly be rooted in honoring something worthwhile and fulfilling? Given that he is a white male, many SJWs would automatically assign sinister motives no matter what his actual motivations.

And in case you were wondering, this firebrand Villegas uses the gender-neutral *actor* to mean both male and female performers. That's part of the political madness language spillover we discussed earlier. To date, no one has been able to articulate, as far as I've seen, just what is wrong with the distinct words *actor* and *actress*. It must gall activists that all the major awards shows still use these terms—though don't be surprised if that's the next to fall.

I see on Villegas's resume two things of interest. First, on the front page she provides a tutorial about how to pronounce her name: "Vee YAY! Gahs." While I understand the basic dignity that the correct pronunciation of one's name provides, she seems to take militant pleasure in 1) assuming people are going to pronounce it incorrectly, and 2) preemptively correcting them. I am assuming that when she refers to foreign places like Rome she also says "Roma" and Hawaii is "Ha-VAH-ee" and insists that others do the same. We live in America. The diversity you espouse means, by definition, that we do things that align with our own broad vocal background, not your preferences or idiosyncrasies. Second, I note that Villegas portrayed Mary Magdalene in *Jesus Christ Superstar*, someone who is not Latinx but Middle Eastern. She also played a Brit in *Mary Poppins*. Good for her.

There is no denying that, however brilliant, Othello should no longer be played *solely* by an Orson Welles or a Laurence Olivier in makeup. But to deny white actors access to roles while giving actors of color a hall pass to every role is exactly the kind of hyphenated America that Teddy Roosevelt and Woodrow Wilson warned against. It is the kind of hysterical overreach that has crippled and scarred Americans for more than five centuries.

It is also racism. In the summer of 2017, the theatrical union Actors Equity teamed with Project Am I Right? in an unapologetic act of overt discrimination. They put on a production in New York called *My Whitelist Cabaret (AKA Roles I Could Get If I Was White/Cis/Non-Disabled)*. The union, which is supposed to stand for the rights of *all* stage actors, subsequently tweeted, "What an incredible event! The future looks pretty good. Let's make it come soon."

Being "of color" does not give anyone the right to act with willful contempt for law and decency. Being "of color" is not a license to practice segregation. The SJWs who are seeking not just parity but retribution are tearing us apart. They are no different than those who abused Reconstruction for their own gain. Just as those repercussions echo to this day, so will the focused hysteria of the rabid hyphenates cause scars that will take generations to heal—if they don't first rip the nation apart.

EIGHT YEARS OF SELF-DESTRUCTION

Being of "anything," whether it is "of color" or "of humble origins," doesn't give you special privileges in America, though many people think it does. This brings us to future mass hysteria, which promises to be no less bilious than that which came before. For example, I saw a chart recently suggesting that college graduates who have been hand-carried through their lives are about to suffer a big blow. They have already taken on decades of student debt, except for the quota-driven people of color and illegal residents who were granted scholarships to add diversity to the university Web pages. They are already unable to find jobs, despite President Trump's efforts to create new ones. Eight years of the new plantation owners at Facebook, Apple, and other firms outsourcing to India and China and a brain-drain resulting, in part, from Obama's gutting of NASA, have left the United States with frighteningly few opportunities for scientists, mathematicians, and engineers even though we have been told that this is the direction of the future. Even with Trump's revitalization of NASA, we are still presently forced to pay Russian $710 million every time we put an astronaut into space on board one of their rockets. That's how far behind we are.

Students who are unemployed and financially underwater were among the many desperate youths who rallied behind Bernie Sanders in 2016 with his utopian fantasies. He tapped their desperate hysteria and turned it into primary votes. These kids did not vet him from the windowless rooms in their parents' basements, since they didn't learn how to think, only to memorize, work on their tablets or smartphones, and react like little automatons. Again, that is the perfect breeding ground for hysteria. No thought, just reaction.

Well, for these people the future looks worse and their hysteria will increase accordingly. Every year, four million Americans turn eighteen, graduate from high school, and head off to college for four years of smoking dope, listening to radical professors, protesting against conservatives (who are, in fact, looking to protect their future), and finally majoring in *something* for their remaining time in school. Meanwhile, during the eight years of the Obama administration, the United States of America permitted an average of one million *legal* immigrants each year to apply for and work at jobs within our borders. The very administration that was hailed by leftists as the future of our nation with Obama as our savior was allowing for—even encouraging—the destruction of an entire generation's worth of viable work and workers.

That's not all. Washington provides around three million short-term work permits to aliens every year. So right there, while these kids were partying and occasionally studying for eight years, the market has been inundated with twenty-four million or so workers who will not only work for less, but will send a portion of that money home. And make no mistake, they are and will continue to be hired. Corporations like to put photographs of women, people of color, and pride-marching employees in their annual reports to prove that they are Equal Opportunity Employers. If you see bank ads or cereal commercials, you would think that this is a nation of exclusively interracial marriages. That is not a knock on interracial marriages but on the institutions that fawn on virtue-signaling and targeted demographics for the sake of profits and pandering rather than from any genuine place of celebrating real families.

Several years ago, I wrote a book called *Trickle Down Tyranny*. (You can find it on Amazon, I'm sure, though I'm also betting the company hasn't removed the personal attack reviews the way they did by cutting nine hundred negative reviews of Hillary Clinton's *What Happened*.) These practices demonstrate exactly how that concept works. Washington imports far more foreign workers than we export. Corporations pay less for this labor and their profits go up. With all the crying about a glass ceiling for women, the Census Bureau's annual report on income has demonstrated that salaries for men have stayed put since 1973 while the numbers of men *earning* those wages has plummeted. Meanwhile, the unemployed drive up the tax burden on every town, every state, the entire nation. The future of the country becomes dependent on these foreign workers. At the same time, many of the unemployed turn to pot and opioids to deal with the depression of unemployment and living with mom and dad.

If you think you're hearing students whine hysterically now, it's nothing. If you're of a certain age, you'll remember when parents were free to discipline and your mother or father would say, "I'll give you something to cry about!" Not any longer. Spanking, which for generations was the accepted way to teach children to stay away from hot stoves and sharp knives, as well as to keep them from throwing fits when they don't get their way, can now get parents reported to Child Protective Services. And children know this. Wait until 2020 or 2024, when their numbers are sufficient to start electing progressive senators like Elizabeth Warren or Cory Booker to the Oval Office. The whiners will be promised everything and put on welfare (or its equivalent with single-payer health care, food stamps, and other programs that you and I will pay for—including student loan forgiveness that will be passed on to the families of better-to-do

students or those students who dedicated themselves to responsible spending and saving in order
to pay back whatever loans they may have accrued).

That is where, when, and how the carcass of the
once-great United States will become nothing more
than carrion for the masses. As China and India rise,
we will sink deeper. And we may well do it without
hysteria because Americans, traditional Americans,
hardworking roll-up-your-sleeves Americans, will be
too tired, feel too consistently betrayed, too dispir-
ited to fight back.

But there is also good news. As we have seen
throughout this journey, hysteria is not a self-
sustaining quality. It is founded in the vaporous quality of emotion, not mind, and eventually disburses
with the light of fact and reason. That is why organizations funded by anarchists like George Soros must
morph quickly from Occupy to Black Lives Matter
and AntiFA. The potheads who beat defenseless citizens, loot, and riot (and flee when motorcycle gangs
show up swinging chains; that's not an endorsement,
it's just a fact) are children who have to be constantly
entertained and distracted, or else they go back into
their college dorms to roll more joints.

While these lamebrains rouse themselves for
a day or a week at most before retreating to their

subsidized lives, the mainstream media—the outlets that hysterically tout their deeds and briefly give them legitimacy—is itself fading. While my audience of loyal, thoughtful listeners grows on the Internet streams, CNN and Fox News and MSNBC see their audiences dwindling. Part of that is an audience becoming unplugged and turning to distractions on their devices; part of that is the loss of responsible journalists in favor of personalities in short skirts and catering to the idea of diversity rather than, say, someone who is white, older, and may be better qualified due to experience, if nothing else...someone who may know that Edinburgh is pronounced "Edin-burrow," not "Edin-burg," which I recently heard on the evening news. With all that the progressives claim to do, addressing the rampant problem of ageism is a major failure on their part. We'd rally, I suppose, if we weren't too busy supporting our unemployed, the welfare cheats, and governments.

Like dictatorships, hysteria is an extremist concept that cannot survive without the middle, without the Eddies and Ediths of this nation. For the present, while statistics tell us whites are no longer the majority, men and women of the middle are the group that put Donald Trump in the White House. We can rouse that will again.

We *will* do it because we love America and believe it is worth fighting for—not with hysteria but with purpose and resolve. Not with violent protest but with support for the men and women, diverse and wonderful, young and old and in-between, who comprise our law enforcement and military forces. We will fight for America not with bats and fists but with votes and ideas.

We will do this with other Americans from all backgrounds—Asians, blacks, whites, gays, straights, the entire spectrum of our deep cultural pool—who are not part of the hysterical fringes and who are all part of the "we" who love this nation.

We will do this because without us, without our example, there will be no one on earth left to lead. Not Islamified Europe, corrupt Russia, the repressive Arab states, totalitarian China, North Korea, or any other nation that may self-servingly dominate finance and industry but fail to move civilization and humanity forward. I urge the left to consider this when they throw tantrums about our borders, our so-called Dreamers, our "inequality," the pseudoscience of climate change, and all the other shibboleths of the left.

This book has been about the many missteps that accompanied a great adventure that began in 1492. Much of what followed was exemplary.

But I, and any right-thinking human being, must also be, and will continue to be, ashamed of a great deal of it—which is why mass hysteria must always be countered with reason.

Today, that is happening less and less. Remember what I said at the start:

Guns. Donald Trump. Russophobia. The mass hysteria from the left bleeds one into the other, folding in additional insanity like "white privilege" and the myth of man-made climate change. Look at our history and remember that while there are those of us who learn the lessons of mass hysteria, there are others who will exploit those lessons.

When the left has removed all the statues of Columbus, all the Confederate flags, all the monuments to our Founding Fathers; when books like this have been burned and removed from libraries, when we have allowed hysterical cries to terminate or terrorize rational discourse, we will all have become Cotton Mather and Hassan-i Sabbah and those who erected testaments to their own infamy with the bones of others.

In one of his many exquisite plays on words, Benjamin Franklin said of Americans—just before he affixed his signature on the Declaration of Independence—"We must, indeed, all hang together or, most assuredly, we shall all hang separately."

ACKNOWLEDGMENTS

I wish to thank my editor, Kate Hartson, for having the faith to believe in my vision, and Jeff Rovin for his outstanding research and structural conceptualizations.

NOTES

CHAPTER 1: MASS HYSTERIA INFLECTION POINT

1. https://www.independent.co.uk/news/world/americas/us-politics/antifa
-ice-employees-list-immigration-nebraska-github-medium-linkedin-sam
-lavigne-a8412496.html

2. https://www.usatoday.com/story/life/people/2018/06/20/peter-fonda
-apologizes-vulgar-barron-trump-tweet/719504002/

3. https://www.vox.com/2018/6/25/17501450/maxine-waters-trump-pelosi
-civility-sarah-sanders

4. https://www.washingtonpost.com/powerpost/gop-leaders-voice-hope
-that-bill-addressing-family-separations-will-pass-thursday/2018/06/20
/cc79db9a-7480-11e8-b4b7-308400242c2e_story.html?utm_term
=.19742c2f8378

5. https://en.wikiquote.org/wiki/Eric_Hoffer

6. https://books.google.com/books?id=eaRvKpLUf0C&pg=PA43&lpg
=PA43&dq=%22It+is+essential+to+have+a+tangible+enemy,+not
+merely+an+abstract+one.%E2%80%9D%22&source=bl&ots=9jIC
NRnYPW&sig=J7B39CWpWwyh9B0lNdwpyQ6V3SU&hl=en&sa=X
&ved=0ahUKEwj-iPekuKfcAhXDm-AKHahcCCkQ6AEIKTAA#v
=onepage&q=%22It%20is%20essential%20to%20have%20a%20
tangible%20enemy%2C%20not%20merely%20an%20abstract%20
one.%E2%80%9D%22&f=false

7. https://books.google.com/books?id=gMLieJOtWwIC&pg=PA168&lpg
=PA168&dq=Hoffer+japanese+berlin+1932&source=bl&ots=Cjnzi
Pqj-g&sig=PHsD6FqKz6PlXjRSELoY5zRpT6w&hl=en&sa=X&ved

=0ahUKEwjymZjQuKfcAhUiUt8KHVDPAkUQ6AEIezAD#v=one
page&q=Hoffer%20japanese%20berlin%201932&f=false

8. https://www.theguardian.com/books/2013/jun/06/china-war-japan-rana
-mitter-review

9. https://www.intellectualtakeout.org/blog/thomas-jefferson-had-some
-issues-newspapers

10. https://www.brainyquote.com/quotes/samuel_johnson_157371

11. https://en.wikipedia.org/wiki/List_of_Americans_in_the_Venona_papers

12. https://en.wikipedia.org/wiki/Harry_Dexter_White

13. https://www.denverpost.com/2018/06/04/colorado-civil-rights-commis
sion-impact/

14. https://michaelsavage.com/?p=17803

CHAPTER 2: HISTORY OF MASS HYSTERIA

1. https://en.wikiquote.org/wiki/George_Santayana

2. https://www.washingtonexaminer.com/washington-secrets/trump-jokes
-about-launching-nukes-to-radio-host-michael-savage

3. https://www.usatoday.com/story/news/politics/onpolitics/2017/11/02
/poll-trump-russia-election-crime/827907001/

4. https://www.usatoday.com/story/news/politics/2018/05/31/doj-russia
-investigation-costs-near-17-million/661744002/

5. http://thefederalist.com/2018/05/03/manafort-lawyers-claim-leaky
-mueller-probe-has-provided-no-evidence-of-contacts-with-russian
-officials/

6. http://www.businessinsider.com/space-travel-per-seat-cost-soyuz-2016-9

7. https://en.wikipedia.org/wiki/2017_Las_Vegas_shooting

8. https://twitter.com/hillaryclinton/status/914853465926639618?lang=en

9. http://thehill.com/homenews/senate/358884-warren-to-gop-thoughts
-and-prayers-not-enough-after-texas-shooting

10. www.nytimes.com/2017/10/04/us/police-response-mass-shootings.html

11. https://www.newsweek.com/malia-obama-harvey-weinstein-accusa
tions-680950

12. https://www.nbcnews.com/storyline/sexual-misconduct/weinstein-here-s
    -growing-list-men-accused-sexual-misconduct-n816546

13. http://www.nydailynews.com/opinion/panic-not-answer-article-1
    .3651778

14. https://www.nytimes.com/2017/10/19/opinion/metoo-sexual-harass
    ment-men.html

15. https://twitter.com/emilylindin/status/933074980627030016?lang=en

16. https://www.democratandchronicle.com/story/news/2017/11/15/florian
    -jaeger-rochester-harassment-open-letter/866662001/

17. https://www.washingtonpost.com/news/comic-riffs/wp/2017/11/30
    /the-growing-list-of-sexual-harassment-scandals-as-satirized-in-car
    toons/?utm_term=.9f0c39be4b81

18. https://en.wikipedia.org/wiki/Harriet_Tubman

19. www.stageandcinema.com/2012/03/24/the-many-mistresses
    -est-jr/

20. http://nymag.com/daily/intelligencer/2017/12/what-happened-to
    -trumps-16-sexual-misconduct-accusers.html

21. http://www.newsweek.com/trump-scared-germs-needs-drink-straw
    -avoid-contamination-671730

22. https://www.stltoday.com/news/local/govt-and-politics/missouri-senator
    -who-called-for-trump-assassination-running-for-seat/article_dff17c03
    -6ac1-59db-9273-559453aa3636.html

23. https://www.huffingtonpost.com/2012/06/08/obama-effigy-hanged
    -outside-church_n_1581272.html

24. https://www.cbsnews.com/news/stormy-daniels-describes-her-alleged
    -affair-with-donald-trump-60-minutes-interview/

25. https://patriotpost.us/articles/56645-republicans-blast-fbi-bias-exposed
    -in-the-ig-report

26. https://www.nbcnews.com/news/us-news/anthony-weiner-begins-21
    -month-sentence-sexting-underage-girl-n817971

27. https://www.nbcnews.com/news/world/north-korea-s-kim-trump-meet
    -andrea-mitchell-weighs-risks-n855111

28. https://en.wikipedia.org/wiki/Peace_for_our_time

29. https://en.wikipedia.org/wiki/Otto_Warmbier

30. http://thehill.com/homenews/administration/391770-trump-lavishes
-kim-with-compliments-after-historic-summit

31. https://en.wikipedia.org/wiki/Walter_Duranty

32. https://history.nasa.gov/sputnik/sputorig.html

33. https://books.google.com/books?id=vHJ1oWiqUgkC&pg=PA25&lpg
=PA25&dq=%22the+united+states+now+sleeps+under+a+soviet+moon
%22&source=bl&ots=lHbU9yGvw3&sig=bnE0MYRFdZ9-Au-nWB
jz8fLuKAs&hl=en&sa=X&ved=0ahUKEwiLs766z6fcAhUvmu
AKHasLBO0Q6AEIbjAN#v=onepage&q=%22the%20united%20
states%20now%20sleeps%20under%20a%20soviet%20moon
%22&f=false

34. en.wikipedia.org/wiki/National_Advisory_Committee_for_Aeronautics

CHAPTER 3: MASS HYSTERIA

1. https://en.wikipedia.org/wiki/Cave_painting

2. https://www.huffingtonpost.com/robert-brustein/the-new-anarchists_b
_1085909.html

3. https://www10.dict.cc/wp_examples.php?lp_id=1&lang=en&s=Seven
%20against%20Thebes

4. http://www.perseus.tufts.edu/hopper/text?doc=Perseus%3Atext%3A
1999.01.0014%3Acard%3D1032

5. https://en.wikipedia.org/wiki/Gunpowder_Plot

6. https://en.wikipedia.org/wiki/Spartacus

7. https://www.washingtonpost.com/news/the-fix/wp/2018/07/06/the-top
-15-democratic-presidential-candidates-for-2020-ranked-3/?utm_term
=.f01ce0cc73db

8. https://www.c-span.org/video/?320176-5/senate-debate-unaccompanied
-immigrant-children

9. https://en.wikipedia.org/wiki/T._Don_Hutto_Residential_Center

10. https://twitter.com/genmhayden/status/1008035777455026178?lang=en

11. https://agupubs.onlinelibrary.wiley.com/doi/abs/10.1002/2017JB014423

12. https://www.newsmax.com/michaelsavage/border-immigration
-children/2018/06/19/id/867098/

13. https://www.huffingtonpost.com/entry/united-states-global-leader
-asylum-requests_us_5b28eea9e4b0f0b9e9a50f57

14. https://pdfs.semanticscholar.org/presentation/9d76/3f8c2aec3b020
a0fc30a150e88f3d7bdb424.pdf

15. https://en.wikipedia.org/wiki/The_War_of_the_Worlds_(radio
_drama)

16. http://www.bostonmassacre.net/trial/acct-adams3.htm

17. https://en.wikipedia.org/wiki/Tea_Act

18. https://en.wikipedia.org/wiki/The_Day_of_the_Locust;www
.cliffsnotes.com/literature/d/the-day-of-the-locust/summary-and
-analysis/chapter-27

19. https://www.nbcnews.com/news/us-news/google-engineer-fired-writing
-manifesto-women-s-neuroticism-sues-company-n835836

20. https://variety.com/2017/biz/news/trump-president-charlottesville
-1202535835/

21. https://www.reuters.com/article/us-virginia-protests-idUSKCN
1AU0TW

22. https://www.jewishvirtuallibrary.org/hitler-s-threats-against-the-jews
-1941-1945

23. https://en.wikipedia.org/wiki/Black_Hand_(Serbia)

24. https://en.wikipedia.org/wiki/Lying_press#History

25. https://salemwitchmuseum.com/blog/elie-wiesels-salem-witch-trials
-memorial-dedication-speech-1992

26. https://www.nytimes.com/2016/02/26/us/university-of-missouri-fires
-melissa-click-who-tried-to-block-journalist-at-protest.html

27. https://exploringyourmind.com/tell-lie-thousand-times-become-truth/

28. https://www.vox.com/cards/mike-brown-protests-ferguson-missouri
/mike-brown-police-officer-darren-wilson

29. http://www.businessinsider.com/paul-gosar-charlottesville-riots-george
-soros-conspiracy-2017-10

30. https://medium.com/@peacelovetrig/on-the-sexist-etimology-of-hysteria
-and-what-academia-did-about-it-ef98815ddb6c

31. https://warwick.ac.uk/fac/arts/history/students/modules/hi383/syllabus
/topic15/

32. https://history.howstuffworks.com/historical-events/10-strangest-mass
-hysterias1.htm

33. https://en.wikipedia.org/wiki/Mass_hysteria

34. https://en.wikipedia.org/wiki/Mass_hysteria#LeRoy,_New_York
_(2011%E2%80%9312)

35. https://www.everydayhealth.com/healthy-living/0130/erin-brockovich
-investigates-mass-hysteria-mystery-illness.aspx

36. https://en.wikipedia.org/wiki/Freud%27s_seduction_theory

37. https://en.wikipedia.org/wiki/Koro_(medicine)

38. https://en.wikipedia.org/wiki/Jean-Martin_Charcot

CHAPTER 4: FROM PLYMOUTH ROCK TO CITY HALL

1. http://www.nydailynews.com/news/national/yale-offers-rehire-man
-broke-window-showing-slavery-article-1.2717458

2. https://en.wikipedia.org/wiki/El_Cid

3. https://www.jewishvirtuallibrary.org/marranos-conversos-and-new
-christians

4. www.cnn.com/2012/05/20/opinion/garcia-columbus-jewish/index.html

5. http://jewishweek.timesofisrael.com/following-terrorist-attack-barce
lonas-chief-rabbi-says-his-community-is-doomed/

6. https://fullfact.org/news/muslims-uk-viral-poster-factchecked/

7. https://en.wikipedia.org/wiki/Opium_of_the_people

8. https://en.wikipedia.org/wiki/Mayflower

9. https://en.wikipedia.org/wiki/William_Bradford_(Plymouth_Colony
_governor)

10. http://archive.randi.org/site/index.php/swift-blog/2177-the-trial-of
-george-spencer.html

11. http://avalon.law.yale.edu/17th_century/mayflower.asp

12. http://www.slate.com/articles/news_and_politics/history/2015/09/new_haven_colony_bestiality_trial_the_twisted_puritan_origins_of_our_modern.html

13. https://www.vice.com/en_us/article/7bdd74/the-time-a-pilgrim-got-the-death-penalty-for-having-sex-with-a-turkey

14. https://www.theawl.com/2017/08/the-curious-case-of-thomas-hogg/, https://vdocuments.site/things-fearful-to-name.html

15. http://www.damnedct.com/alse-alice-young, https://patriciahysell.wordpress.com/2012/05/26/alse-young/

16. https://books.google.com/books?id=nlcssspLvd8C&pg=PT64&lpg=PT64&dq=%E2%80%9CNeither+do+I.+And+if+I+see+anybody+undesirable+coming+in+here,+I%E2%80%99ll+be+the+first+to+complain.%E2%80%9D&source=bl&ots=z96kfNuvOJ&sig=FXpkX65gOeBMMyLhop1RwjXCZis&hl=en&sa=X&ved=0ahUKEwjHzKT14qfcAhXImuAKHRKrD6QQ6AEIMzAB#v=onepage&q=%E2%80%9CNeither%20do%20I.%20And%20if%20I%20see%20anybody%20undesirable%20coming%20in%20here%2C%20I%E2%80%99ll%20be%20the%20first%20to%20complain.%E2%80%9D&f=false

17. http://www.witchcraftandwitches.com/trials_connecticut.html

18. https://www.catholicnewsagency.com/news/was-the-last-witch-of-boston-actually-a-catholic-martyr-27747 https://en.wikipedia.org/wiki/Ann_Glover

19. https://edwingcoleman.wordpress.com/2002/05/31/its-bluenoses-and-not-bluenosers-may-3102/

20. https://en.wikipedia.org/wiki/Cotton_Mather

21. https://www.si.com/tech-media/2017/08/23/robert-lee-espn-decision-pull-announcer-broadcast

22. https://www.newyorker.com/magazine/1971/02/20/raising-kane-i

23. https://en.wikipedia.org/wiki/Battleship_Potemkin

24. https://www.sfchronicle.com/bayarea/article/Berkeley-mayor-asks-Cal-to-cancel-12104330.php

25. https://en.wikipedia.org/wiki/Columbus_Circle

26. http://gothamist.com/2017/08/23/de_blasio_grant_hate_symbol.php

27. https://en.wikipedia.org/wiki/1868_Democratic_National_Convention

28. https://www.politico.com/blogs/politico44/2012/03/obama-if-i-had
-a-son-hed-look-like-trayvon-118439

29. http://www.foxnews.com/story/2008/02/19/michelle-obama-takes-heat
-for-saying-shersquos-lsquoproud-my-countryrsquo-for.html

30, 31. https://www.indiewire.com/2013/11/review-12-12-12-hurricane
-sandy-relief-concert-doc-featuring-bruce-springsteen-paul-mccartney
-the-rolling-stones-more-91568/

32. https://deadline.com/2017/09/the-x-files-gillian-anderson-david
-duchovny-take-a-knee-colin-kaepernick-nfl-pharrell-williams-stevie
-wonder-social-injustice-1202176894/

CHAPTER 5: FROM SALEM TO CNN

1. https://www.usatoday.com/story/news/nation/2013/08/05/brawley
-begins-to-repay-lawyer-she-falsely-accused/2618399/ https://en.wiki
pedia.org/wiki/Tawana_Brawley_rape_allegations

2. https://www.history.com/this-day-in-history/abigail-adams-urges-hus
band-to-remember-the-ladies

3. http://www.masshist.org/digitaladams/archive/doc?id=L17970213aa

4. http://www.rasmussenreports.com/public_content/lifestyle/general
_lifestyle/august_2017/73_say_freedom_of_speech_worth_dying_for

5. https://en.wikipedia.org/wiki/Salem_witch_trials

6. https://en.wikipedia.org/wiki/Cotton_Mather

7. https://en.wikipedia.org/wiki/King_William%27s_War

8. http://www.famous-trials.com/salem/2074-asal-math

9. https://en.wikipedia.org/wiki/Bridget_Bishop http://www.famous-trials
.com/salem/2043-bridget-bishop

10. https://books.google.com/books?id=kDuboILCZwYC&pg=PA33&lpg
=PA33&dq=%22we+cannot+but+humbly+recommend+unto+the
+government,+the+speedy+and+vigorous+prosecution+of+such+as
+have+rendered+themselves+obnoxious,%22&source=bl&ots=JY2

Z1ffQM5&sig=EqnpTVYcaXl-lNJQVz2QXrTxwAk&hl=en&sa
=X&ved=0ahUKEwiHzbD08KfcAhXIY98KHdQVBF4Q6AEIK
TAA#v=onepage&q=%22we%20cannot%20but%20humbly%20
recommend%20unto%20the%20government%2C%20the%20speedy
%20and%20vigorous%20prosecution%20of%20such%20as%20
have%20rendered%20themselves%20obnoxious%2C%22&f=false

11. https://en.wikipedia.org/wiki/Martha_Corey

12. https://en.wikipedia.org/wiki/Dorothy_Good, https://en.wikipedia.org
/wiki/Sarah_Good

13. https://www.legendsofamerica.com/ma-witches-b/2/

14. https://en.wikipedia.org/wiki/Salem_witch_trials#September_1692

15. https://en.wikipedia.org/wiki/Salem_witch_trials#Accusations_and
_examinations_before_local_magistrates

16. https://www.tulane.edu/~salem/Salem%20and%20Village.html

17. https://en.wikipedia.org/wiki/Iran_hostage_crisis

18. https://en.wikipedia.org/wiki/1983_Beirut_barracks_bombings

19. https://en.wikipedia.org/wiki/TWA_Flight_847

20. https://www.history.com/this-day-in-history/pan-am-flight-103
-explodes-over-scotland

21. https://en.wikipedia.org/wiki/1993_World_Trade_Center_bombing

22. https://en.wikipedia.org/wiki/Khobar_Towers_bombing

23. https://en.wikipedia.org/wiki/1998_United_States_embassy
_bombings

24. https://www.britannica.com/event/USS-Cole-attack

25. https://en.wikipedia.org/wiki/September_11_attacks

26. https://en.wikipedia.org/wiki/War_in_Afghanistan_(2001%E2
%80%93present); https://www.bbc.co.uk/newsround/15214375

27. https://en.wikipedia.org/wiki/Daniel_Pearl

28. https://www.bbc.com/news/world-asia-19881138

29. https://www.washingtoninstitute.org/policy-analysis/view/the-syna
gogue-bombings-in-istanbul-al-qaedas-new-front

30. https://en.wikipedia.org/wiki/Nick_Berg

31. https://en.wikipedia.org/wiki/Boston_Marathon_bombing; https://www.nbcnews.com/slideshow/boston-marathon-bombing-attack-massive-manhunt-followed-n865766

32. https://nypost.com/2015/01/07/gunmen-who-killed-12-at-newspaper-were-calm-controlled/

33. https://www.imdb.com/title/tt0012136/quotes/?ref_=tx_sq_sr_40

34. https://en.wikipedia.org/wiki/Ancient_Roman_cuisine#Foods_and_ingredients

35. https://www.wnd.com/2017/09/roman-empire-ominous-parallels-with-modern-america/

36. https://www.wnd.com/2016/09/lessons-for-america-from-the-fall-of-rome/

37. https://www.fda.gov/downloads/AboutFDA/History/FOrgsHistory/EvolvingPowers/UCM593437.pdf

38. https://en.wikipedia.org/wiki/Huey_Long

39. https://www.pbs.org/wgbh/pages/frontline/shows/dope/etc/cron.html

40. https://en.wikipedia.org/wiki/Reefer_Madness

41. https://en.wikipedia.org/wiki/Marihuana_(novel)

42. https://www.history.com/this-day-in-history/actor-robert-mitchum-is-released-after-serving-time-for-marijuana-possession

43. https://en.wikipedia.org/wiki/Sam_Phillips

44. https://1965book.com/2014/11/05/november-19-the-berkeley-barb-publishes-allen-ginsbergs-essay-demonstration-or-spectacle-as-example-as-communication-or-how-to-make-a-marchspectacle-which-extols-the-use-of-flowers-in-pro/

45. http://fortune.com/2018/01/04/sessions-on-marijuana/

46. https://www.denverpost.com/2017/08/25/marijuana-impairment-testing/

47. Lifson quotes from a private communication between Lifson and Savage 1/1/18.

48. https://www.heritage.org/crime-and-justice/report/legalizing-marijuana-why-citizens-should-just-say-no

49. https://www.washingtonpost.com/business/economy/claims-that
-fish-oil-boosts-health-linger-despite-science-saying-the-opposite/2015
/07/08/db7567d2-1848-11e5-bd7f-4611a60dd8e5_story.html?utm_term
=e7d51fb1a25b

CHAPTER 6: FROM ASSASSINS TO GENERALS

1. https://en.wikipedia.org/wiki/Hassan-i_Sabbah https://en.wikipedia
.org/wiki/Assassins http://disinfo.com/2012/07/hasan-bin-sabbah-and
-the-secret-order-of-hashishins/ https://erowid.org/plants/cannabis
/cannabis_info4.shtml

2. https://www.scientificamerican.com/article/the-hidden-harm-of
-antidepressants/ https://www.bmj.com/content/352/bmj.i65

3. https://www.telegraph.co.uk/science/2016/03/14/antidepressants-can
-raise-the-risk-of-suicide-biggest-ever-revie/

4. https://www.telegraph.co.uk/science/2016/03/14/antidepressants-can
-raise-the-risk-of-suicide-biggest-ever-revie/

5. https://www.cbsnews.com/news/antidepressant-use-soars-65-percent
-in-15-years/

6. https://www.reuters.com/article/us-health-suicide-drugs/rise-in-u-s
-suicides-highlights-need-for-new-depression-drugs-idUSKCN1J42TO

7. http://www.history.com/topics/american-revolution/stamp-act https://
en.wikipedia.org/wiki/Stamp_Act_1765 http://www.history.org/history
/teaching/tchcrsta.cfm

8. https://en.wikipedia.org/wiki/Sons_of_Liberty

9. http://mastatelibrary.blogspot.com/2016/08/the-loyal-nine-secret-pre
cursor-to-sons.html

10. https://en.wikipedia.org/wiki/Virginia_Resolves

11. https://books.google.com/books?id=ZrMsDwAAQBAJ&pg=PA31&lpg
=PA31&dq=%E2%80%9CI+have+a+large+store+of+goods+and+seldom
+less+than+twenty-thousand+pounds+currency+value+in+it+with
+which+the+populace+would+make+sad+havoc.%E2%80%9D
&source=bl&ots=ecGeJJ1crp&sig=LmRBIhqA5n822sLDguicg3B
HmqA&hl=en&sa=X&ved=0ahUKEwj2r6HvnqjcAhWkg-
AKHQYHCoMQ6AEILzAB#v=onepage&q=%E2%80%9CI%20

have%20a%20large%20store%20of%20goods%20and%20seldom%20
less%20than%20twenty-thousand%20pounds%20currency%20value
%20in%20it%20with%20which%20the%20populace%20would%20
make%20sad%20havoc.%E2%80%9D&f=false

12. https://allthingsliberty.com/2016/10/truth-george-washington-hemp/;
    https://books.google.com/books?id=w0qvkVGO0sgC&pg=PA131&lpg
    =PA131&dq=%22What+was+done+with+the+Seed+saved+from+the
    +India+Hemp+last+summer?%22&source=bl&ots=DpY90FFGQx&sig
    =2goiBLbObqu6gf5mFTOYHHLnrwQ&hl=en&sa=X&ved=0ah
    UKEwjckYmAoKjcAhUDMt8KHQDtArsQ6AEIMTAC#v=onepage
    &q=%22What%20was%20done%20with%20the%20Seed%20
    saved%20from%20the%20India%20Hemp%20last%20summer%3F
    %22&f=false https://hightimes.com/culture/11-us-presidents-who
    -smoked-marijuana/ https://www.mountvernon.org/george-washington
    /the-man-the-myth/george-washington-grew-hemp

13. https://en.wikipedia.org/wiki/Expulsion_of_the_Loyalists

14. https://books.google.com/books?id=SRxWAAAAMAAJ&q=commit
    tee+of+safety+tar+and+pitch+%22necessary+for+the+public+use+and
    +safety%22&dq=committee+of+safety+tar+and+pitch+%22necessary
    +for+the+public+use+and+safety%22&hl=en&sa=X&ved=0ahUKEwjxr
    5baoajcAhVCGt8KHVq0CbgQ6AEIMzAC

15. https://books.google.com/books?id=XwPFDgAAQBAJ&pg=PA113
    &lpg=PA113&dq=%22riding+the+rails%22+israel+putnam&source
    =bl&ots=2Wnh9cLWYK&sig=NMiISVwoJXUMOd_lNWank2on
    CNY&hl=en&sa=X&ved=0ahUKEwimlJGNoqjcAhWxmOAKHTS
    jBUIQ6AEIQTAK#v=onepage&q=%22riding%20the%20rails%22
    %20israel%20putnam&f=false

16. https://www.smithsonianmag.com/history/divided-loyalties-107489501/

17. http://www.toriesfightingfortheking.com/Punishing.htm

18. https://www.npr.org/2015/07/03/419824333/what-happened-to-british
    -loyalists-after-the-revolutionary-war http://www.ushistory.org/us/11b
    .asp http://philadelphiaencyclopedia.org/archive/loyalists/ https://
    en.wikipedia.org/wiki/Loyalist_(American_Revolution)

19. Occupy stories: personal testimony from a Michael Savage associate.

CHAPTER 7: FROM WAR TO PEACE

1. https://en.wikipedia.org/wiki/List_of_recessions_in_the_United_States

2. https://en.wikipedia.org/wiki/Copper_Panic_of_1789

3. http://www.ohiohistorycentral.org/w/Panic_of_1819 https://www.u-s -history.com/pages/h277.html

4. https://en.wikipedia.org/wiki/Panic_of_1819

5. https://en.wikipedia.org/wiki/Nullification_Crisis

6. https://books.google.com/books?id=AbsOAAAAYAAJ&pg=PA453&lpg =PA453&dq=%E2%80%9Cthe+tariff+was+only+a+pretext,+and +disunion+and+southern+confederacy+the+real+object.+The+next +pretext+will+be+the+negro,+or+slavery+question.%E2%80%9D &source=bl&ots=7nHEeigMzB&sig=745ZOEaybYK1yp6Hs8Uhq 71Cbqo&hl=en&sa=X&ved=0ahUKEwizu7DHqKjcAhUPhuAKHV stC5kQ6AEIbTAM#v=onepage&q=%E2%80%9Cthe%20tariff%20 was%20only%20a%20pretext%2C%20and%20disunion%20and%20 southern%20confederacy%20the%20real%20object.%20The%20 next%20pretext%20will%20be%20the%20negro%2C%20or%20 slavery%20question.%E2%80%9D&f=false

7. https://www.essence.com/news/harriet-tubman-20-bill-Josh-Malina

8. https://en.wikipedia.org/wiki/Chinese_Exclusion_Act

9. https://en.wikipedia.org/wiki/Catholic_Church_in_the_Thirteen _Colonies

10. https://en.wikipedia.org/wiki/Germans_in_the_American_Revolution

11. https://en.wikipedia.org/wiki/Irish_Americans#17th_to_mid-19th _century

12. https://www.catholicleague.org/pope-pius-ix/

13. https://en.wikipedia.org/wiki/Pope_Pius_IX_and_the_United_States

14. http://teachingresources.atlas.illinois.edu/chinese_exp/introduction04 .html

15. https://en.wikipedia.org/wiki/Johannes_Bapst

16. https://ir.library.louisville.edu/cgi/viewcontent.cgi?article=3542&con text=etd

17. https://books.google.com/books?id=hmI3CwAAQBAJ&pg=PA24
&lpg=PA24&dq=%22shone+in+the+world+there+was+no+reli
gious+freedom.%E2%80%9D%22&source=bl&ots=nAqput
Ws8U&sig=Wrmu7J-bN0jg-w8dY8KQ_VQ4KMU&hl=en&sa
=X&ved=0ahUKEwi2pM3bsKjcAhXjRd8KHS2mCJkQ6AEIK
TAA#v=onepage&q=%22shone%20in%20the%20world%20
there%20was%20no%20religious%20freedom.%E2%80%9D%22
&f=false

18. https://books.google.com/books?id=vR4WNNkWHKMC&pg
=PA233&lpg=PA233&dq=%E2%80%9CLet+the+foreigners
+keep+their+elbows+to+themselves%22&source=bl&ots=aAUyf
7NRr2&sig=arS_s-jIEn8h-twcXvOQ2EQp7C4&hl=en&sa=X
&ved=0ahUKEwjdgO7-sKjcAhXDVt8KHZURD8oQ6
AEIKTAA#v=onepage&q=%E2%80%9CLet%20the%20
foreigners%20keep%20their%20elbows%20to%20themselves
%22&f=false

19. http://www.counterfire.org/history/16271-lincoln-slavery-and-the
-american-civil-war

20. https://civilwartalk.com/threads/london-times-reacts-to-lincolns
-emancipation-proclamation.110202/ The London Times: October 7,
1862

21. https://www.jstor.org/stable/2715371 https://books.google.com
/books?id=-Hw8-RmhEuYC&pg=PA4&lpg=PA4&dq=If+Lincoln
+is+elected+to-day,+you+will+have+to+compete+with+the+labor
+of+four+million+emancipated+negros&source=bl&ots=QmkBY
emv6O&sig=VaEvsFhpkn8EyAAzf_hdSDas-L8&hl=en&sa
=X&ved=0ahUKEwiRvtX_sajcAhVPT98KHU5BCpIQ6AEIPz
AD#v=onepage&q=If%20Lincoln%20is%20elected%20to-day
%2C%20you%20will%20have%20to%20compete%20with%20
the%20labor%20of%20four%20million%20emancipated%20
negros&f=false

22. https://www.nytimes.com/2016/02/18/nyregion/remembering-a-vile
-civil-war-act-on-fifth-avenue.html

23. https://blackdoctor.org/513476/dr-james-mccune-smith-the-nations
-first-black-doctor/2/

24. https://www.stereogum.com/1997383/wynton-marsalis-says-rap-is
-more-damaging-than-a-statue-of-robert-e-lee/wheres-the-beef/

25. http://www.latimes.com/business/la-fi-wall-street-bull-20170914-story
.html; https://www.nbcnewyork.com/news/local/Charging-Bull-Statue
-Covered-Blue-Paint-Wall-Street-444421073.html

26. https://en.wikipedia.org/wiki/Joseph_Smith_and_the_criminal_justice
_system

27. https://www.lds.org/manual/church-history-in-the-fulness-of-times
-student-manual/chapter-thirty-three-a-decade-of-persecution-1877
-87?lang=eng

CHAPTER 8: FROM PEACE TO WAR

1. https://www.roadsideamerica.com/story/17994

2. https://www.pbs.org/wgbh/americanexperience/features/grant-kkk/

3. The Opelousas incident is recounted in https://www.jstor.org/stable
/4231556

4. https://www.history.com/this-day-in-history/birth-of-a-nation-opens
https://en.wikipedia.org/wiki/The_Birth_of_a_Nation

5. https://books.google.com/books?id=L8AQAAAAIAAJ&pg=PA571&lpg
=PA571&dq=was+%E2%80%9Cthe+darkest+hour+of+the+life+of+the
+South,+when+her+wounded+people+lay+helpless+amid+rags+and
+ashes,%E2%80%9D&source=bl&ots=Evb-gnh0ZY&sig=uNeC
sDVJmIQyiQjv-tvZgR2lZLk&hl=en&sa=X&ved=0ahUKEwi6tsW
_v6jcAhWsVt8KHdSlCSUQ6AEIKTAA#v=onepage&q=was%20
%E2%80%9Cthe%20darkest%20hour%20of%20the%20life%20
of%20the%20South%2C%20when%20her%20wounded%20people
%20lay%20helpless%20amid%20rags%20and%20ashes
%2C%E2%80%9D&f=false

6. https://www.history.com/topics/gold-rush-of-1849

7. http://www.pbs.org/wned/klondike-gold-rush/home/

8. http://old.seattletimes.com/special/klondike/pacific13b.html

9. https://www.nps.gov/klgo/learn/historyculture/tonofgoods.htm

10. http://jack-and-the-klondike.blogspot.com/

CHAPTER 9: FROM REGIONAL WAR TO PROHIBITION

1. https://en.wikiquote.org/wiki/Citizen_Kane

2. https://www.azquotes.com/quote/705003

3. For the Spanish-American War in general, see: http://www.history.com /topics/spanish-american-war; https://en.wikipedia.org/wiki/Time line_of_the_Spanish%E2%80%93American_War#1896; and https:// en.wikipedia.org/wiki/Rough_Riders; also https://history.state.gov /milestones/1866-1898/yellow-journalism; and https://en.wikipedia.org /wiki/Propaganda_of_the_Spanish%E2%80%93American_War

4. https://www.pbs.org/crucible/tl7.html

5. http://www.iancfriedman.com/?p=29

6. https://digitalcollections.nypl.org/items/84ea964f-4861-b09d-e040-e00 a18066a1d

7. http://www.newworldencyclopedia.org/entry/Spanish-American_War

8. https://en.wikipedia.org/wiki/Operation_Wetback

9. http://mentalfloss.com/article/19061/get-your-country-out-my-happy -meal-liberty-cabbage-freedom-fries-and-other-product

10. https://en.wikipedia.org/wiki/Anti-German_sentiment

11. http://crookedtimber.org/2006/12/07/liberty-cabbage-and-pinochle/

12. https://en.wikipedia.org/wiki/Hyphenated_American

13. https://en.wikipedia.org/wiki/American_entry_into_World_War_I

14. http://library.sewanee.edu/c.php?g=118671&p=773217

15. https://en.wikipedia.org/wiki/Internment_of_German_Americans #World_War_I

16. https://www.npr.org/2017/04/07/523044253/during-world-war-i-u-s -government-propaganda-erased-german-culture

17. https://en.wikipedia.org/wiki/United_States_home_front_during _World_War_I#Civil_liberties

18. http://library.sewanee.edu/c.php?g=118671&p=773217

19. http://www.americanrhetoric.com/speeches/wilsonleagueofnations.htm

20. https://www.wnd.com/2015/05/minnesota-muslims-brutally-honest-we -want-shariah/

21. https://www.wnd.com/2015/05/minnesota-muslims-brutally-honest-we -want-shariah/

22. http://digitalexhibits.libraries.wsu.edu/exhibits/show/prohibition-in -the-u-s/introduction

23. https://www.americanhistoryusa.com/topic/american-temperance -society/

24. http://digitalexhibits.libraries.wsu.edu/exhibits/show/prohibition-in-the -u-s/introduction

25. https://en.wikipedia.org/wiki/Carrie_Nation#.22Hatchetations.22

26. https://en.wikipedia.org/wiki/Prohibition_in_the_United_States

27. https://books.google.com/books?id=FtbnIe103p4C&pg=PA50&lpg =PA50&dq=%22We+will+turn+our+prisons+into+factories%22 &source=bl&ots=pVvDXbbc3F&sig=TJaLRCL8Sj5S950RAtuglnY Ln6Q&hl=en&sa=X&ved=0ahUKEwiJ8feV0ajcAhXEmuAKHQ 6PAVcQ6AEIMDAB#v=onepage&q=%22We%20will%20turn%20 our%20prisons%20into%20factories%22&f=false

28. https://vinepair.com/articles/jewish-prohibition-bootlegging/

29. http://leben.us/kkk-wctu-partners-prohibition/

30. http://www.druglibrary.org/schaffer/Library/homrate1.htm

31. https://dp.la/exhibitions/exhibits/show/spirits/unintended-consequences

32. https://en.wikipedia.org/wiki/Mothers_Against_Drunk_Driving

33. https://www.ncbi.nlm.nih.gov/books/NBK216414/

CHAPTER 10: FROM REDS TO FASCISTS

1, 2. https://www.thoughtco.com/1920-wall-street-bombing-terrorism-in -america-3209275 https://en.wikipedia.org/wiki/Wall_Street_bombing

3. https://variety.com/2018/legit/news/robert-de-niro-trump-tonys -1202839957/

4. www.usa-anti-communist.com/ard/pdf/Overman-Committee-NYT -1919.pdf; and http://depts.washington.edu/depress/fish_committee .shtml

5. https://www.britannica.com/topic/Palmer-Raids

6. https://en.wikipedia.org/wiki/A._Mitchell_Palmer

7. https://en.wikipedia.org/wiki/Red_Scare

8. https://en.wikipedia.org/wiki/History_of_Japanese_Americans

9. https://en.wikipedia.org/wiki/History_of_Japanese_Americans#Japa
nese_American_history_before_World_War_II

10. https://en.wikipedia.org/wiki/Internment_of_Japanese_Americans

11, 12. https://en.wikipedia.org/wiki/Japanese-American_life_before
_World_War_II#Japanese-American_life_under_U.S._policies_during
_World_War_II

13. https://en.wikipedia.org/wiki/Niihau_incident

14. https://www.theatlantic.com/photo/2011/08/world-war-ii-internment
-of-japanese-americans/100132/

15. https://en.wikipedia.org/wiki/Internment_of_Japanese_Americans

16. https://en.wikipedia.org/wiki/442nd_Infantry_Regiment_(United
_States)

17. http://www.pbs.org/thewar/at_home_civil_rights_japanese_american
.htm

18. https://www.npr.org/sections/codeswitch/2013/08/09/210138278/japa
nese-internment-redress

19. https://en.wikipedia.org/wiki/Der_Fuehrer%27s_Face

20. http://www.dvdbeaver.com/film2/DVDReviews49/confessions_of_a
_nazi_spy.htm

21. https://en.wikipedia.org/wiki/Internment_of_German_Americans

22. https://www.chicagoreader.com/Bleader/archives/2017/09/06/george
-takei-on-his-childhood-in-japanese-internment-camps-his-career
-after-imprisonment-and-ugh-donald-trump

CHAPTER 11: FROM COMMIES TO COMICS

1. http://libertyhangout.org/2017/05/mccarthy-was-right-there-were
-communist-infiltrators-in-america/

2. http://spartacus-educational.com/USAhuac.htm

3. https://en.wikipedia.org/wiki/Fellow_traveller

4. https://variety.com/2015/film/awards/trumbo-and-five-facts-you-didnt-know-about-the-hollywood-blacklist-1201590187/

5. http://spartacus-educational.com/USAhammett.htm

6. https://www.imdb.com/name/nm0822034/bio

7. http://www.digitalhistory.uh.edu/disp_textbook.cfm?smtid=2&psid=3416

8. https://www.history.com/topics/cold-war/huac

9. https://en.wikipedia.org/wiki/Committee_for_the_First_Amendment

10. https://www.military.com/veteran-jobs/career-advice/military-transition/famous-veteran-jimmy-stewart.html

11. http://www.angelfire.com/my/mighty8th/hwood18.html

12. https://en.wikipedia.org/wiki/Henry_Fonda

13. https://www2.gwu.edu/~erpapers/myday/displaydoc.cfm?_y=1947&_f=md000796

14. https://en.wikipedia.org/wiki/Hollywood_blacklist

15. https://en.wikipedia.org/wiki/Communist_Control_Act_of_1954

16. https://en.wikipedia.org/wiki/Motion_Picture_Alliance_for_the_Preservation_of_American_Ideals

17. https://en.wikipedia.org/wiki/McCarthyism

18. https://www.history.com/this-day-in-history/fbi-report-names-hollywood-figures-as-communists https://en.wikipedia.org/wiki/Committee_for_the_First_Amendment

19. http://articles.latimes.com/1996-01-28/entertainment/ca-29491_1_director-edward-dmytryk-named-names

20. https://en.wikipedia.org/wiki/The_Bridge_on_the_River_Kwai

21. https://en.wikipedia.org/wiki/Dalton_Trumbo

22. www.americanthinker.com/articles/2009/10/all_the_presidents_mao.html

23. https://www.bloomberg.com/news/articles/2017-11-06/get-rid-of-capitalism-millennials-are-ready-to-talk-about-it

24. https://en.wikipedia.org/wiki/Joseph_McCarthy

25. https://en.wikipedia.org/wiki/Joseph_McCarthy

26. https://en.wikipedia.org/wiki/Millard_Tydings

27. https://en.wikipedia.org/wiki/Joseph_McCarthy

28. https://www.politico.com/story/2013/06/this-day-in-politics-093127

29. https://en.wikipedia.org/wiki/Joseph_McCarthy

30. https://en.wikipedia.org/wiki/Venona_project

31. https://en.wikipedia.org/wiki/Joseph_McCarthy

32. https://en.wikipedia.org/wiki/Joseph_McCarthy

33. https://en.wikipedia.org/wiki/Joseph_McCarthy

34. https://en.wikipedia.org/wiki/Joseph_McCarthy

35. https://en.wikipedia.org/wiki/Joseph_McCarthy

36. https://en.wikipedia.org/wiki/Joseph_McCarthy

37. https://uclanlg.wordpress.com/about/

38. https://en.wikipedia.org/wiki/Joseph_McCarthy

39. https://books.google.com/books?id=HuZgDQAAQBAJ&pg=PT16
    &lpg=PT16&dq=maxwell+ginsburg+comics&source=bl&ots
    =W-sKVohKT&sig=hyf_pQFvRii8x4R08BhK3REllDI&hl=en&sa
    =X&ved=0ahUKEwihk63Y_KjcAhWpm-AKHWoBCPQQ6AEIO
    zAC#v=onepage&q=maxwell%20ginsburg%20comics&f=false

40. https://en.wikipedia.org/wiki/Max_Gaines

41. https://www.comicconnect.com/bookDetail.php?id=293749; https://
    comics.ha.com/itm/golden-age-1938-1955-/cartoon-character/famous
    -funnies-carnival-of-comics-nn-eastern-color-1933-cgc-vf-nm-90-off
    -white-pages-widely-regarded-as-the-second/a/809-2232.s; https://
    en.wikipedia.org/wiki/Famous_Funnies

42. https://en.wikipedia.org/wiki/Tales_from_the_Crypt_(TV_series)

43. https://en.wikipedia.org/wiki/Seduction_of_the_Innocent

44. http://dc.wikia.com/wiki/Harriet_Cooper_(Earth-One)

45. https://en.wikipedia.org/wiki/United_States_Senate_Subcommittee
    _on_Juvenile_Delinquency

46. http://www.thecomicbooks.com/gaines.html

47. https://en.wikipedia.org/wiki/William_Gaines

CHAPTER 12: FROM THE CATHOLICS TO FLOWER POWER

1. https://www.jfklibrary.org/JFK/JFK-in-History/JFK-and-Religion.aspx
2. https://www.jfklibrary.org/JFK/JFK-in-History/JFK-and-Religion.aspx
3. http://www.americanrhetoric.com/speeches/jfkhoustonministers.html
4. https://www.jfklibrary.org/JFK/JFK-in-History/JFK-and-Religion.aspx
5. https://www.politico.eu/article/pope-francis-heretic-vatican-liberal -conservative-war/
6. http://www.citymayors.com/society/muslims-europe-cities.html
7. https://en.wikipedia.org/wiki/Don_Black_(white_supremacist)#The _Ku_Klux_Klan_and_Operation_Red_Dog
8. https://en.wikipedia.org/wiki/Nikita_Khrushchev#Leader_(1953%E2 %80%931964)
9. https://en.wikipedia.org/wiki/We_will_bury_you
10. https://en.wikipedia.org/wiki/Shoe-banging_incident
11. https://en.wikipedia.org/wiki/More_popular_than_Jesus
12. https://en.wikipedia.org/wiki/More_popular_than_Jesus
13. https://www.history.com/topics/black-panthers
14. https://en.wikipedia.org/wiki/Ballad_of_the_Green_Berets
15. https://en.wikipedia.org/wiki/Victor_Lundberg#Hit_record
16. https://en.wikipedia.org/wiki/Waist_Deep_in_the_Big_Muddy
17. https://thestonewallinnnyc.com/

CHAPTER 13: FROM GAS LINES TO REAGAN

1. http://www.opec.org/opec_web/en/
2. http://www.nola.com/travel/index.ssf/2016/06/40_years_ago_summer _road_trips.html
3. https://en.wikipedia.org/wiki/1973_oil_crisis
4. http://www.washingtontimes.com/news/2006/may/15/20060515 -122820-6110r/
5. http://www.businessinsider.com/gas-signs-1970s-2011-8#-6

6. http://www.washingtontimes.com/news/2006/may/15/20060515
   -122820-6110r/

7. https://www.theatlantic.com/politics/archive/2016/05/american-oil
   -consumption/482532/

8. https://timeline.com/gas-crisis-levittown-riot-9a7705c4deb4

9. https://www.mercurynews.com/2016/10/30/the-year-daylight-saving
   -time-went-too-far/

10. http://flashbak.com/scared-america-8-crises-and-collective-panics-of
    -the-1970s-27236/

11. https://en.wikipedia.org/wiki/1973_oil_crisis

12. http://www.washingtontimes.com/news/2006/may/15/20060515
    -122820-6110r/

13. https://en.wikipedia.org/wiki/1973_oil_crisis

14. https://en.wikipedia.org/wiki/1973_oil_crisis

15. https://en.wikipedia.org/wiki/1979_energy_crisis

16. http://content.bangtech.com/thinking/jimmycarter1976.htm

17. https://timeline.com/hippies-started-the-peoples-park-but-were
    -confronted-by-violent-police-26df58ae1d44

18. https://en.wikipedia.org/wiki/Meese_Report

19. https://en.wikipedia.org/wiki/President%27s_Commission_on
    _Obscenity_and_Pornography

20. https://supreme.justia.com/cases/federal/us/354/476/

21. https://kipdf.com/fordham-intellectual-property-media-and-enter
    tainment-law-journal_5ab504aa1723dd339c8105be.html

22. https://www.dissentmagazine.org/article/not-safe-for-work-feminist
    -pornography-matters-sex-wars

23. http://www.radicalwomen.org/activityShare4-19-12.shtml

24. https://www.ncjrs.gov/App/abstractdb/AbstractDBDetails.aspx?id
    =109837

25. http://www.lasvegasworldnews.com/gilberto-valle-sicko-cannibal-wann
    abe-nypd-officer-wanted-to-cook-and-eat-women/6859/

26. https://listverse.com/2014/02/22/10-incredibly-insane-cases-of-mass
    -hysteria/

27. https://www.cdc.gov/mmwr/preview/mmwrhtml/00001618.htm

28. https://en.wikipedia.org/wiki/McMartin_preschool_trial

29. https://en.wikipedia.org/wiki/Martensville_satanic_sex_scandal

30. https://timeline.com/cabbage-patch-craze-867ce8d076c

31. http://www.mortaljourney.com/2011/01/1980-trends/cabbage-patch
    -kids-dolls

32. https://timeline.com/cabbage-patch-craze-867ce8d076c

33. https://timeline.com/cabbage-patch-craze-867ce8d076c

34. https://www.youtube.com/watch?v=VaQuxCWWTaI

35. https://www.nytimes.com/1989/07/13/business/company-news-hasbro
    -s-purchase-of-coleco-s-assets.html

36. https://en.wikipedia.org/wiki/Coonskin_cap

37. http://harvardpolitics.com/united-states/phrase-flux-history-political
    -correctness/

38. https://en.wikipedia.org/wiki/Antonio_Gramsci

39. https://writing.wisc.edu/Handbook/GenderNeutralPronouns
    .html

40. http://www.dailymail.co.uk/news/article-4372224/Now-students-lose
    -marks-using-he.html

41. https://books.google.com/books?id=p3c7oO7LsAcC&pg=PA335&lpg
    =PA335&dq=%22western+culture+has+got+to+go%22+Jesse&source
    =bl&ots=HycPl30ABC&sig=P27rJylyuxFG5QByYlq7O0H7uTo
    &hl=en&sa=X&ved=0ahUKEwjv1-ubqKncAhXmTN8KHQ4UA
    -8Q6AEINzAD#v=onepage&q=%22western%20culture%20has%20
    got%20to%20go%22%20Jesse&f=false

42. https://archive.nytimes.com/www.nytimes.com/books/98/10/04/nnp
    /kimball-radicals.html

43. https://www.nbcnews.com/news/us-news/teen-accepted-stanford-after
    -writing-blacklivesmatter-100-times-application-n742586

44. https://www.nytimes.com/1991/05/05/us/excerpts-from-president-s
-speech-to-university-of-michigan-graduates.html

45. https://studybreaks.com/news-politics/should-ebonics-be-used-in-an
-educational-setting/

46. https://www.nationalreview.com/2016/07/lgbt-history-second-graders
-californias-new-education-guidelines/

47. https://www.nationalreview.com/2015/05/university-study-certain
-rooms-are-microaggressions-themselves-katherine-timpf/

48. https://www.self.com/story/yoga-indian-cultural-appropriation

49. https://www.theatlantic.com/politics/archive/2015/12/the-food-fight-at
-oberlin-college/421401/

50. https://nypost.com/2017/09/18/woman-freaks-out-over-hobby-lobbys
-raw-cotton-display/

51. https://www.washingtontimes.com/news/2018/may/2/david-hogg-leads
-new-wave-anti-gun-activists-again/

52. https://en.wikipedia.org/wiki/Nidal_Hasan

53. https://www.npr.org/2018/05/29/615263473/thousands-of-starbucks
-stores-close-for-racial-bias-training

54. https://variety.com/2018/tv/news/roseanne-revival-without-roseanne
-barr-abc-1202829682/

55. https://www.npr.org/2016/08/26/491531869/university-of-chicago
-tells-freshmen-it-does-not-support-trigger-warnings

CHAPTER 14: FROM CONSUMABLES TO CLIMATE CHANGE

1. https://www.beyondceliac.org/celiac-disease/facts-and-figures/

2. https://www.verywellhealth.com/how-many-people-have-gluten
-sensitivity-562965

3. www.academia.edu/3266702/You_are_what_you_eat...............Nutrition

4. https://hellogiggles.com/lifestyle/food-drink/gluten-is-not-the-enemy
-why-you-might-want-to-reconsider-cutting-certain-carbs/

5. http://ossfoundation.us/projects/environment/global-warming/milan
kovitch-cycles

6. https://www.scientificamerican.com/article/sun-spots-and-climate
   -change/

7. https://www.skepticalscience.com/volcanoes-and-global-warming.htm

8. https://insideclimatenews.org/news/07052018/atlantic-ocean-circulation
   -slowing-climate-change-heat-temperature-rainfall-fish-why-you
   -should-care

9. https://en.wikipedia.org/wiki/The_Climate_Reality_Project

10. http://cdiac.ess-dive.lbl.gov/trends/co2/vostok.html

11. www.fitsnews.com/2017/10/04/hurricane-hysteria-here-we-go-again/

CHAPTER 15: FROM TREASON TO TOMORROW

1. https://ebooks.adelaide.edu.au/f/franklin/benjamin/autobiography
   /chapter12.html

2. https://1776united.com/products/rebellion-to-tyrants

3. https://en.wikipedia.org/wiki/Chelsea_Manning

4. https://www.washingtonpost.com/news/grade-point/wp/2017/09/14
   /former-cia-directors-shun-harvard-after-the-school-invites-chelsea
   -manning-to-campus/

5. https://pjmedia.com/trending/cop-hating-antifa-professor-finally-ter
   minated-john-jay-college/

6. https://investigaterussia.org/about-us

7. https://www.nytimes.com/2017/07/27/theater/mandy-patinkin-oak
   -onaodowan-great-comet.html

8. https://www.laurenvillegas.com/pair.html

ABOUT THE AUTHOR

In 2016, after twenty-two years on the air, Michael Savage was inducted into the National Radio Hall of Fame, an honor that Dr. Savage calls "the capstone of my life."

The Savage Nation, the country's #1 streaming radio show, is one of the top programs in America, with millions of listeners and broadcast on over 230 stations, including WABC and KSFO. A prolific *New York Times* bestselling author, Dr. Savage has been profiled in *Playboy* and *The New Yorker*, and he has been awarded the Freedom of Speech Award from *Talkers* magazine. He received his PhD in epidemiology and nutrition sciences from the University of California at Berkeley.